THE

DIVINE LIFE:

A Book of Facts and Histories.

BY THE

REV. JOHN KENNEDY.

M.A., F.R.G.S.

"The words of Christ assure us that the communication of the life of God to men was the greatest of all miracles, the essence and aim of all; and further, that it was to be the standing miracle of all after ages."

NEANDER.

PHILADELPHIA:
PRESBYTERIAN BOARD OF PUBLICATION,
No. 821 CHESTNUT STREET.

STEREOTYPED BY
JESPER HARDING & SON,
NO. 57 SOUTH THIRD STREET, PHILADELPHIA.

PREFACE.

It has been well said that "a man's religion is the chief fact with regard to him." "The thing a man does practically lay to heart, and know for certain, concerning his vital relations to this mysterious universe, and his duty and destiny there, that is in all cases the primary thing for him, and creatively determines all the rest." It follows that "the thing a man does practically lay to heart," the formative principle of spiritual character, if it be error, will poison the soul, —if truth, it will bring health and life. Instead of its being a matter of indifference whether we worship "Jehovah, Jove, or Baal," false religion is, to use the words of Vinet, "a disordered spirit, which, in the ardour of its thirst, plunges, all panting, into fetid and troubled waters; it is an exile, who, in seeking the road to his native land, buries himself in frightful deserts."

What, then, is truth? The question is a very old one. It was asked and discussed among the pastoral chiefs of Arabia three and thirty centuries ago. "Where shall wisdom be found? and where is the place of understanding? The depth saith, It is not in me: and the sea saith, It is not with me. It cannot be gotten for gold, neither shall silver be weighed for the price thereof. . . . Whence then cometh wisdom? and where is the place of understanding?"

This volume is designed to be a small contribution towards an answer to this momentous inquiry. And it is hoped that the facts and histories which it contains, will, through the blessing of God, guide not a few to HIM who is the Way, the Truth, and the Life. The facts and histories are left for the most part to teach their own lesson, and when the principles which are involved in them are formally deduced and illustrated, it is more frequently in the words of others, than in those of the Author, that thus testimony may be borne to the existence of a wide and scriptural harmony among different communions as to what the Divine Life is, and how it is produced.

"——From his bright pavilion,
Like eastern bridegroom clad,
Hailed by earth's thousand million,
The Sun sets forth, right glad.
So pure, so soul restoring,
Is Truth's diviner ray ;
A brighter radiance pouring
Than all the pomp of day :
The wanderer surely guiding,
It makes the simple wise ;
And evermore abiding,
Unfailing joy supplies."

CONTENTS.

INTRODUCTION.

Page

Modern Science—Spiritual Facts—These fit subjects of investigation—Their importance and interest—The Divine Life; what is it?—Language of the Apostle Peter - 7—12

PART I.

ITS NATURE.

The Religious Faculty—Bechuanas—Heathenism—Mohammedanism—Asceticism—Saul of Tarsus—Luther, Loyola, Latimer, Col. Gardiner, Urquhart, Birrell, Caroline Fry—Conclusions—Quotations from Howe, Bullar, and Butler - - - - - - - - - - 13—106

PART II.

ITS ORIGINATION.

Diversity and Unity—Remarks of Wilberforce, Chalmers, and Fletcher—Miracles of Christ—Changes in Nature—First class of Instances; John Foster, R. Morrison, Knibb—Second class; Bengel, Blackader, J. J. Gurney, Fletcher, Mrs. Graham—Third class; Paul, Philippian Jailor, C. Anderson—Fourth class; Bilney, Archer Butler, M. Boos—Fifth class; Lyttleton, West, Dykern, Rochester, Wilson, H. K. White—Sixth class; Inspiration and Constitutional Peculiarities, Jonathan Edwards, Mrs. Phelps—Remarks - - - - - - - 107—212

PART III.

PROVIDENTIAL OCCASIONS.

Page

Events divided into Two Classes—The Casual, a Storehouse of Divine Weapons—Gifford—Bunyan—Alderman Kiffin—Lady Huntingdon and Capt. Scott—Robinson—Simeon—Wilberforce—Legh Richmond—Chalmers—Doddridge—R. Haldane—Students in Geneva—John Williams—Dr. Judson—Budgett—Hewitson—Dr. Hope—Narrative by Dr. Malan—The Influence of Affliction—Howels—Cecil—Waldo—John Newton—Remarks by Tholuck—The Finger of God. - - - - - 213—288

PART IV.

TRUE MEANS.

Pilgrim and the Cross—Allegory by Dr. James Hamilton—Moravian Missions—Testimony of John Williams—Cannibal Priest—Rammohun Roy—Banerji—Experience of Dr. Duff—John Wesley—C. Wesley—Whitefield—Kingswood Colliers—David Hume—Hervey—Walker—Toplady—Berridge—Baxter—A. Fuller—Dr. MacAll—Quotations from Isaac Taylor, Chalmers, and Professor Butler - - - - - - - - 289—359

CONCLUSION.

Standing Miracle—Argument for Divinity of the Gospel—What Conversion does not do—What it is not—Am I a Partaker of the Divine Life?—Dying Young Lady—"The Sand and the Rock." - - - - 360—375

INTRODUCTION.

It is the boast of modern science that its decisions are based on facts. Three centuries ago, lord Bacon taught men to abandon their mere conjectures and fancies about the properties of matter and the laws of the universe, and to go into the school of nature as little children. Would we understand the material world, he said, we should not consult our imagination, but should rather bring together facts and instances, examine them in all possible lights and aspects, and then draw from them such general truths as are involved in them. Before this rule a host of wild theories vanished at once. It was by a rigid adherence to it that sir Isaac Newton concluded that the descent of a tile from a house, or an apple from a tree, is produced by the same cause which keeps the planets in their paths round the sun. And now science accepts of no theory, even the most captivating and brilliant, that is not a proper induction from ascertained and acknowledged facts.

The inner world of man's spiritual nature has its facts as well as the outer and material; and to the examination of one class of them this book is devoted, in the hope of finding in them some help towards understanding wherein the divine life consists, and how it is produced. The name by which the facts in view are ordinarily designated, conversion, is offensive to many; but the wise man, who would make good his title to be a follower of lord Bacon, will examine them without prejudice; he will not conclude at once that all who use this term are fools or hypocrites, but will seek to ascertain dispassionately the true character of the phenomenon (if we must use scientific language) which occupies so prominent a place in religious history.

The facts to which we appeal are of both ancient and modern date. The history of Christianity is full of them. They have been faithfully recorded by those who had personal knowledge of them, or who received their information from credible witnesses. They occur, in larger or smaller numbers, in every congregation of human beings to which the gospel of Jesus Christ is continuously preached. And, although they belong to the invisible region of the soul, they are made palpable by various means which bring them within the reach of our knowledge. We can look at them in all the phases which they assume, we can trace their progress in the very act of occurrence, we can examine the means which produce them, and we can observe the results in which they issue. If real, these facts must be important. Transformations of human character transcend in interest any transformations of which material substances are capable. The laws which affect the progress of a spirit out of a state of sin into one of holiness, are incomparably more momentous than those which affect the growth of the body or the cure of natural disease. "All the variations of fortune in her wildest caprices, lifting peasants to a throne, and depressing kings to a dungeon, are idle as the changeful shadowings of an evening cloud, when compared with that solitary hour, when He who 'stands at the door and knocks' is first consciously admitted by the loving heart of a repentant believer." "The moral history of a beggar, which faithfully revealed the interior movements of his mind, and laid open the secret causes which contributed to form and determine his character, might enlarge and enlighten the views of a philosopher."

The reader is not asked, however, to accept without question our averment that there are spiritual facts of this order as real as any which occur in the material world, nor do we ask him to accept without question our interpretation of them. The more rigidly men apply lord Bacon's principle of induction to our histories the better. They will thus distinguish between appearances and realities, between accidental resemblances and essential oneness; they will penetrate through the diversities of form which these facts assume, and ascertain for themselves the common principle which pervades them. Only, in doing this, let them remember that they are in a better position than the student of material nature. Their inquiries have been anticipated by a Book which reveals the philosophy they are in search of. This Book describes the spiritual occurrences which take place in the history of man's soul, and is itself the means of their production; and it furnishes criteria, though not formally, by which to distinguish the genuine from the counterfeit. To reject its aid in our investigation were to grope our way through a naturally dark labyrinth, under the guidance of our own senses of sight and touch, when we might traverse its most remote and intricate recesses with the illumination of a bright sun and the direction of an unerring guide.

The divine life—what is it? All things, we know, are, in a sense, divine, because all things are of God. This obvious truth, however, has, by the help of ambiguous language, been worked into a form which, under the guise of beautiful sentiment, strikes at the foundations of religion. Everything that is beautiful or great is freely spoken of as "divine." Genius, especially, is "divine," if not divinity itself, and its possessors are gods. So that there are both divine mountains and divine men. A Divine Being, distinct from all other beings; possessing a nature peculiarly and exclusively his own; himself, by his personal will and power, the creator and supporter of other beings—this is a God that many dreamers will not know or confess. Their divinity is some mystic essence which, unseen and subtle, spreads itself universally, pervades and penetrates the whole creation. It is not exactly light, nor air, nor electricity, nor magnetism; but it is something of the like kind. It is not peculiar to the intellectual and intelligent universe; it belongs to the material as well. So that we may say there is more of divinity in the sunbeam than in the dull clod of the valley, and more in the majestic eagle, which soars in mid-heaven, and gazes in the face of the sun's brightest blaze, than in the earthworm which dwells in the darkness of its native soil.

With some persons the ascription of "divinity" to everything good and great may be nothing more than poetic sentiment, but with others it is the very spirit of atheism; in this polite form, they bow the Creator out of his own universe. To make everything divine, is to make nothing divine; to find essential divinity in everything, a part of everything, or an attribute of everything, is to deprive it of that personal, intelligent, self-conscious, and almighty existence which constitutes Godhead.

The Bible, happily, never exhibits one truth as the antagonist of another, and never so cherishes and exaggerates one truth as to make it destructive of another. According to the apostle Peter, men may be made "partakers of the divine nature;"* but there is no truth more fundamental to Christianity, none of which it takes a firmer grasp, or presents a bolder view, than the existence of a divine nature which is peculiar to one great and glorious Being, to which there is no approximation, and of which there can be no participation. "I am God, and besides me there is none else," are the words in which this great ONE isolates himself from all other beings. He thus draws around himself a circle within which no one else dwells. Beyond this circle there is a universe, immense and various, but it is no part of him—it is only his workmanship. And of his ineffable nature, with its omniscience and omnipotence, neither angels nor men are partakers.

The language of the apostle Peter is at no variance with this first truth. He expounds himself. To be a "partaker of the divine nature," is to have "escaped the corruption that is in the world through lust." And this, too, his "beloved brother Paul also, according to the wisdom given unto him," indicates, when he says that the Father of our spirits chastens us that we may be "partakers of his holiness." On the same authority we are taught that the "new man" which is "after God," or "after the image of God," is "created in righteousness and true holiness." And this "true holiness" is "the glory of the Lord" into

* 2 Peter i. 4.

which Christians are transformed.* To be morally godlike, is to be a "partaker of the divine nature" and of the divine life.

The life of sense which animates the body is a divine life, in that it is the gift of God. The life of intelligence which animates the intellect is, for the same reason, a divine life. And both of them, common as they are, are mysteries which have been hid from past ages, and are not likely to be unveiled to those that are to come. But *the* divine life of which we speak, is something higher and better still. It is the life of godly principle and godly affection in the soul. It is that from which springs "true holiness," and which, when it animates a man, makes him godlike in purity and love.

A divine life, then, is not a figure of speech, but a truth and reality, the highest form of moral existence, whether in beings that tread this earth, or in spirits that people heaven. Without attempting, at present, any further definition of it, we will endeavour to feel our way towards a better knowledge both of what it is and of how it is produced.

* Heb. xii. 10; Eph. iv. 22—24; Col. iii. 9, 10; 2 Cor. iii. 18.

PART THE FIRST.

THE DIVINE LIFE: ITS NATURE.

FACTS.

CONTENTS.—The Religious Faculty—Bechuanas—Heathenism—Mohammedanism — Asceticism — Saul of Tarsus — Luther, Loyola, Latimer, Col. Gardiner, Urquhart, Birrell, Caroline Fry—Conclusions— Quotations from Howe, Bullar, and Butler.

"Every religion is false, which has not for its leading tenet, to adore one God as the first principle of all things; and its moral system, to love one God only and supremely in all things."—PASCAL.

"Any one understanding the real nature of man, must perceive that a true religion ought to be based in our nature; ought to know its greatness and its degradation, and the causes of both the one and the other. What religion but Christianity exhibits such a knowledge as this?"—PASCAL.

"There is a phenomenon in the moral world for which no adequate natural cause has ever yet been assigned,—I mean a great and sudden change of temper and character, brought about under a strong impression of scriptural truths—a change in many cases from habitual vice and malignity to the sweetness and purity of the Christian spirit, and continuing to manifest itself in a new character through life, accompanied, if you will believe the subjects, with new views of God and Christ, and Divine things in general, and with new feelings towards them. . . . Thousands who are not mad, but cool, dispassionate, and wise, the ornaments of society and learning, whose word would be taken in any other case, and who certainly ought to be regarded as competent judges, tell you that they have had opportunity to see both sides, as the revilers of this doctrine have not; that they once looked upon the subject with the eyes of their opponents, but have since seen for themselves, and do assuredly know that there is such a thing as a spiritual change of heart. And what witnesses can you oppose to these? Men who offer mere negative testimony—who can only say, they know of no such thing."—Dr. Edward D. Griffin.

THE DIVINE LIFE:

ITS NATURE.

"We may travel the world," said Plutarch, "and find cities without walls, without letters, without kings, without wealth, without coin, without schools and theatres; but a city without a temple, without worship, without prayers, no one ever saw." These words of the ancient Greek are as true now as they were eighteen centuries ago. The discovery of a new world beyond the Atlantic, and of innumerable islands in the Pacific, has only supplied fresh evidence of the fact that religion, in some form, is the common attribute and possession of mankind. The progress of geography has revealed new modes of civilization and of barbarism, but has not informed us of nations that practise no worship, or at least that have proved incapable of being taught to worship.

The missionary, Robert Moffat, sought in vain, he tells us, to find among the Bechuanas and Bushmen a temple, an altar, or a single emblem of heathen worship. No fragments remained of former days, as mementoes to the present generation, that their ancestors ever loved, served, or reverenced a being greater than man. Their religious system, like those streams in the desert which lose themselves in the sand, had entirely disappeared. And the missionary could make no appeals to legends, or to altars, or to an unknown God. They had faith in a rain-maker, but the missionary does not regard this faith as involving in it any idea of the supernatural.

In these degraded tribes, apparently exceptional to the common rule, and just because they are exceptional, we have what may be regarded as the very best means of an experiment to determine whether the religious faculty is as universal as the rational. They were in a state of ignorance from which was excluded every ray of Divine truth, every notion of Godhead and immortality; were they likewise incapable of apprehending and receiving religious ideas? They were without the knowledge of God—of any god; were they likewise without a capacity to know God? The means were used which should determine this question. The fitting test was applied when the missionary declared to them the being and character of God, and preached to them the facts of the Christian revelation, especially the love of God to man as manifested in the gospel. When thus tested, the Bechuanas awoke from the slumber of generations. Their hearts responded to the appeal. And it was proved that even in their souls there lay unextinguished, though unexercised, the most distinctive character of humanity, the faculty of knowing, loving and serving God. Many of them are now enlightened and spiritual worshippers of the Most High.

Admitting the universal existence of the religious faculty, it becomes a question of great interest how it is to be exercised in order to the divine life in a man's soul. The Chinese worship their ancestors. The Hindoos reckon their gods by hundreds of millions. One half of the human race are pantheists, who confound nature with its God and Maker. These have not attained to the knowledge which even the Sunday-school child receives from the first verse of the Bible —"In the beginning God created the heavens and the earth." The "beginning" of the heavens and the earth is, in their imagination, as ancient as the beginning of God himself. A personal God, distinct from the creation, and not its soul or animating principle—eternal, intelligent, and self-conscious—has no place in their faith. And pantheism either descends into atheism, as in the case of cold-hearted speculators, or grows into polytheism, and, ascribing divinity to every part and attribute of nature, worships all outward things, from the reptile that crawls on the earth, to the sun that shines in the heavens. From this spirit, so rife in both ancient and modern heathendom, Mohammedanism strongly recoils, and builds itself on the doctrine of one living invisible God who doeth all things after the counsel of his eternal will. Christianity associates the doctrine of one living personal God with his incarnation in *Jesus Christ, and the* atoning death which Christ endured on the cross. Now, we would inquire, May the divine life be produced indifferently by all these systems?

If the life of God in the soul consisted in the mere fervent exercise of the religious faculty, we should answer this question in the affirmative. There is no object of worship that has ever been named, which has not had power to excite the fervour of its votaries. The ancient Egyptians, twenty centuries ago, crowding along the sacred Nile, seven hundred thousand in number, according to Herodotus, to the festival of the cat-headed Bubastis; the modern Hindoos, hasting from all parts of India to their holy city, Benares, to worship its sacred bulls, and wash in its sacred river;

the followers of Mohammed going on pilgrimage from all lands to Mecca; the so-called followers of Jesus Christ, of the Greek and Roman rites, rushing down the banks of the Jordan on Easter-day, and plunging themselves into its waters—have this in common, that their religious practices are honoured with the utmost fervour of their nature. But it is a fervour which is compatible with the profoundest ignorance, and with a moral condition so low and debased, that those who have the means of knowing it, frequently decline to inform the world what they have seen and heard.

Sincerity in religion is often indolently regarded as having power to cover both a multitude of errors, and a multitude of sins. And if sincerity be fanned into earnestness, it is a popular theory that it may dispense with the element of religion altogether, and that, even if it does, the earnest man is the great man to whom all others of mortal form are to render homage. This principle will not only place superstition, enthusiasm, and fanaticism, side by side with enlightened piety, as equally forms of the divine life, but will exalt Satan himself to a throne from which he may lawfully claim our worship. There is, perhaps, not a more earnest created being in the universe than he. He knows and believes much of the most important truth, but hates it all with an intensity of which man is not capable. What the absolute amount of his power is we do not know, but we know that his energies are in constant and restless action. Let it be indifferent whether earnestness be associated with purity or impurity, benevolence or malevolence, and it will not diminish the devil's claims to honour, that he is earnestly engaged in works of dishonour to God and ruin to man; it would be our duty to admire him as truly great, and to protest against the bad opinion which is commonly entertained of his character. But our moral sense revolts against a theory which leads to such conclusions.

In feeling our way to a true notion of the divine life, we may dismiss from our thoughts all the systems which are condemned in the law—"Thou shalt not make unto thee any graven image, or any likeness of any thing that is in heaven above, or that is in the earth beneath, or that is in the water under the earth: thou shalt not bow down thyself to them, nor serve them."* "Graven images" may have been originally the symbols of divine attributes, and, even when the popular mind had become so debased and ignorant as to regard them as in themselves divinities, there may have been in most countries a select few who maintained in secret the knowledge and belief that they were only symbols. But whether regarded as symbolical or as properly divine, their worship is incompatible with just conceptions of the Godhead.

Historically, indeed, we know nothing of idolatry as a pure symbolical system. It has existed, and still exists, only as a gross materialism, the worship of outward things, which were held to be, not representative of divine attributes, but possessed of them. "That men should have worshipped their poor fellow man as a god, and not him only, but stocks and stones, and all manner of animate and inanimate objects; and fashioned for themselves such a distracted chaos of hallucinations by way of theory of the universe—all this looks like an incredible fable. Nevertheless, it is a clear fact that they did it."

The refined and learned Greeks were "fools" in

* Exod. xx. 4, 5.

this matter equally with the most ignorant and barbarous people; at least, so thought the apostle Paul. He regarded the heathen, not as children giving expression to infantine and immature conceptions of God in visible forms, but as the inheritors of a deep degeneracy which had originated in the aversion of men to the true character and rule of the Eternal and Holy One. He could not but remark the contrast between their intellectual and religious condition. Their oratory, and poetry, and architecture, showed genius and advancement. But their religion! Within temples, whose glory, as works of art, is not yet forgotten, he found altars, on which burned incense to the meanest reptiles, or to the mere image of wood or stone. And, bending in prostrate homage before those altars, he saw men, the fame of whose genius is still fresh in the world. They were no children, but men of mighty and cultivated intellect. And Paul found in their worship, not the strivings of great and uninstructed souls to realize all that is godlike in man and nature, but the blindness and fatuity which our moral apostasy from our Maker has inflicted on mankind.

History has preserved one specimen of the way in which this great apostle of truth argued with educated idolaters the great question of the spirituality of the Godhead. Standing on Mars' Hill among the assembled philosophers and areopagites of Athens, he quoted the saying of one of their own poets—"We are the offspring of God"—a saying which involves the scriptural idea that man is made in the image of God, and, consequently, that there is a God other and higher than man's hands can fashion. "Forasmuch then," argued Paul, "as we are the offspring of God, we ought not to think that the Godhead is like unto gold, or silver, or stone, graven by art or man's device."* It can be only in our spiritual nature that we are the offspring of God. The Godhead, man's Father, the Father of man's spirit, must therefore be spiritual, and can only be dishonoured and misrepresented by an image of gold or silver, or wood or stone. The apostle took hold of the highest and purest religious sentiment which was to be found in the literature of Greece to strike at the root of the popular worship. The sentiment was rare even among the poets. Paul could have drawn from their writings descriptions of gods and goddesses, the very recital of which might have covered his learned audience with shame. But he wisely availed himself of the saying of Aratus, to lift their thoughts to sublimer and truer conceptions of the Godhead, and addressed himself, not to the masses who practically regarded the graven image as itself a god, but to the learned assembly then before him, who might be supposed to regard the image as only the likeness or symbol of a divinity that was unseen. But even this higher and more refined theory Paul did not regard as capable of producing or sustaining a true divine life. "I perceive that in all things ye are very much given to religion," he said—for such is the meaning of his words. Their religiousness was excessive. It was in active and fervent and constant exercise. "When any public calamity was not removed by the invocation of the gods known to the laws, it was customary to let the victims loose into the fields, or along the public ways, and wherever they stopped there to sacrifice them to the 'propitious unknown god.'" But Paul was not content. The religiousness of Athens had not the

* Acts xvii. 22—31.

enlightenment and guidance of truth in its exercise, and possessed no power to purify those whose breasts it filled. It was not the divine life. And the apostle preached to them not new and better gods than their own, but THE ONLY ONE GOD, who giveth to all life, and breath, and all things.

There is one species of idolatry which stands forth as of a somewhat higher order than all others. The Persians erected neither statues, temples, nor altars, but regarded them with contempt: for, as we are told by Herodotus, they did not believe, like the Greeks, that the gods had human forms. The name of Zeus (or Jupiter) they applied to the entire vault of heaven. They sacrificed to the sun and moon, to the earth, fire, water, and the winds. And who can wonder that these men of the east, having once ceased to retain God in their knowledge, should fall down and worship as the Supreme, that Sun whose face was hidden from them by the excess and splendour of his light? Not the work of their own hands, not their weak fellow, they saw in him the very type of majesty, sublimity, and glory, the nearest approximation to ubiquity, and a power to both curse and bless, before which it was natural to stand in awe. And if their thoughts were still earthly, and if they as well as other idolaters, sought the living among the dead, and the infinite among the finite, we cannot charge them with the grossness and absurdity of worshipping gold, and wood, and stone. Still it was the creature, and not the Creator, these Persians worshipped, and in such worship their souls found no divine life.

When we cut off the vast domains of idol worship, we greatly circumscribe the limits within which we are to look for the divine life. We have to do now only with those systems whose central doctrine is the unity, and spirituality, and invisibility of God. But we cannot assume that even all these systems are capable of producing or fostering the true life of God in the human soul. It may be, for aught we can determine beforehand, that most or all of them are mixed with elements that not only do not produce it, but are fatal to its existence. For instance, it is possible to conceive of a god—one, spiritual and invisible—that is malignant, and that delights in wrong and suffering. The state of mind which the worship of such a god will produce, must be essentially different from that which is produced by the worship of the God of love. In each case the maxim will be found true, "Like God, like worshipper." And the mental opposites thus produced cannot be alike the divine life.

But even where there is no distinct apprehension of God as malignant, the truth may be associated with errors either in the way of excess or of defect, that shall effectually prevent its proper action on the soul. "A knowledge of God is found," says Mr. Isaac Taylor, "to avail little apart from the knowledge of ourselves; and unless some genuine emotions of contrition have broken down the pride of the heart, the abstract truth of the Divine unity seems only to inflame our arrogance, and to prepare us to be inexorable and cruel. So it was in the system of Mohammed; it had no true philanthropy, because it had no humiliation, no penitence, and no method of propitiation. The Koran does indeed teach and inspire a profound reverence toward God; and it has actually produced among its adherents, and in an eminent degree, that prostration of the soul in the presence of the Supreme Being which becomes rational creatures. But at this point it stops: Moslem humiliation has no tears, and as it does not reach the depths of a heartfelt repentance, so neither is it cheered by that gratitude which springs from the consciousness of pardon. No sluices of sorrow are opened by its devotions; the affections are not softened; there is a feverish heat among the passions; but no moisture. Faith and confidence toward God are bold rather than submissive, and the soul of the believer, basking in the presumption of the Divine favour, might be compared to the scorched Arabian desert, arid as it is, and unproductive, and liable to be heaved into billows by the hurricane."

"All religious history," says the same author, "may be appealed to in attestation of this averment, that the Christian doctrine of the forgiveness of sins is the only one which has ever generated an efficacious and tender-spirited philanthropy. It is this doctrine, and no other, that brings into combination the sensitiveness and the zeal necessary to the vigour of practical good-will toward our fellow-men. Exclude this truth, as it is excluded by sceptical philosophy, and then philanthropy becomes vapid matter of theory and meditation. Distort it with the church of Rome, and the zeal of charity is exchanged for the rancour of proselytism. Quash it, as the Koran does, and there springs up in the bosoms of men a hot and active intolerance. The Christian, and he alone, is expansively and assiduously compassionate; and this not merely because he has been formally enjoined to perform the seven works of mercy, but because his own heart has been softened throughout its very substance; because tears have become a usage of his moral life; and because he has obtained a vivid consciousness of that

Divine compassion, rich and free, which sheds beams of hope upon all mankind."

There may have been a period in the mental history of Mohammed, a period of meditation and fermentation, when the presentation of a New Testament, or the exhibition of a pure Christianity in a practical form, might have saved him from those delusions by which he deceived first himself and then others, and have made him an apostle of Christ with no sword but that of the Spirit. And it is certain that, however much of imposture was mingled with his pretensions, Mohammed "kindled, from side to side of the eastern world, an extraordinary abhorrence of idol worship, and actually cleansed the plains of Asia from the long-settled impurities of polytheism." But it is equally certain that he failed to awaken in himself, or in his followers, a divine life, if that life involves in it the elements of humility and love, and does not consist in a tyrannous, burning, and malignant fanaticism.

Nor can we regard all the religiousness that is found within Christendom, and which possesses some Christian element, as necessarily constituting a divine life. The mere formalist who says his prayers at certain times, and at all other times forgets that there is a God, and the devout man who gives to God his heart, and does it in the market-place as well as in the closet; the Italian bandit who goes forth to rapine and murder, and returns to his unhallowed cave to give thanks to the virgin Mary for his successes, and the humble, honest, hard-working man who acknowledges the kindness of Providence in the driest crust upon his table, and confides in the love of that Saviour to whom he has entrusted the most precious interests of his soul; the self-righteous Pharisee who proudly thanks God that he is better than other men, and the penitent publican who dares not lift his eyes to heaven, but cries, "God be merciful to me a sinner;" the bitter, relentless persecutor, whose eyes glare with the lustre of hatred while he applies his torch to the fagots that are to consume his victim, and the martyr, fastened to the stake, with love to his enemies in his heart and prayer for their forgiveness on his lips; these cannot be spiritually one. They may bear the Christian name in common, but in real character they are separated from each other as far as the east is distant from the west.

There is one species of religiousness which has prevailed much under a Christian form, as well as under others, and which has made large pretensions to be the divinest life of all—we mean the ascetic. The description which Cowper gives of the life of a monk, and his argument on its true character, are sufficient for our present purpose:—

"His dwelling a recess in some rude rock;
Book, beads, and maple-dish, his meagre stock;
In shirt of hair and weeds of canvass dressed,
Girt with a bell-rope that the Pope has blessed;
Adust with stripes told out for every crime,
And sore tormented long before his time.

His works, his abstinence, his zeal allow'd,
You think him humble—God accounts him proud.
High in demand, though lowly in pretence,
Of all his conduct this the genuine sense—
My penitential stripes, my streaming blood,
Have purchased heaven, and prove my title good."

The inspired records of Christianity make no reference to asceticism except to condemn it. The apostle Paul speaks of the "neglecting of the body" as "having a show of wisdom."* It was one of "the command-

* Col. ii. 18, 23.

ments and doctrines of men" against which he solemnly warned the church of Christ. It had originated in one of the vain philosophies of the east, which taught that the present world had derived its existence from two causes or principles, the one good and the other evil. The former was identified with light, or was regarded as its parent and the parent of spirit. The latter was identified with darkness, or was regarded as its parent and the parent of all matter. Matter was, therefore, essentially evil, and the inference was direct that the salvation of man involved in it the mortification of his material frame, if not its ultimate destruction. This theory insinuated itself, even in the days of the apostles, into the modes of thinking and feeling among Christians, and at a later period acquired an almost universal ascendency. "The voluntary (or artificial) humiliations—the worshipping of angels—the sanctimonious abstinences—the human traditions—the specious piety, and the idle tormenting of the body; in a word, all the elements of the great apostasy are designated by Paul in the most distinct manner; or as if the many-coloured corruptions of the tenth century had vividly passed before the eye of the writer. How healthy is that piety and that morality which he recommends in opposition to all such absurdities!"

The practices which the spirit of asceticism has generated in the Christian church, have not been more salutary, morally, than those to which it has given rise in heathendom. "Turn eastward now"—we resume the quotation from Cowper:—

"Turn eastward now, and fancy shall apply
To your weak sight her telescopic eye.
The Bramin kindles on his own bare head
The sacred fire, self-torturing his trade.

His voluntary pains, severe and long,
Would give a barbarous air to British song;
No grand inquisitor could worse invent,
Than he contrives to suffer well content.

"Which is the saintlier worthy of the two?
Past all dispute, yon anchorite, say you.
Your sentence and mine differ. What's a name?
I say the Bramin has the fairer claim.
If suffering Scripture nowhere recommends,
Devised by self to answer selfish ends,
Give saintship, then all Europe must agree,
Ten starveling hermits suffer less than he."*

Saul of Tarsus; born about B. C. 2; died A. D. 66.

But let us now see whether we may not find a historical example of the true divine life. The name of SAUL of TARSUS, PAUL the APOSTLE, is familiar to us as a household word, and presents itself at once, as one which exhibits a most instructive instance; first, of a spurious religiousness, and then of a true divine life. It furnishes a test of the fictitious and the genuine. And we have only to study the very complete portrait which he has drawn of himself to have a good understanding of both.

* The following statement is from the pen of an East Indian missionary in 1854. "On approaching a ghât leading down to the river, a miserable object arrested our attention. It was a devotee seated by the embers of a slow fire. His right arm presented a sickening spectacle. It was erect over his head, and was shockingly emaciated. The hand was closed, but the nails of the fingers stretched beyond it five or six inches. In this erect position the limb had remained rigidly fixed for eleven years, and by this act of self-mortification the wretched man vainly hoped to be saved.

"On descending the steps we passed another devotee, who was standing with one foot on the ground and the other on a swing raised from two to three feet high. Here he stands night and day. He shifts his feet occasionally, and thus prevents the two limbs from becoming immovable. He never lies down, nor obtains rest or sleep except such as he can obtain here. Both these victims of idolatry imagined that by such practices of asceticism they would acquire boundless merit, so that their sins would be forgiven and themselves admitted into heaven."

Though born in Tarsus, and familiar from childhood with heathen spectacles, Saul, the son of a Jew who was a "Pharisee of the Pharisees," was brought up from his twelfth or thirteenth year amid the associations of the holy city, and under the tuition of one who could appreciate his ingenuous, bold, and inquiring disposition. He read the history of his fathers, the most wonderful that has ever been lived or written, in the very streets of Jerusalem, in the hills whereon it stood, and in the valleys by which it was intersected and surrounded. And his susceptible heart was subjected, probably for twenty years, to the influence of these scenes; while his active mind gave all its energy to the study of the Scriptures, and of the traditional interpretation of them, of which Gamaliel was the expounder. We have his own testimony that he outstripped his cotemporaries in the school of Gamaliel in zeal for the traditions of the elders, and in the knowledge of that Judaism which was more traditional than biblical.

Saul comes before us historically first, in connection with the stoning of Stephen, the proto-martyr of the Christian church. He gave his "vote" against this early confessor of the Christian faith; being, not improbably, already a member of the sanhedrim. And we are at once struck by the contrast which he now presents to his preceptor. "Refrain from these men," Gamaliel had said a few weeks or months before, "and let them alone: for if this counsel or this work be of men, it will come to nought: but if it be of God, ye cannot overthrow it; lest haply ye be found even to fight against God." But Saul was "exceeding mad" against the followers of Jesus, and "made havoc of the church." Whether the contrast is simply that between prudent age and impetuous youth, or that between a timid worldly policy and a fearless godly zeal, or that between the large and liberal views of a far-reaching mind and the bitter intolerance of an honest but unenlightened spirit; or whether it is simply a matter of constitutional temperament, it is only such as often appears between master and disciple. If in nothing else, yet in practical zeal for the Judaism which Saul had learned from Gamaliel, the disciple in this instance excelled the master as he did his fellow-disciples.

Having done his utmost in Jerusalem, Saul hastened to Damascus to execute a mission of destruction there. But he entered the Syrian capital a very different man from what he was when he left the capital of Judea. He was now a new man; no longer a Pharisee, but a Christian. The most obvious difference between the old man and the new is, that the old man disbelieved the claims of Jesus of Nazareth to be honoured as the Messiah; the new believed in them implicitly. And so far it may be called a change of opinion, his old opinions having been held as honestly as his new. But we shall find that with this change of opinion, there was an entire revolution in the moral habit of his soul—a revolution which is best expressed in his own words—"If any man be in Christ, he is a new creature; old things are passed away; behold, all things are become new." Before his conversion to Christianity he was a fanatic of the highest order. The fervid passion which filled his breast was one of malignant and murderous hatred. The passion which filled his breast after his conversion, and which impelled him from shore to shore to preach Christ, was equally fervid; but it was one of pure, intense, and unwearied love. And herein consists the difference between fanaticism and piety. Before his conversion he was proud, stood erect before God, as one that was blameless touching the righteousness which the law, as he then understood it, required of him; after his conversion, and in all his subsequent life, there is no trait of his character more marked than the deep humility with which he prostrated his soul before God; and that not merely as a creature conscious of his littleness, but as a transgressor of the Divine law, conscious of his sins. To some this change in the hidden man of the heart may seem a small thing; but they who have any insight into the springs of action, and can appreciate the leavening power of hatred and pride on the one hand, and of love and humility on the other, will require no justification of Paul's words—"Old things are passed away; behold, all things are become new."

But yet there are several characteristics of the earlier religion of Saul of Tarsus which may seem to raise it to the honour of a divine life. His morals were blameless. His "manner of life from his youth" was such as to bear the scrutiny of the most keen-eyed malice. There were no youthful follies or indiscretions whose memories could be raked from the dust to dishonour him. His time and thoughts had been engrossed by his studies and his religious duties. More than this, he was not only virtuous, but, in a sense, godly. His religion was no heartless formalism; he was "zealous towards God." And the God toward whom he was moved with zeal was not such a deity as the fanatical populace of Ephesus were zealous for when they shouted, "Great is Diana of the Ephesians;" it was the One, True, Everlasting; the Jehovah of the Old Testament, in whom we live, and move, and have our being. Shall we then deny the credit of a divine life to one whose virtue is blameless, and whose heart is the seat of a burning zeal for God?

Let us hear his own judgment on this question: "I was a blasphemer, and a persecutor, and injurious." True, his apologist may reply, you blasphemed, you spoke evil of a name which you conscientiously regarded as identified with false pretensions. True, you persecuted those who believed in that name, but you did it with a good conscience; you verily thought with yourself that you ought to do it, and in doing it you sincerely imagined that you were doing God service. True, you were injurious; but if the sect of the Nazarenes were what you judged it to be, that would be no reproach; the more injury you inflicted on it the better. The worst that can be said of you, Paul, is that you were too hasty in your judgment, and yielded too readily to the impetuosity of your nature; even if your opinion of the Nazarenes were correct, it would have been wiser to have followed the counsel of Gamaliel, and to have "let them alone," for a season at least, that it might be seen whether their doctrine were of men or of God; but as it is, even your failings leaned to virtue's side; it was the fire of a true godliness that burned on the altar of your heart, and all that you have to reproach yourself for is an error of judgment.

To this apology Paul's only reply is severely brief and conclusive: "I was the chief of sinners." Many others have described themselves in the same words, and in his case as well as in theirs, the words may not imply an absolute supremacy in guilt, but a deep consciousness of such guilt as one can scarcely imagine to exist, where he cannot see it as he sees the evil that is in his own bosom. We accept this interpretation, and do not account that Paul meant to say, that of all the sinners that have ever trodden this earth he was absolutely the greatest. But at the least he meant to say that, religious as he was in some sense, earnestly religious as he was, his early life was exceeding sinful; his opposition to the name and followers of Christ was deeply criminal. But how could that be? It is true that he cursed the name of Jesus, that he pronounced on it all the anathemas of the law and of Jewish tradition; and the rude insolence of those who spat on the face of the Son of God and buffeted him, was in reality nothing to the malignity with which he pursued it. But then he acted in unbelief, and his unbelief sprang from ignorance; had he known the Lord of glory, he would have worshipped and served him.

At this point the question arises, whether his ignorance was innocent or criminal. So far as a man does not possess the means of knowledge, he cannot be accountable for the want of it. But if a man's ignorance result from his neglect of means or from an indisposition to receive the truth, he must be held responsible before God. Now where was Saul of Tarsus all those years that Jesus taught and wrought mighty works in the synagogues and cities of Judea and Galilee? Was he still in the school of Gamaliel, so intent on the study of the traditions of the fathers, that he knew nothing of the great and wonderful things that were taking place at his very door, and that were moving the heart of his nation to its inmost depths? Or had he gone to Tarsus to live with his kindred, and to exercise the functions of a rabbi in a foreign synagogue? We cannot tell. He may, or he may not have seen the face of Jesus, radiant as it ever was with love, or heard from his lips the words of a higher wisdom than Gamaliel ever uttered, or witnessed some of those miracles which declared him to be the Son of God. But the works of Jesus were not done in a corner, and it might be said to Saul, "Art thou only a stranger in Jerusalem, and hast not known the things which are come to pass there in these days?" He could not fail to know enough to impose on him the obligation of inquiry. Public report might be very imperfect; but even its tales, distorted as they were, contained presumptive evidence that Jesus of Nazareth was a teacher sent from God; and the heart in which there was no secret or sinful disinclination to the truth of God, would long to know whether God was not about to redeem his people. Christ has told us the issue of a single-minded and unbiassed inquiry—"If any man will do his (the Father's) will, he shall know of the doctrine, whether it be of God, or whether I speak of myself."

But what evil bias, or other moral cause of error, could there have been in the heart of one so conscientious and so zealous towards God, as was Saul of Tarsus? We need not imagine any other than that which was common to his countrymen, intensified, perhaps, by his constitutional earnestness. "I bear them record," he wrote many years after his conversion, "that they have a zeal of God, but not according to knowledge. For they being ignorant of God's righteousness, and going about to establish their own righteousness, have not submitted themselves unto the righteousness of God. For Christ is the end of the law for righteousness to every one that believeth."* Saul, and his countrymen in general, felt a proud confidence in the Divine call by which they were separated from the nations, and in their descent from Abraham, and were ignorant of their own deep sinfulness before God. Their self-love and earthliness veiled from them the purity and spirituality of the moral law under which they were placed. And no wonder that, thus blinded and ignorant, they laboured to establish a ground of their own whereon they might stand just before God, and resented and repelled a teaching whose faintest whispers were sufficient to forewarn them that, when fully known, it would humble them in the dust.

But those states of mind to which we thus ascribe the ignorance of the Jews—pride, self-love, and earthliness—are in themselves criminal. The "lusts" which unconverted men "fulfil" include "the desires of the flesh and of *the mind*"—an expression on which some light may be thrown by certain words that are used by the apostle James. He speaks of a wisdom which cometh not down from above, but is "earthly, sensual, devilish."† The devil's sins are very different in kind from those that are committed by the felons and fornicators of this world, and yet he may be denominated, without reserve, "the chief of sinners." His sins are pride and hatred, and those courses hostile to God and man to which these evil passions drive him. Pharisaism was commonly earthly and sensual; but above all it was—(and if the expression seem too strong, we plead the authority of the apostle James) it was devilish; its prevailing characters were pride and hatred.

* Rom. x. 2—4. † James iii. 15.

One almost trembles to carry this thought to its legitimate conclusion; but we must. Who then, of all mankind is likest to the devil? Not the man who wallows in the mire of sensuality—for that the devil cannot do—but he who is most proud and most full of hatred to God and man, whose intellect rebels most fiercely against God's truth, and whose heart is most opposed to God's will. The "chief of sinners" among mankind are not the tenants of gaols and penitentiaries, but those who most resemble the first sinner in "fulfilling the desires of the mind."

When Paul knew himself and understood the law of God, he did not plead, in arrest of judgment on his character, that his morals were blameless in all the social relations of life, that he was sincere in all his religious duties, yea, that in his most violent proceedings against the name of Jesus, he was moved by zeal for God. His charge against himself was not that he was all the time unenlightened;—the mere absence of knowledge would not have made him the chief of sinners;—nor was it that his best doings were imperfect and mixed with sin; it was virtually that in him there had dwelt no good thing, that the root and spring of his then spiritual life was unmixed evil. He had no outward criminalities to palliate and no hypocrisy to be ashamed of. But now that the light of God's law and love had shone upon his soul, he saw that he was filled with spiritual pride and self-righteousness, and consequent hatred to the true will of God. And now he was not less disposed than the publican in our Lord's parable, to smite upon his breast and exclaim, "God be merciful to me a sinner."

On either side of the great crisis by which the

history of the Pharisee is separated from the history of the Christian in Saul of Tarsus, we find several things that are common to both—outward virtue, entire sincerity, a certain zeal for God, and constitutional ardour. But these, springing from the soil of Pharisaism, inspired and impelled by its pride and selfishness, produced only a bitter fanaticism; springing from the soil of Christianity, inspired and impelled by its humility and love, they were the manifestations and instruments of a pure divine life.

The nature of the crisis itself, in which the Pharisaism of Saul perished and his Christianity was born, will instruct us further in the difference between a spurious religiousness and a true piety. The outward prodigies which accompanied it are well known. The young rabbi, fresh from the school of Gamaliel, with less worldly wisdom than his master, or less breadth and comprehensiveness of view, or whatever else it was, was hasting to Damascus, in an agony of soul, to destroy the followers of that Jesus whom they affirmed to be alive and in glory. When the towers and gardens of the great city burst upon his view, he was without misgiving or mental conflict in reference to the purpose of his journey. His victims seemed already in his hand, when suddenly there shone round about him a light of unearthly brightness, transcending the glare of the noontide sun. "To his fellow-travellers nothing more was vouchsafed than the perception of a supernatural splendour and sound coming from the heavens, yet for himself there stood forth in the midst of the brightness a personal form, and the sound shaped itself into distinct words in the Hebrew tongue." And the words were, "Saul, Saul, why persecutest thou me?" The central point of the whole inner being of Saul up to this moment was the conviction that he ought to persecute unto the death what he regarded as an impious sect. And "precisely on this centre do the words of Jesus strike like a thunderbolt." "Saul might, he had thought, well hope to receive the blessing and approbation of God on his holy work, and now behold it is accursed! He is apprized that his supposed zeal for Jehovah the Lord of heaven was in fact a zeal against the Lord of heaven, for with his own ears, and in his inmost soul, he hears that the Lord of heaven is Jesus of Nazareth. In the disciples of Jesus he had hitherto seen the enemies of Jehovah, the schismatics who blasphemed and sought to overthrow the law and the sanctuary; and now he is constrained to hear, and could not withdraw from the sound of the words that penetrated his very inmost soul, declaring that these supposed enemies of Jehovah were so wonderfully and intimately associated with the Lord of heaven that he speaks of them not merely as his people, or his, but so identifies himself with them, although gleaming in the light of heaven and casting to the earth all that opposes itself, he yet designates as his own the sufferings inflicted on those who acknowledged him."

All that the history informs us of the immediate result of the vision and words of Jesus on the mind of Saul, is the fact of the unreserved surrender of himself to that Lord who had thus marvellously arrested him: "Lord, what wilt thou have me to do?"

The humbled man rose from the earth, and, finding himself actually "blinded by excess of light," he was led by the hand, gentle as a lamb, into the city which he expected to have entered as a very lion. And there "he was three days without sight, and neither did eat nor drink." Whether his abstinence was entire or partial, whether it was the voluntary expression of his soul's humiliation, or resulted from a physical indisposition to food, produced by mental agitation, we know not. But these three sightless days spent in solitude and silence, were spiritually the most eventful and important of his life. While outward vision was denied him, his prayer was doubtless like that of the blind poet of a later age :—

> "So much the rather Thou, celestial Light,
> Shine inward, and the mind through all her powers
> Irradiate; there plant eyes, all mist from thence
> Purge and disperse, that I may see and tell
> Of things invisible to mortal sight."

And God, who commanded the light to shine out of darkness, shone in his heart, to give him the light of the knowledge of his glory in the face of Jesus Christ. This is not our conjecture, but his own statement. Writing to the churches of Galatia many years after, he said, "I certify you, brethren, that the gospel which was preached of me is not after man. For I neither received it of man, neither was I taught it, but by the revelation of Jesus Christ. . . . When it pleased God, who separated me from my mother's womb, and called me by his grace, to reveal his Son in me, that I might preach him among the heathen; immediately I conferred not with flesh and blood."*

The period of this "calling" by the grace of God, and of that "revelation" which was made to him by Jesus Christ without the intervention of any human teacher, is identified in the passage from which we quote with his first stay at Damascus. It was then, and especially during those three days which preceded

* Gal. i. 11, 12, 15, 16.

the visit of Ananias, that Saul was "called," by the grace of God, and infallibly taught by Christ himself that gospel which he ever afterwards preached among the Gentiles. We cannot describe the fermentation of his thoughts when Old Testament Scriptures crowded into his mind in their new and true light. We cannot follow his inner man step by step in its progress out of the kingdom of Satan into the kingdom of God's dear Son. The veil has not been withdrawn from those dark mysterious struggles through which Saul passed in his new birth; but enough has been intimated to enable us to discern the secret which it shrouds. The law of Moses had been the end and aim of all his thoughts and efforts, and now that which, measured by that standard as he understood it, he had held to be the best and holiest course, had been branded as an impious crime.* Had he then really not understood that which had been the subject of so much study and the object of so fervent a devotion? His startled soul must have cast an anxious glance at the law, and then it must have been clear to him that hitherto he had only looked upon the curtains, but had never penetrated the sanctuary itself. It had happened unto him, as unto the sect of the Pharisees generally, who with their prejudices and additions had made void its holy meaning, who had taken the outward things of the law to be its most essential requirements, while they lightly regarded its great commands which were directed to the heart. But now at length he becomes aware that the law is not satisfied with works of outward righteousness, but demands a temper pure and free from evil desires. The brief com-

* Several thoughts and sentences in this paragraph are taken in substance from Baumgarten on the Acts of the Apostles, vol. i. 228.

mandment, "Thou shalt not covet," now became to him so highly significant, that by occasion of it he discerned the true nature of the law as spiritual, and of sin as having its seat in the heart.* While his soul confronted these discoveries of the true import and requirements of the Divine law, he became conscious of the intense opposition of his self-will to the will of God; and at the same time he felt himself a dead man, for "Cursed is every one that continueth not in all things which are written in the book of the law to do them." The conclusion was inevitable that by the deeds of the law no flesh could be justified before God. And now for the first time Saul's eyes were opened to the chasm that yawned between him and God; for himself, he feels that he is lying at the bottom of the abyss, but Jehovah he beholds at the immeasurable height of his heavenly holiness. How shall man be just with God?

The answer to this question was given to Paul, "not by man, but by the revelation of Jesus Christ." He who knew no sin was made sin for us, that we might be made the righteousness of God in him: Christ hath redeemed us from the curse of the law, being made a curse for us: We are justified freely by the grace of God, through the redemption that is in Christ Jesus, whom God hath set forth to be a propitiation through faith in his blood, to declare his righteousness for the remission of sins: that he might be just, and the justifier of him who believeth in Jesus. These sayings are taken from three of the Epistles of Paul,† and the doctrine which they embody is the very life-blood of the gospel which he preached

* Rom. vii. 7.

† 2 Cor. v. 21; Gal. iii. 13; Rom. iii. 24—26.

among all nations. And such was the importance which he attached to it, that when certain teachers led the Galatians, not indeed to deny it, but to add to it what he regarded in essence inconsistent with it (namely, the doctrine of the necessity of certain rites in order to acceptance with God), he denounced the compound as "another gospel, which is not another."*

It was in those sad, sightless days which Saul spent at Damascus that the doctrine of an atonement by the death of the Son of God, and of the free pardon of sin through that atonement, shone into his mind by the "revelation of Jesus Christ," and immediately he counted as loss those things which heretofore he had deemed his gain—his pure Hebrewism, his earnest Pharisaism, his moral and ritual blamelessness—and cast away all his confidence in them that he might be found in Christ, not having on his own righteousness, but that which is by the faith of Christ.†

This gospel was the means of a two-fold deliverance to his soul; it removed the burden of guilt which oppressed his conscience, and at the same time slew the pride and self-will of his heart. Being justified by faith, he had peace with God through his Lord Jesus Christ. He was a new man. Henceforward the love of Christ constrained him to live not unto himself, but unto him who had died for him. And we know how zealous for God, how tender towards man, that love made him. The divine life, as he now experienced it, cannot be better described than in his own words:—"We are the circumcision—the true Israel and church of God—which worship God in the spirit, and rejoice in Christ Jesus, and have no con-

* Gal. i. 6, 7.

† Phil. iii. 4, 9.

fidence in the flesh." "God hath not given us the spirit of fear; but of power, and of love, and of a sound mind."*

At the distance of more than fourteen centuries from the time of Paul, there was born in Germany one whose name is only less widely known than his, and in whose inner history we find a remarkable re-acting of the experiences through which the apostle passed into the enjoyment of the divine life. The plains of Mansfeldt and the banks of the Vipper were the scenes of the earliest sports and activities of MARTIN LUTHER. During the earliest years of his life his parents were very poor. They were worthy and virtuous people, but their domestic discipline was severe. On one occasion Martin's mother whipped him for a mere trifle till the blood came. And at school the poor child was treated with equal severity. His master flogged him fifteen times in one day. "It is right," said Luther, relating this fact, "it is right to punish children, but, at the same time, we must *love* them." With such an education Luther early learned to despise the attractions of a self-indulgent life.†

Martin Luther; born at Eisleben, November 10th, 1483; died at the same place, February 17th, 1546.

Martin was taught in the school of Mansfeldt, the heads of the Catechism, the Ten Commandments, the Apostles' Creed, and the Lord's Prayer, with some other forms of prayer and some hymns. But the only religious feeling which he manifested at this time was fear. Every time he heard Christ spoken of he turned

* Phil. iii. 3; 2 Tim. i. 7.

† In this sketch we follow mainly the narrative of D'Aubigné.

pale with terror, for he had been represented to him only as an angry Judge. This servile fear is far removed from true religion.

John Luther, in conformity with his predilections, resolved to make his son a scholar, and sent him, when fourteen years old, to the school of the Franciscans at Magdeburg. Martin's life at Magdeburg was a severe apprenticeship. Without friends or protectors, he trembled in the presence of his masters, and in his play hours he and some children, as poor as himself, with difficulty begged their bread. It was the same afterwards at Eisenach, where he was obliged to go with his schoolfellows and sing in the streets to earn a morsel of bread—a custom which still exists in many towns in Germany. Often the poor, modest boy, instead of bread, received nothing but harsh words. More than once, overwhelmed with sorrow, he shed many tears in secret, and he could not look to the future without trembling.

One day in particular, after having been repulsed from three houses, he was about to return fasting to his lodgings, when having reached the Place St. George, he stood before the house of an honest burgher, motionless, and lost in painful reflections. Must he, for want of bread, give up his studies, and go and work with his father in the mines of Mansfeldt? Providence had something else for him to do. The wife of Conrad Cotta had more than once remarked young Martin at church, and had been affected by the sweetness of his voice and his apparent devotion. She heard the harsh words with which the poor scholar had been repulsed. She saw him overwhelmed with sorrow before her door, came to his assistance, beckoned him to enter, and supplied his wants.

Under the roof of this good Shunammite, Luther found a home. And here he enjoyed a tranquil existence, exempt from care and want; his mind became more calm, his disposition more cheerful, and his heart more enlarged. His whole nature was awakened by the sweet beams of charity, and began to expand into life, joy, and happiness. His prayers were more fervent; his thirst for learning became more ardent; and, under the tuition of John Trebonius especially, he made rapid progress in his studies.

On attaining his eighteenth year, Luther was sent to the university of Erfurth, in 1501. His father, who was now in better circumstances, required him to study the law. Full of confidence in his son's talents, he desired to see him cultivate them, and make them known in the world. At Erfurth, Luther outstripped his schoolfellows. Gifted with a retentive memory and a vivid imagination, all that he had heard or read remained fixed on his mind; it was as if he had seen it himself. But even at this early period the young man of eighteen did not study merely with a view of cultivating his understanding. There was within him a spirit of serious thoughtfulness. He felt that he depended entirely on God, and fervently invoked the Divine blessing on his labours. Every morning he began the day with prayer; then he went to church; and afterwards commenced his studies, which he prosecuted all day without intermission. One would almost say of him that he lacked nothing.

When Luther had been two years at Erfurth, he saw a Bible for the first time. It was in the university library. On opening it he was filled with astonishment to find in it more than those fragments of the gospels and epistles which the church had selected to be read to the people in their places of worship. Till then he had thought that these were the whole word of God. With eagerness, and indescribable feelings, he turned over the leaves of this Latin Bible. He read and re-read, and then, in his surprise and joy, he went back to read again.

In this same year Luther was laid on a sick bed. Death seemed at hand, and serious reflections filled his mind. All were interested in the young man. "It was a pity," they thought, "to see so many hopes so early extinguished." Nor were they extinguished. Luther recovered, and seemed to himself to have been called to a new vocation. But yet there was no settled purpose in his mind. He resumed his studies, and, in 1505, was made doctor in philosophy. Encouraged by the honours which were heaped upon him on this occasion, he prepared to apply himself entirely to the study of the law, agreeably to the wishes of his father. But God willed otherwise.

Whilst Luther was engaged in various studies and beginning to teach in the university, his conscience incessantly reminded him that religion was the one thing needful, and that his first care should be the salvation of his soul.

He had learned God's hatred of sin; he remembered the penalties that his word denounces against the sinner; and he asked himself tremblingly, if he was sure that he possessed the favour of God. His conscience answered, "No."

His character was prompt and decided; he resolved to do all that depended on himself to insure a well-grounded hope of immortality. Two events occurred, one after another, to rouse his soul and confirm his resolution. Amongst his college friends there was one named Alexis, with whom he was very intimate. One morning a report was spread that Alexis had been assassinated. Luther hurried to the spot, and ascertained the truth of the report. This sudden loss of his friend affected him, and the question which he asked himself, "What would become of me if I were thus suddenly called away?" filled his mind with the liveliest apprehension.

During the summer of 1505, Luther visited the home of his childhood at Mansfeldt, and on his return to the university, he was within a short distance of Erfurth, when he was overtaken by a violent storm. The thunder roared; a thunderbolt sank into the ground at his side. Luther threw himself on his knees: his hour is perhaps come: death, judgment, eternity, are before him in all their terrors, and speak with a voice which he can no longer resist; encompassed with the anguish and terror of death, as he himself says, he makes a vow, if God will deliver him from this danger, to forsake the world, and devote himself entirely to his service. Risen from the earth, having still before his eyes that death which must one day overtake him, he examines himself seriously, and inquires what he must do. The thoughts that formerly troubled him return with redoubled power. He has endeavoured, it is true, to fulfil all his duties; but what is the state of his soul? Can he with a polluted soul appear before the tribunal of so terrible a God? He must become holy. He now thirsts after holiness as he had thirsted after knowledge; but where shall he find it? How is it to be attained? The university has furnished him with the means of satisfying his thirst for knowledge. Who will assuage this anguish, this vehement desire that consumes him now? To what school of holiness can he direct his steps? He will go into a cloister; the monastic life will insure his salvation. How often has he been told of its power to change the heart, to cleanse the sinner, to make men perfect! He will enter into a monastic order. He will there become holy. He will thus ensure his eternal salvation.

Such were the resolutions and hopes which filled the breast of Luther as he re-entered Erfurth. His resolution was unalterable. Still it is with reluctance that he prepares to break ties that are so dear to him. One evening he invites his college friends to a cheerful and simple repast. Music once more enlivens their social meeting. It is Luther's farewell to the world. At the moment when the gaiety of his friends is at its height, the young man can no longer repress the serious thoughts that occupy his mind. He speaks. He declares his intention to his astonished friends. They endeavour to oppose it; but in vain. And that very night Luther, perhaps dreading their importunity, quits his lodgings. Leaving behind his books and furniture, and taking with him only Virgil and Plautus (he had not yet a Bible), he goes alone, in the darkness of the night, to the convent of the hermits of St. Augustine. He asks admittance. The door opens and closes. And, not yet two-and-twenty years old, he is separated from his parents, his companions and the world.

Luther imagines himself now with God and safe. His decision and renunciation of the world are commended by the monks, and reprobated by his father and friends. As for himself, he is quite in earnest. The ring he received when made doctor of philosophy, he returns to the university, that nothing may remind him of the world he has renounced. Within his new home he performs the meanest offices. And then when the young monk, who was at once porter, sexton, and servant of the cloister, had finished his work, "With your bag through the town!" cried the brothers; and, loaded with his bread-bag, he was obliged to go through the streets of Erfurth, begging from house to house, and perhaps at the doors of those very persons who had been either his friends or his inferiors. But he bore it all. Inclined, from his natural disposition, to devote himself heartily to whatever he undertook, it was with his whole soul that he had become a monk. Besides, could he wish to spare the body? to regard the satisfying of the flesh? Not thus, he thought, could he acquire the humility, the holiness that he had come to seek within the walls of a cloister.

The prior of the convent, upon the intercession of the university, freed Luther, ere long, from the mean offices which the monks had imposed upon him; and the young monk resumed his studies with fresh zeal. The works of the fathers, especially St. Augustine, attracted his attention. Nothing struck him so much as the opinions of this father upon the corruption of man's will, and upon the grace of God. He felt, in his own experience, the reality of that corruption, and the necessity for that grace. The words of Augustine found an echo in his heart. He loved above all to draw wisdom from the pure spring of the word of God. He found in the convent a Bible, fastened by a chain, and to this chained Bible he had constant recourse. He understood but little of the word; but still it was his most absorbing study.

Burning with a desire after that holiness which he

had sought in the cloister, Luther gave himself up to all the rigour of an ascetic life. He endeavoured to crucify the flesh by fastings, macerations, and watchings. Shut up in his cell, as in a prison, he was continually struggling against the evil thoughts and inclinations of his heart. A little bread, a single herring, were often his only food; and for days together he would go without eating or drinking. Nothing was too great a sacrifice, at this period, for the sake of becoming holy to gain heaven. Never did a cloister witness efforts more sincere and unwearied to purchase eternal happiness. Had they lasted much longer, he would have become a martyr literally, he declared afterwards, through watchings, prayer, reading, and other labours.

At this point we may pause to inquire where Luther is spiritually, and what he has attained. Is he a partaker of the divine life? Comparing him with Saul of Tarsus, Martin Luther is now what Saul was when he sat at the feet of Gamaliel, and there outstripped his fellows in zeal for the traditions of his fathers. He is a very Pharisee. Like Saul he is blameless in his morals, intensely earnest in the performance of ritual observances, heartily zealous to serve God with such service as he then imagined to be pleasing to his Maker. But like Saul, too, he was only "going about to establish his own righteousness." This is an endeavour which is often as plainly and prominently exemplified among professing Christians, as it ever was by the most zealous adherents of the Mosaic ritual. "There are other materials," says Dr. Chalmers, "besides those of Judaism, which men may employ for raising a fabric of self-righteousness. Some of them, even among Protestants, as formal in their character, as the sabbaths and sacraments of Christianity; others of them, with the claim of being more substantial in their character, as the relative duties and proprieties of life; but all of them proceeding on the same presumption, that man can, by his own powers, work out a meritorious title to acceptance with God, and that he can so equalize his doings with the demands of the law, as to make it incumbent on the Lawgiver to confer on him the rewards and the favour which are due to obedience. . . . The question of our interest with God is no sooner entertained by the human mind, than it appears to be one of the readiest and most natural of its movements to do something for the object of working out such a righteousness. The question of, How shall I, from being personally a condemned sinner, become personally an approved and acceptable servant of God? no sooner enters the mind, than it is followed up by the suggestion of such a personal change in habit or in character as it is competent for man, by his own turning and his own striving, to accomplish."

Never did human soul obey this natural impulse to essay his own redemption, both from guilt and from sin, with more promptness and earnestness than did Luther's. In his agony of mind, he had recourse to all the practices of monkish holiness. When temptations assailed him, "I am a lost man," he said, and then resorted to a thousand methods to appease the reproaches of his heart. "I confessed every day. But all that was of no use. Then, overwhelmed with dejection, I distressed myself by the multitude of my thoughts. See, said I to myself, thou art envious, impatient, passionate; therefore, wretch that thou art, it is of no use to thee to have entered into this holy order." One day, overcome with sadness, he shut himself in his cell, and for several days and nights suffered no one to approach him. At last the door was broken open, and Luther was found stretched on the floor in unconsciousness and without any sign of life. And there, through mental suffering and bodily self-mortification, he would have perished, but for those who rescued him by a gentle violence.

What, we repeat the question, was Luther's religion at this time? Was it superstition or fanaticism? It was certainly not the divine life, for it was the very "spirit of bondage and fear," and not "of power, of love, and of a sound mind." How he became a partaker of the divine life, our narrative will tell.

The superior of the Augustinian order was a man of enlightened mind. The study of the Bible and of St. Augustine, the knowledge of himself, the war which he, like Luther, had to wage with the deceitfulness and lusts of his own heart, had led him to the Saviour. And he found, in faith in Christ, peace to his soul. This good man, John Staupitz, found Luther reduced by study, fasting, and watching, so that you might count his bones. He saw, in his countenance, the expression of a soul agitated with severe conflicts, but yet strong and capable of endurance. He approached him affectionately, and endeavoured to overcome the timidity of the novice. The heart of Luther, which had remained closed under harsh treatment, at last opened and expanded to the sweet beams of love. He felt that the vicar-general understood him, and did not refuse to open to him the cause of his sadness.

"It is in vain," said the dejected Luther, "that I

make promises to God; sin is always too strong for me." "Oh! my friend," answered the vicar-general, "I have vowed to the holy God more than a thousand times that I would live a holy life, and never have I kept my vow. I now make no more vows; for I know well I shall not keep them. If God will not be merciful to me for Christ's sake, and grant me a happy death when I leave this world, I cannot, with all my vows and good works, stand before him. I must perish." The young monk was terrified at the thought of Divine justice. He confessed all his fears. The unspeakable holiness of God, his sovereign majesty, filled him with awe. "But why," said Staupitz, "do you distress yourself with these speculations and high thoughts? Look to the wounds of Jesus Christ, to the blood which he has shed for you; it is there you will see the mercy of God. Instead of torturing yourself for your faults, cast yourself into the arms of your Redeemer. Trust in him, in the righteousness of his life, in the expiatory sacrifice of his death. Do not shrink from him; God is not against you; it is you who are estranged and averse from God."

But Luther could not find in himself the repentance which he thought necessary to his salvation; he answered, "How can I dare to believe in the favour of God, so long as there is in me no real conversion? I must be changed before he can receive me." His venerable guide endeavoured to show him that there can be no real conversion, so long as man fears God as a severe Judge. "What will you say, then," cried Luther, "to so many consciences, to whom are prescribed a thousand insupportable penances in order to gain heaven?" The answer to this question seemed to him a voice from heaven. "There is," said Staupitz, "no true repentance but that which begins in the love of God and of righteousness. That which some fancy to be the end of repentance is only its beginning. In order to be filled with the love of that which is good, you must first be filled with the love of God. If you wish to be really converted, do not follow these mortifications and penances. Love Him who has first loved you." These words penetrated the heart of Luther. Guided by this new light, he consulted the Scriptures. He looked to all the passages which speak of repentance and conversion, words which were no longer dreaded but became the sweetest refreshment. Those passages of Scripture which once alarmed him, seemed now, he says, to run to him from all sides, to smile, to spring up, and play around him.

"Before," he exclaims, "though I carefully dissembled with God as to the state of my heart, and though I tried to express a love for him, which was only a constraint and a mere fiction, there was no word in the Scripture more bitter to me than *repentance*. But now there is not one more sweet and pleasant to me. Oh, how blessed are all God's precepts, when we read them, not in books alone, but in the precious wounds of the Saviour!" Luther was at this time probably unacquainted with the words of the psalmist, "I will run the way of thy commandments, when thou shalt enlarge my heart." But he was beginning to realize their meaning. The spirit of bondage and fear was giving way before the blessed truth of God's free grace to man through the death and mediation of his beloved Son, and in its stead there was springing up a spirit of filial confidence and obedience.

This change, however, was not instantaneous, but gradual. "Oh! my sin! my sin! my sin!" he cried one day, in the presence of the vicar-general, and in a tone of the bitterest grief. "Well, would you be only the *semblance* of a sinner," replied the latter, "and have only the *semblance* of a SAVIOUR? Know that Jesus Christ is the Saviour of those even who are *real* and *great* sinners, and deserving of utter condemnation." To the doubts of his conscience were added those of his reason. He wished to penetrate into the secret counsels of God—to unveil his mysteries, to see the invisible, and comprehend the incomprehensible. Staupitz checked him. He persuaded him not to attempt to fathom God, but to confine himself to what he has revealed of his character in Christ. "Look at the wounds of Christ," said he, "and you will there see shining clearly the purpose of God towards man. We cannot understand God out of Christ. 'In Christ you will see what I am and what I require,' hath the Lord said; 'you will not see it elsewhere, either in heaven or on earth.'"

The conscience of the young Augustinian did not, however, find solid repose without further conflict. His health at last sank under the exertions and stretch of his mind. He was attacked with a malady which brought him to the gates of the grave. And all his anguish and terrors returned in the prospect of death. His own impurity and God's holiness again disturbed his mind. One day (it was now the second year of Luther's abode at the convent), when he was overwhelmed with despair, an old monk entered his cell and spoke kindly to him. Luther opened his heart to him, and acquainted him with the fears which disquieted him. The old man uttered in simplicity this article of the Apostles' Creed:—"I believe in the forgiveness of sins." These simple words, ingenuously recited at a critical moment, shed sweet consolation in the mind of Luther. "*I* believe," repeated he, to himself, on his bed of suffering, "I believe in the remission of sins." "Ah," said the monk, "you must not only believe that David's or Peter's sins are forgiven: the devils believe that. The commandment of God is, that all men believe that sins are remitted to them."

"From that moment," says D'Aubigné, "the light shone into the heart of the young monk of Erfurth. The word of grace was pronounced, and he believed it. He renounced the thought of meriting salvation, and trusted himself with confidence to God's grace in Christ Jesus. He did not perceive the consequence of the principle he admitted; he was still sincerely attached to the church of Rome, and yet he was thenceforward independent of it; for he had received salvation from God himself; and Romish Catholicism was virtually extinct to him. From that hour Luther went forward; he sought in the writings of the apostles and prophets for all that might strengthen the hope which filled his heart. Every day he implored help from above, and every day new light was imparted to his soul."

The history of the Reformation lies beyond our present theme. But it is important to remark that Luther did not assail the errors of Romanism in detail until after he was grown to a mature stature in the knowledge and enjoyment of THE TRUTH. When he did assail them, it was because he had already felt their incompatibility with THE TRUTH. "He reasoned always," to use the words of Mr. Isaac Taylor, "from the centre outward; not as from without toward the centre. He threw off the errors of the church, article by article, from the interior force of a spiritual vitality; or as a husk which the ripened fruit rejects. The false principles and corrupt usages in which he had been bred, and to which he had been most firmly attached, *shaled* away one by one from his mind, from his conduct, from his creed, as *exuviæ* which the energy of a genuine piety could no longer endure."

In the history of Luther, as we have traced it, we have found a two-fold conversion; first, from the mere secularity of earthly ambition to an earnest and self-crucifying Pharisaism, and then from this Pharisaism to a pure and spiritual Christianity. The turning point of the former was the death of his friend Alexis, and the thunderbolt which burst at his feet as he was entering Erfurth. He ceased to be a Pharisee and became a Christian through the instructions of John Staupitz and the humbler agency of the old monk who reminded him, in an hour of mental disquietude, of the doctrine of the forgiveness of sins. And now a Christian, the divine life shines forth, not in the spirit of bondage and fear; but in the spirit of power and of love, and of a sound mind. As in the case of his prototype, Saul of Tarsus, the gospel of God's love to men through the Mediator Jesus Christ not only freed him from the burden of guilt which oppressed his conscience, but inspired his heart with new and stronger motives to holiness. He was no longer a slave impelled by the fear of punishment to serve a hard master, but a son constrained by love and gratitude to do the will of his heavenly Father.

Ignatius Loyola; born 1491; died near Rome, July 31, 1556.

In bold contrast with the name of Luther stands out that of IGNATIUS LOYOLA, and yet in his history, too, we likewise learn much that will help us in studying the true character of the divine life. "A Spanish gentleman, of bold bearing, and who courts every chivalrous distinction, and breathes at once a nice honour and a gallantry less nice, is grievously wounded and thrown upon his bed, where he endures weeks of anguish and months of languor. Spoiled for war and pleasure by the hurt he has received, and fired in a moment by a new ambition, he breaks from his home, and sets forward as a Christian fakir, to amaze the world by feats of wild humility. He undergoes mental paroxysms, he sees visions, and exists thenceforward in a condition of intense emotion, resembling, in turns, the ecstasies of the upper, and the agonies of the nether world. He dedicates himself, body and soul, to the service of the blessed virgin—the queen of angels; he sets out on a preaching pilgrimage to convert the Mohammedan world, and he contemns all prudence and common sense in applying himself to an enterprise so immensely disproportioned to his abilities. In the course of a year or two he has merited canonization—if fervent pietism can ever merit it."*

What approaches Loyola made to the divine life, as we have seen it in Paul and in Luther, and in what respects he came short of it, will soon appear.

Ignatius Loyola was the son of a Spanish noble, and at an early age was sent as a page to the court of

* Loyola and Jesuitism in its Rudiments. By Isaac Taylor.—We are indebted to this interesting and able work for the materials of our sketch of Ignatius Loyola.

Ferdinand and Isabella. Though he put little restraint upon the passions of youth, he was distinguished among his companions by his abstinence from profane language, by his reverence towards the ministers of religion, and by his dislike of gambling. Still he pursued a career of pleasure and worldly ambition till he had completed his twenty-ninth year, when circumstances occurred which turned the current of his thoughts into other channels.

France and Spain were, at this time, contending for the possession of the border provinces. Pampeluna was invested by a French force, and the garrison meditated surrender. The gallant Loyola retired into the citadel, where he incited those who held it to maintain their position to the last. A breach in the walls was, however, soon effected; and while Loyola was stopping the way, along with a few brave companions, he was struck by a ball on the right leg, and by a splinter from the wall on the left, and fell in the breach. The French, with considerate kindness, sent their heroic prisoner, with all care, to be nursed in his paternal castle not far distant.

Loyola thus found himself at home, with every aid at hand which love and skill could furnish. But the cure of his wounds was tardy. Violence, frightful to think of, but which the patient endured with the calm fortitude of a soul strong in will, was oftener than once applied to the fractured limb. He sustained too much injury to allow him to indulge the hope of ever again shining, as heretofore, in chivalrous array, or in the shows and revelries of a court. His return to the world being thus cut off, his after-formed resolution to turn his eye for ever from its glare was, no doubt, rendered so much the less difficult to adopt, and to adhere to.

To beguile the tedious hours of languishing, Ignatius called for some of those tales of chivalry which he had been accustomed to peruse. But none were at hand, or he soon exhausted the entertainment of such as the castle could furnish. Two books of devotion now fell in his way—a Life of Christ, probably some meagre and decorated compilation from the evangelists, and some ascetic memoirs or legends of the desert.

"These books," to use the words of Mr. Isaac Taylor, "looked into at first with listless vexation, soon set on fire the very soul of Ignatius. As every fresh page was turned, sparks fell thick, and thicker still, upon materials so combustible as were those of this soldier's nature. That greatness which the soul draws upon itself by the habitual contemplation of infinitude; the steady purpose, too, and the unconquerable will, and the unearthly abstraction, and the lofty contempt of whatever the world most admires and covets—all these rudiments of spiritual heroism won the admiration of a spirit like Loyola's, sensitive and generous, and now broken off by a sudden violence from the incitements of worldly passions, although in no degree sickened of them."

From the reading of monastic legends Loyola arose a changed, if not a new man. "Why should not I," he exclaimed, "with the help of God, emulate the holy Dominic or the holy Francis?" "These breathings of a new ambition were, however, still mingled with sighs and groans, produced by the struggle of earthly passions in his bosom. The bright enticements which hitherto had engaged all his thoughts and desires, continued to exert their unabated influence over him, and his inmost soul was racked by the alternate sway of those opposite forces. It seemed as if his very spirit must have been riven by the grasp, on either hand, of mighty powers, 'contrary the one to the other.'"

This great battle between the spirit of the world and the spirit of the monastery was decided in favour of the latter, and forthwith he addicted himself to the most self-denying practices. Soon after he left home, and on his journey to the Benedictine monastery at Montserrat, he chastised his flesh nightly with the lash. At this famous monastery, in order to obtain more effective aids in the preservation of an inviolate purity, he placed himself in a formal and solemn manner under the immediate guardianship of the virgin Mary. His next business was to make confession of the sins of his past life, a recital of which, from his written memoranda, occupied the hours of three entire days. He next surrendered the remaining contents of his purse to the use of the poor; bestowed upon a ragged mendicant, under favour of the night, the costly garb he had lately worn; and with eager haste took to himself the pilgrim gear which he had just provided —a long hempen cloak of the most rugged texture, a tunic, a rope for a girdle, shoes of matted Spanish broom, a pilgrim's staff turned at the end, and a drinking bowl. His right foot, being still in a swollen state he indulged with a shoe; the left was bare, and his head also. "Moreover, as it was the usage with those who were about to enter any order of knighthood to pass one entire night, armed, in a church, he resolved, in his own case, to adopt this practice on the occasion of his formally dedicating himself to the Christian warfare. Thus minded, and having suspended his sword and dagger in the church, he spent the whole night in front of the altar of the virgin—

now standing—now on his knees, with all humility, imploring pardon for his past offences; devoting himself to the divine service, and not ceasing especially, with earnest supplication, to propitiate the 'blessed mother of God.'"

In all this Loyola was thoroughly in earnest. We see him the Spanish gentleman in sumptuous attire no more, but painfully limping along the roads, one foot naked, the other swollen and clouted, his head bare, his hair matted and foul, his beard rough, his nails grown like eagles' claws, his visage sunken and squalid. At Manresa, a small town about nine miles from Montserrat, he spent some time, and each day begged a morsel of bread from door to door. Three times every day he smartly chastised his bare shoulders with the lash; thrice every day he attended prayers at church, besides seven hours of private devotion; and every week confessed and received the sacrament. At the same time he gave all diligence to the care of his spirit, so that the habiliments of poverty and self-denial might truly symbolize the condition of the inner man.

The reader will at once be reminded of Luther in the convent of Erfurth. How like the picture! and how similar the result of these endeavours to obtain peace and purity! Loyola's toils were as vain as had been those of Luther a few years before. "In his perplexity he began to doubt if the elaborate three days' confession of the sins of his life, which he had lately effected, had indeed been complete. The black catalogue of crime was perhaps wanting in some one particular, on behalf of which the wrath of heaven continued to follow him. Day and night he wept; he went over, again and again, the ground of his late confession; and, as one who has dropped an invaluable jewel on his way, turns back, and with trembling diligence scrutinizes every inch of the ground he has trodden, and renews the desperate search day by day, so did Ignatius retrace the path of his past life, even up to the commencement of his moral consciousness, anxiously searching among the almost effaced impressions of memory for the lost crime. To think too much of his sins was not Loyola's mistake; but it was his misfortune to know so little as he knew of the only mode of release from the anguish of an awakened conscience."

In the midst of his wretchedness he was seized with despair, and meditated self-destruction. Withheld from this purpose, he resolved, with the hope of vanquishing or appeasing the Divine justice, to abstain absolutely from all food until he should win back the peace and joy which he had lost. Would that, in this crisis of his soul's agony, he had met with a Staupitz to direct him to the Saviour; or with that Book which taught Luther that the blood of Jesus Christ cleanseth from all sin! But it was not so. Intermitting no services and no penances, he fasted a day—and two days—and three—and four—nay, an entire week; and he would have persisted in his resolution had not his confessor commanded him to abandon so presumptuous an endeavour as that of contending with the Almighty. For a time he regained some tranquillity, but soon relapsed into the same condition of inward distress, and was tempted at once to renounce his ascetic purposes, and to return to the world and to its enjoyments. His deliverance from this state of mind is ascribed to a resolute act of will. He suddenly came to the conclusion, that "the mystery of confession," attended to in the manner and for the purposes for which he used it, was not good, but evil. At once, therefore, and without any further hesitation, he resolved to consign the entire delinquencies of his past life to perpetual oblivion. And thus, by a convulsive effort, he disengaged himself from the load of his past sins.

Though from the time when, by this strong act of will, he emancipated himself from his despair, he could be a mere ascetic no longer, he still maintained ascetic practices, and attached to them a virtue and efficacy which belong only to the atonement of our Lord Jesus Christ. When he approached the throne of offended justice, "he undertook there the desperate task of expiating the guilt of past years by bodily torments, such as the most renowned saints had themselves practised and had applauded." Occasionally he seemed to rise above the absurdity of such practices; but he persevered in them, sometimes perhaps from motives of policy, but mainly from an idea of their virtue.

Whatever opinion we form of the order of Jesuits, no one will deny that its founder was in earnest. His soul had a capacity for government which it is difficult to understand or to fathom. And all his religious undertakings were prosecuted with a fervour the most intense and consuming. If zeal has virtue of its own, irrespective of the object it aims to accomplish, and of the means which it uses, the divine life has seldom appeared in more vigorous action than in the person of Ignatius Loyola. But if we consent to be taught by the apostle Paul, we must believe that there was only a "show of wisdom" in that "voluntary humility" which made him a beggar for his daily bread when plenty was within his reach in other and more honourable ways; and only "a show of wisdom," likewise, in that "neglecting of the body," and in those self-inflicted penances which emaciated his frame and covered it with disease. If we accept Paul as a model, we shall not forget that he worked with his own hands to provide for his necessities, but never begged to exhibit his humility; and that while the love of Christ constrained him to endure the stripes which the enemies of Christ inflicted on him, he never lifted his own hand to do himself harm. Such practices Paul traced distinctly to a heathen source—and heathen they must ever be, whether they are followed by a Hindoo fakir, or a Mohammedan dervish, or a so-called Christian devotee. They are no signs of the divine life; this best and heavenliest principle developes itself in far other fruits and ways.

We are now in a position to compare Paul, Luther, and Loyola. All of them constitutionally ardent and active, they were all, likewise, religiously sincere, earnest, and self-denying. But up to a certain period these attributes were Pharisaic, not Christian. And more thorough disciples than these men Pharisaism cannot boast. Paul is introduced to us at the very beginning of his history as a Pharisee. Luther and Loyola begin as men of mere worldly pursuit and ambition; the former a student, and the latter a soldier. But both pass from pure worldliness to an earnest religiousness; the one frightened by the death of his friend Alexis, and the thunderstorm, to flee into the Augustinian convent to save his soul; the other incapacitated to pursue a soldier's life, and enjoy the soldier's pleasure, by the wounds of which he slowly recovered in the home of the lords of Pampeluna. Up to this point the three stand on the same religious platform. And had they all found rest there, their future life might have varied in form, but would have been identical in spirit and principle; they would have been earnest-minded Pharisees and nothing more. Paul, however, became a Christian, not by the mere intellectual conviction that Jesus is the Christ, far less by the mere practice of Christian rites, but by the grace which taught him to find peace with God, and a fountain of inward purity and strength, in the mediation of Him who died, the just for the unjust. The Pharisee, Martin Luther, became a Christian when he was withdrawn from confidence in his own inward conflicts and outward mortifications, and beheld and confided in the Lamb of God that taketh away the sin of the world. In the Christian Paul and Luther, the divine life manifests itself not in mere earnestness and zeal, but in the spirit of trustful, rejoicing, filial love to their God and Father. But what shall we say of Ignatius Loyola? In the hour of his distress there was no Staupitz at hand to say to him, "Look to the wounds of Jesus Christ, to the blood which he has shed for you; it is there you will see the mercy of God. Instead of torturing yourself for your faults, cast yourself into the arms of your Redeemer. Trust in him; in the righteousness of his life, in the expiatory sacrifice of his death." There was no Bible at hand to tell him, "Believe in the Lord Jesus Christ, and thou shalt be saved." "In Christ Jesus neither circumcision availeth anything, nor uncircumcision; but faith which worketh by love." And when the Holy Scriptures fell into his hands, we do not find that he recognized in them those first truths which imparted peace and life to Paul and Luther, delivered them from the spirit of bondage and fear, and created within them a spirit, not of power merely, but of love and of a sound mind likewise. So far as the conversion of Loyola can be traced, it left him at a distance from the home of evangelical peace, and ignorant of the true principles of evangelical obedience.

The effect of the doctrine of Christ's atonement, as our peace with God, is to produce a spirit of obedience to God at once earnest and filial. "There is nothing that so chains the inactivity of a human being as hopelessness," says Dr. Chalmers. "There is nothing that so paralyzes him as the undefined but haunting insecurity and terror which he cannot shake away. . . . The truth that Christ died for our sins, so far from a soporific, is a stimulus to our obedience; and it is when this truth enters with power into the heart, that the believer can take up the language of the psalmist and say, 'Thou hast enlarged my heart, and I will run the way of thy commandments.'" The spirit in which they obey who have obtained pardon and peace through the blood of the cross, and in which they obey who are looking for pardon and peace through the virtue of their obedience, is essentially different, even when they perform the same acts. The one is the spirit of the child, the other of the slave. "As sons, we do them from the feeling of love; as servants, we do them by the force of law. It is the spontaneous taste of the one; it is the servile task of the other. The meat and drink of the servant lie in the hire which is given for the doing of his master's will. The meat and drink of the son lie in the very doing of that will. He does not feel it to be a service, but the very solace and satisfaction of his own renovated spirit."

Of the principles which have been elicited from the experience of Paul and Luther, and, by contrast, from that of Ignatius Loyola, we shall furnish another illustration in the history of the English bishop Latimer.

Latimer; born in Leicestershire, in 1491; suffered martyrdom at Oxford in 1556.

The first character in which we know HUGH LATIMER is that of a genial, merry lad. He had followed the pursuits of a yeoman's life without stain of vice or dishonour. At the age of fourteen he was sent to the university of Cambridge, and took as much interest in the amusements as in the studies of the place. He was fond of pleasure and of cheerful conversation, and mingled frequently in the festivities of the youthful crowd around him. At what age the transition took place from light-heartedness to asceticism, we are not aware; but he was still young, and the circumstances have been recorded. When Latimer and a company of his fellow-students were dining together, one of the party exclaimed in the Latin of the Vulgate translation of Eccl. iii. 12, "There is nothing better than to be merry and to do well." "A vengeance on that *do well!*" replied a monk of impudent mien; "I wish it were beyond the sea; it mars all the rest." Young Latimer was startled. "I understand it now," he said; "that will be a heavy *do well* to these monks when they have to render God an account of their lives." Forsaking pleasure, the yeoman's son threw himself, heart and soul, into the practices of superstition, and became distinguished for his asceticism and enthusiasm. He learned to attach the greatest importance to the merest trifles. As the missal directs that water should be mingled with the sacramental wine, often while saying mass he would be troubled in his conscience for fear he had not put sufficient water. And this fear never left him a moment's tranquillity during the service. He became notorious for his ardent fanaticism, and his zeal was rewarded by the appointment of cross-bearer to the university. And in this capacity he was conspicuous for seven years, amidst the chanting priests and splendid shows of every religious procession. A more religious man than he was, in his own way, there could not be—not Saul of Tarsus, not Luther in the Augustinian monastery, not Ignatius Loyola. Was he now a true convert to Christ? Was his religion the divine life?

At this time the university of Cambridge was greatly agitated by the publication of the Greek New Testament, with a Latin translation by Erasmus. And there was no one to whom the hopes of the enemies of this book looked so confidently as to the cross-bearer of the university. This young priest combined a biting humour with an impetuous disposition and indefatigable zeal. He followed the friends of the word of God into the colleges and houses where they used to meet, debated with them, and pressed them to abandon their faith. On occasion of receiving the degree of bachelor of divinity, he had to deliver a Latin discourse in the presence of the university, and chose for his subject, "Philip Melancthon and his doctrines." Latimer's discourse produced a great impression. At last, said his hearers, Cambridge will furnish a champion for the church that will confront the Wittenberg doctors, and save the vessel of our Lord.

Among the cross-bearer's hearers on this occasion was Thomas Bilney, almost hidden through his small stature. Bilney easily detected Latimer's sophisms, but at the same time loved his person and conceived the design of winning him to what he believed to be the truth. He reflected, prayed, and at last planned a strange plot.* He went to the college where Latimer resided. "For the love of God," he said, "be pleased to hear my confession." The confessor expected to hear a recantation of Bilney's new doctrines. My discourse against Melancthon has converted him, he thought. The pale face and wasted frame, and humble look of his visitor, seemed to indicate that he would still be one of the ascetics of Rome. And Latimer at once yielded to his request. Bilney, kneeling before his confessor, told him, with touching simplicity, the anguish he had once felt in his soul, the efforts he had made to remove it, their unprofitableness, and the peace he had felt when he believed that Jesus Christ is the Lamb of God that taketh away the sin of the world. He described to Latimer the Spirit of adoption he had received, and the happiness he experienced in being able to call God his Father. Latimer listened without mistrust. His heart was opened, and the voice of the pious Bilney penetrated it without obstacle. From time to time the confessor would have chased away the new thoughts which came crowding into his bosom; but the penitent continued. His language, at once so simple and so lively, entered like a two-edged sword. At length the penitent rose up, but Latimer remained seated, absorbed in thought. Like Saul on the way to Damascus, he was conquered, and his conversion like the apostle's, was instanta-

* D'Aubigné's "Reformation in England."

neous. He saw Jesus as the only Saviour given to man: he contemplated and adored him. His zeal for the superstitions of his fathers he now regarded as a war against God, and he wept bitterly. Bilney consoled him—"Brother, though your sins be as scarlet, they shall be white as snow." Latimer received the truth, and was henceforward a changed man. His energy was tempered by a divine unction, and he ceased to be superstitious. His conversion, as of old the miracles of the apostles, struck men's minds with astonishment. To the hour of his martyrdom he proclaimed Jesus Christ as him who, having tasted death for every man, has delivered his people from the penalty of sin. With this blessed doctrine Bilney and Latimer explored even the gloomy cells of the madhouse to bear the sweet voice of the gospel to the infuriate maniacs. They visited the miserable lazar-house without the town, in which several poor lepers were dwelling; they carefully tended them, wrapped them in clean sheets, and wooed them to be converted to Christ. The gates of the jail at Cambridge were opened to them, and they announced to the poor prisoners that word which giveth liberty. Before princes and people they testified the gospel of the grace of God. And many years after they sealed their testimony with their blood.

These instances of the divine life—experimental facts by which its reality is ascertained, and from which its nature may be inferred—have, it will be observed, much in common. But it may be supposed that they have peculiarities which remove them to a certain extent from the experience of men in ordinary society, and in our country and times. It will be seen, however, on the examination of the instances to which we now proceed, that these peculiarities do not affect the substance of christian truth, or its practical results in the heart and life of those who receive it.

The first example which we select of a more common class of conversions than that of monks and ascetics, possesses a bold and definite outline. And we place it first because the change which its subject underwent was so obvious and visible, that the blindest eye must see it.

Colonel Gardiner, born January 10th, 1688; died at Preston-Pans, September 21st, 1745.

JAMES GARDINER was born in the year of the English revolution, 1688. Such was his reckless daring that he had fought three duels before he attained to the stature of a man. In the first of his country's battles in which he was engaged, he was left among the wounded on the field of action, and his conduct in this melancholy position shows how godless and hardened his heart was. He was now in the nineteenth year of his age. His life had already been steeped in licentiousness, but he had no thoughts of repentance; his one concern was how to secure the gold which he had about him. Expecting to be stripped by the enemy, he took a handful of clotted gore, placed his gold in the midst of it, shut his hand, and kept it in that position till the blood so dried and hardened that his hand would not easily fall open if any sudden surprise overtook him. The next morning he lay faint and exhausted, through loss of blood, and overheard one Frenchman say to another, "Do not kill that poor child." And when he was able to open his fevered lips, the first thing he did was to tell a deliberate falsehood, namely, that he was nephew to the governor of

Huy, a neutral town in the neighbourhood. His sufferings the following night were such that he begged those who were carrying him to Huy to kill him outright; but still he had no thoughts of God. And when his recovery was perfected, and he was restored to his country, it was only to plunge into all manner of excesses. The most criminal intrigues formed the staple of his existence from this period till the thirtieth year of his age. By his military companions he was called "the happy rake." But he was not happy. On one occasion while his profligate associates were congratulating him on his criminal successes, a dog happened to enter the room, and the young soldier (as he well remembered afterwards) could not forbear groaning inwardly, "Oh that I were that dog!" "His continual neglect of the great Author of his being, of whose perfections he could not doubt, and to whom he knew himself to be under daily and perpetual obligations, gave him, in some moments of involuntary reflection, inexpressible remorse, and this, at times, wrought upon him to such a degree, that he resolved he would attempt to pay him some acknowledgments." Accordingly, for a few mornings he repeated some passages of Scripture, and bent his knees before the throne of God. But the remonstrances of reason and conscience soon yielded to the power of temptation; and hairbreadth escapes by sea and land only confirmed his alienation from God.

In the thirty-first year of his age, however, Gardiner became the subject of a moral change as thorough and striking as any which human history can present, while the singularity of the circumstances in which it occurred has seldom been equalled.

Towards the middle of July, 1719, he spent an

evening of folly with some of his gay associates. The company broke up about eleven, and at twelve he had made a criminal appointment. The intervening hour must be bridged over by some employment. A pious mother had, without his knowledge, slipped into his portmanteau Watson's "Christian Soldier, or Heaven taken by Storm." The title attracted him, and he expected some amusement from its military phraseology. He took it and read, but it produced no seriousness nor reflection. While the book was yet in his hand, however, impressions were made on his mind, the fruit of which must be regarded as the best index to whence they came. Whether he was asleep or awake at the time, he felt it afterwards difficult to determine. But if asleep, so vividly was what he saw and heard impressed on his mind, that it seemed to be a waking reality. "He thought he saw an unusual blaze of light fall on the book while he was reading, which he at first imagined might happen by some accident in the candle. But, lifting up his eyes, he apprehended, to his extreme amazement, that there was before him, as it were suspended in the air, a visible representation of the Lord Jesus Christ upon the cross, surrounded on all sides with a glory; and was impressed, as if a voice, or something equivalent to a voice, had come to him to this effect, 'O sinner! did I suffer this for thee? and are these the returns?'" Affected as were Daniel and John by the supernatural visions they saw, "there remained hardly any life" in colonel Gardiner, and he continued, he knew not how long, insensible, but when he opened his eyes, he saw nothing more than usual.

It were easy to dismiss this tale as the dream of

an enthusiast, but such a proceeding would be far too summary to be worthy of inquirers after truth. If Gardiner had returned to his evil courses, we should have treated his vision as the mere offspring of an excited imagination and a disturbed conscience. And, as it is, it need not be doubted that imagination and conscience were both at work; but then, they were called to their work, and guided in the part which they performed, by some power foreign to the man's own soul. This we infer from the results. And what that power was, they will not doubt who are willing to be guided by the Book in their interpretation of spiritual changes. "It cannot in the course of nature be imagined," says his biographer, "how such a dream should arise in a mind full of the most impure ideas and affections, and, as he himself often pleaded, more alienated from the thoughts of a crucified Saviour than from any other object that can be conceived; nor can we surely suppose it should, without a mighty energy of the Divine power, be effectual to produce not only some transient flow of passion, but so entire and so permanent a change in character and conduct."

The dreamer arose from his seat, after a period of unconsciousness, and walked to and fro in his chamber under a tumult of emotions, "till he was ready to drop down in unutterable astonishment and agony of heart, appearing to himself the vilest monster in the creation of God, who had all his lifetime been crucifying Christ afresh by his sins. With this was connected such a view both of the majesty and goodness of God, as caused him to loathe and abhor himself, and to repent as in dust and ashes. He immediately gave judgment against himself, that he was most justly worthy of eternal damnation, and he was astonished that he had not been immediately struck dead in the midst of his wickedness." For several months after, it was a settled point with him that the wisdom and justice of God almost necessarily required that such an enormous sinner should be made an example of everlasting vengeance, and he dared hardly ask for pardon. His mental sufferings were now extreme, but he often testified afterwards that they arose not so much from the fear of hell "as from a sense of that horrible ingratitude he had shown to the God of his life, and to that blessed Redeemer who had been in so affecting a manner set forth as crucified before him." Those licentious pleasures which had before been his heaven, became now absolutely his aversion. "And, indeed," says his biographer, "when I consider how habitual all those criminal indulgences were grown to him, and that he was now in the prime of life, and all this while in high health, too, I cannot but be astonished to reflect upon it, that he should be so wonderfully sanctified in body as well as in soul and spirit, as that, for all the future years of his life, he, from that hour, should find so constant a disinclination to and abhorrence of those criminal sensualities, to which he fancied he was before so invariably impelled by his very constitution, that he was used strangely to think and to say that Omnipotence itself could not reform him without destroying that body and giving him another."

At length the heavy burden fell from off this weary pilgrim, as from others, when he saw the cross. His peace came by means of that memorable Scripture, "Whom God hath set forth to be a propitiation through faith in his blood, to declare his righteousness for the remission of sins;—that he might be just, and the justifier of him which believeth in Jesus."* He had used to imagine that the justice of God required his eternal death. But now he saw that the Divine justice might be vindicated, and even glorified, in saving him by the blood of Jesus Christ. "Then did he see and feel the riches of redeeming love and grace in such a manner as not only engaged him, with the utmost pleasure and confidence, to venture his soul upon it, but even swallowed up, as it were, his whole heart in the returns of love, which from that blessed time became the genuine and delightful principle of his obedience, and animated him with an enlarged heart to run in the way of God's commandments."

The future life of colonel Gardiner, from the hour of his conversion till he fell at Preston Pans in defence of the House of Hanover—a period of twenty-six years—was one of distinguished excellence. The "new man" was virtuous and pure and godly as the "old" had been licentious and profane. The change is a spiritual fact of deep interest; and if it be in any sense mysterious when viewed in the light of Christian truth, it would be not only mysterious, but unaccountable, if that truth be denied.

We select for our SECOND EXAMPLE a spiritual change, which presents a contrast to that of colonel Gardiner in all respects but in that essential oneness which will be found to unite all true conversions.

When Dr. Chalmers was professor of moral philosophy in the university of St. Andrews, the fame of his eloquence attracted to his classes young men of a

* Rom. iii. 25, 26.

superior order from all parts of the kingdom. Of one of these, who died young, the professor wrote in 1827: "He had the amplitude of genius, but none of its irregularities. He was neither a mere geometer, nor a mere linguist, nor a mere metaphysician; he was all put together; alike distinguished by the fulness and the harmony of his powers. . . . He far outpeered all his fellows; and, in a class of uncommon force and brilliancy of talent, shone forth as a star of the first magnitude." From the class thus described have arisen some of the most eminent men who now adorn both the pulpit and the bar. And the youth who outpeered these men, and elicited this encomium from so illustrious a teacher, must have been a person of no common order.

John Urquhart; born in Perth, June 7th, 1808; died in Glasgow, January 10th, 1827.

This was JOHN URQUHART, the son of a goldsmith in the ancient city of Perth. From his childhood he enjoyed the inestimable privilege of enlightened parental care, and of pastoral instruction of a high order. He was constitutionally affectionate and amiable. Among his schoolfellows he was a pattern of all outward goodness at least. One of them—now Dr. Duff, missionary in Calcutta—testifies that his superior intellectual attainments commanded their admiration, and his simplicity and guileless innocence their love. "You never heard him utter a harsh or unbecoming expression; you never saw him break forth into a violent passion; you never had to reprove him for associating with bad companions, nor for engaging in improper amusements. In every innocent pastime for promoting the health, in every playful expedient for whetting the mental powers, none more active than he; but in all the little brawls and turmoils that usually agitate youthful associations, there was one whom you might safely reckon upon not having any share. The love of what was good, and abhorrence of what was evil, had been so habitually inculcated from childhood, that the cherishing of these feelings might seem to have acquired the strength of a constitutional tendency, and the abandonment of them would have been like the breaking up of an established habit."

Can such a youth need conversion? See him at school, and he stands foremost morally as well as intellectually; see him at home, and he is the idol of parental affection; see him in the playground, and with all the zest with which he enjoys it there are intermingled none of its evil passions; see him in the sanctuary, and none, so far as eye can judge, more devout than he; see him in the morning, and you will find him with the rising sun, pacing the beautiful banks of the Tay, "like a shadow wholly unbound to the surface, sometimes in the attitude of deepest meditation, and sometimes perusing the strains of the Mantuan bard;" see him in the evening, and not the haunt of wickedness, but the family hearth and the quiet study are his resort. We follow him to the university of St. Andrews, while he is yet a boy, having only completed his fourteenth year, and he is unchanged. Steady and persevering in all his habits, he is ardently set on rising to eminence in some honourable department of life. Possessed of a generous and self-denying spirit, he nobly sacrifices everything which it is possible for him to give up, that the expenses of his education may affect as little as possible the other members of his father's family. Exposed to new and formidable dangers, his conduct is uniformly correct; his attendance on divine worship is regular; the private reading of the Holy Scriptures is not neglected; and morning and evening are sanctified by prayer. Can such a youth need conversion? "In a case like his," his biographer justly remarks, "no very marked or visible transition could take place." But John Urquhart was led to judge that he needed a change as deep and real as any poor prodigal who has wasted his substance with riotous living. And during the second year of his university course he gave the following account of what he hoped was such a change, to his pastor and friend, and afterwards his biographer, the Rev. William Orme:—

"My first impressions of danger, as a sinner, were caused by a sermon you preached about a year and a half ago. At the time I was very much affected; it was then, I think, that I first really prayed. I retired to my apartment, and with many tears confessed my guilt before God. These impressions were followed by some remarkable events in the providence of God, which struck me very forcibly. About that time I had a proof of the inability of earthly wisdom and learning to confer true happiness, by the melancholy death of my grammar school teacher. On leaving my father's house to come here, shortly after, I felt myself in a peculiar manner dependent on Jehovah. I was removed from the care of my earthly father, and from the intercourse of my earthly friends; and I felt great pleasure in committing myself to Him, who is the father of the fatherless, and a friend to those that have none. My companion used to join me morning and evening in the reading of the Scriptures and prayer. In these, and in attending on the more public exercises of God's worship, I had some enjoyment, and from them, I think, I derived some advantage. On my return home, however, last summer, I began to feel less pleasure in these employments; they began to be a weariness to me, and were at last almost totally neglected. My soul reverted to its original bent, and the follies of this world wholly engrossed my attention. Had I been left in that state, I must have inevitably perished. But God is rich in mercy; he delighteth not in the death of the wicked. In his infinite mercy he has again been pleased to call my attention to the things of eternity. For some months back I have been led to see the utter worthlessness of earthly things; to see that happiness is not to be found in any earthly object; that

> "Learning, pleasure, wealth and fame,
> All cry, 'It is not here.'"

And I think I have been led to seek it where alone it is to be found, in 'Jesus crucified for me.' I have felt great pleasure in communion with God; and I have felt some love, though faint, to the Saviour and to his cause. I have had a long struggle with the world. I have counted the cost, and I have at last resolved that I will serve the Lord."

In pursuance of this holy purpose, formed not in his own strength, John Urquhart took his place publicly among the followers of Christ in the sixteenth year of his age. And well did his life sustain the character which he thus assumed. "His crowning excellence," said Dr. Chalmers, "was his piety. This religious spirit gave a certain ethereal hue to all his college exhibitions." Young Urquhart looked forward solemnly to "life" as the "test" of the genuineness of the professions which he now made. "May God perfect his strength in my weakness," he said, "and may he enable me to live henceforth not to myself, but to Him who died for me, and who rose again; to offer my body a living sacrifice, and to devote all the faculties of my mind to his service." "Talents which," to use the words of Dr. Chalmers, "would have raised him to the highest summits of learning and philosophy" were thus unreservedly consecrated to the honour of his Divine Lord and Saviour. "Length of days" was not given to him to test his fidelity; but he lived long enough, although he died in the nineteenth year of his age, to have it said of him, as it was of Henry Martyn, that "his symmetry in the Christian stature was as surprising as its height."

Our THIRD EXAMPLE differs in many respects both from colonel Gardiner and from John Urquhart.

EBENEZER BIRRELL was trained in the fear of God.

Ebenezer Birrell; born at Kirkaldy, July 17th, 1820; died in London, December 30th, 1841.

During his boyhood there was much in his moral deportment to awaken the interest and hopes of his kindred. In the sixteenth year of his age he was the subject of deep religious impressions. Uniting with his brother and a sister's family in the morning reading of the Holy Scriptures, when some observations were made on the danger of stifling serious impressions, his countenance assumed an appearance altogether unusual. "It became pale and full of dread," says his brother, "and we quickly finished the engagement by earnest prayer, under the persuasion that that was the most suitable course. An unusual tenderness appeared in his conduct, during the few minutes that I saw him, before retiring to rest at night. Not long, however, after having done so, I heard a voice in his chamber. On rising, I found him kneeling on his bed, weeping and trembling with the greatest violence; and, on asking the cause of his emotion, he answered that he dreaded the consequences of being left to final hardness of heart. After acquiring some composure, we knelt together, and cried, in that solemn night season, for the mercy and grace of God." But the result was transient. Years afterwards, he said of it—"At this time I remember to have experienced, for the first time, the impression that religion was a matter with which *I* had to do. I became alarmed and impressed, but, after continuing rather serious for a few days, I again sank back into my former indifference."*

Soon after this period, he entered a house of business in the metropolis. Most of the young men in the same house were, like himself, related to pious families, and had received a religious education. But, "to nearly all of them London was full of novelty, and life apparently intended only for enjoyment." Birrell's disposition was in the highest degree sociable; his manners were frank and affable, and his powers of communicating amusement were singularly great. "First," he writes, "one part of the Sunday, and then the whole, was given to pleasure." Those sentiments which form the shield of the sanctity of the day of rest were gradually obliterated, and it became as secular as any other. "It would but unnecessarily recal unpleasant feelings," he writes in his diary, "were I to recount the steps by which I was led so far over the threshold of morality and right principle, as that theatres and Sunday excur-

* Memoir by his brother, the Rev. Charles Birrell.

sions should at last become familiar to me. But for nearly three years, avoiding the path of wisdom, I wandered far into the ways of sin."

But early habits are not easily abandoned. Fresh from places of exciting and sinful amusement, Ebenezer Birrell would kneel down before God, and pray that he would change his heart. On another fact which is told of him, the Rev. Thomas Binney has beautifully remarked: "What a mysterious, magical, divine thing is a mother's love! How it nestles about the heart, and goes with the man, and speaks to him pure words, and is like a guardian angel! This young man could never take any money that came to him from his mother, and spend that upon a Sunday excursion, or a treat to a theatre. It was a sacred thing with him; it had the impression and inscription of his mother's image, and his mother's purity, and his mother's piety, and his mother's love. It was a sacred thing to him; and these pleasures, which he felt to be questionable or felt to be sinful, were always to be provided for by other resources, and by money that came to him by other hands." In his attendance on public worship at the Weigh-house chapel, this young man often heard his character described and his sentence pronounced, but his heart would not yield. "Such convictions were usually stifled, by resorting to the idea of predestination. He attempted to believe that his conversion would be produced, or prevented, by the efficacy of a direct purpose on the part of his Creator, without respect, in any sense, to his own conduct. 'This principle I applied, also,' he remarks, 'to death; so that I went calmly to bathe, or row, in dangerous parts of the Thames, believing that the day of my death was settled, and die then I should, whatever

I was doing, or wherever I was.' It was thus that he struggled to master and to extinguish the very instinct of responsibility, and to provoke the God of truth to give him over to permanent hardness of heart. But the termination of the contest drew near." In February, 1839, he heard a sermon on the claims of the Bible to the faith and obedience of mankind, which left on his mind a deep impression of his own neglect of the blessed book, but effected no reformation. Exactly at the same time, one of his sisters, not at all aware of the state of his heart, put down his name in the list of Sabbath school teachers at a new chapel in Lambeth. The displeasure which this awakened in his breast was "as the observation of a planet to the navigator—it indicated the position of his soul in relation to God." On the evening of the day on which he heard what his sister had done, he went to York-road chapel, to hear the Rev. Samuel Martin preach. And the result will be best described in his own words:—

"Mortified to think that I should soon have to give up a considerable portion of my leisure time on the Sunday, and miserable in the reflection that I should have to keep up a show of religion in my heart, and to teach the children to observe what I was living in open violation of myself, I entered that chapel with a heart burning with greater enmity to God than I had ever experienced. The preacher's text was—'They all with one consent began to make excuse.' As he proceeded, my bitter feelings were gradually softened down, and I left that sanctuary very different from what I had entered it—serious and thoughtful. There was no particular part of the discourse with which I was impressed; but the whole set me on a train of thought respecting my present condition and my future prospects. On the one hand I loved my sins and the ways of the world; and when I reflected upon them, it appeared impossible that I could give them up. On the other hand I felt, deeply felt, that I was unhappy. I knew, I saw, that God's people were happy, and that I might be converted if I proceeded in the right way. These, and such as these, were my thoughts, until I was brought in some measure to see what a sinner I was in the sight of God. I remembered how I had resisted his Holy Spirit, when he had formerly spoken to me; that he was speaking to me again, and that now it might be for the last time; so I asked myself—'Why should I wish to be excused?' All along Blackfriars-road a conflict between opposite principles went on in my mind, and as I stepped on the bridge, I was led, by the grace of God, to determine to cease from sin; to open that volume which had never been opened with a sincere desire for knowledge; and, imploring God's blessing, to seek the way of salvation with full purpose of heart. From that moment I perceived that God was strengthening me; for, from that time, I had no difficulty in doing what before appeared to me so difficult—giving up my outward sins. In this state of mind I got home, and immediately retired to my room, and, God directing me, the book I took up was one which you [his brother] had given me, but which I had laid aside, not expecting to have any use for it—'James's Anxious Inquirer,' which I began to read in the manner he recommends, with earnest prayer to God that it might be blessed to my soul. I read the first three chapters that night, together with some of the first chapters of Matthew, and rose up in the morning still determined to be the Lord's, and feeling happy in my determination; at the same time I was sorry and downcast that I did not feel enough the enormity of my sins, nor had shed tears (as formerly I had done while under impressions), nor been much agitated; but, on the contrary, calm and composed. When night came I again retired to my room, still very unhappy for these reasons. The next chapter in the 'Anxious Inquirer' was on Repentance; and how can I describe the feelings with which I read: 'You are not to suppose that you do not repent, because you have never been the subject of overwhelming horror and excessive grief. Persons in the first stages of religious impression are sometimes cast down and discouraged, because they do not feel those agonizing and terrifying convictions that some whom they have heard or read of have experienced. Others, again, are greatly troubled, because they do not and cannot shed tears, and utter groans, under a sense of sin, as some do. If they could either be wrought up to horror, or melted into weeping, they should then take some comfort, and have some hope that their convictions were genuine.' I returned thanks to God that that chapter had ever been written. Feeling much easier, I went on to read the next chapter, on Faith. I read there: 'You are never safe, reader, until you have faith.' Anxiously I inquired, What is faith? I read again: 'Faith, in general, means a belief in whatever God has testified in his word; but faith in Christ means the belief of what the Scriptures say of him—of his person, offices, and work. You are to believe that he is the Son of God—God manifest in the flesh, God-man, Mediator; for how can a mere creature be your saviour? In faith you commit your soul to the Lord Jesus. What! into the hands of a mere creature? The Divinity of Christ is thus not merely an article of faith, but enters also into the foundation of hope. You are required to believe in the doctrine of the atonement, that Christ satisfied Divine justice for human guilt, having been made a propitiation for our sins, and that now his sacrifice and righteousness are the only ground or foundation on which a sinner can be accepted or acquitted before God. You are to believe that all, however previously guilty and unworthy, are welcome to God for salvation, without any exception, or any difficulty whatever.' 'Well,' I said to myself, 'I believe that Jesus Christ was the Son of God, that he came down from heaven to this earth, and that he died on the cross that sinners might be saved;' but, notwithstanding this, I seemed waiting in expectation of something—some visible and perceptible change—something indicative of the Spirit of God coming upon me; but I felt nothing—I was the same as before. I turned to Matthew and read there, in the ninth chapter, of the woman who had the issue of blood, and whose faith had made her whole; and I read other instances of the efficacy of faith, but they did not seem to me to apply to my case. They had exercised faith, certainly, but then they saw Christ with their eyes, and felt that they had been healed. Now I felt nothing of this sort; I could see nothing by which I might know I was cured. With these perplexing thoughts, I returned again to the 'Anxious Inquirer,' and read: 'Faith is not a belief in your own personal religion, this is the assurance of hope; but it is a belief that God loves sinners, and that Christ died for sinners, and for you among the rest.

It is not a belief that you are a real Christian; but that Christ is willing to give you all the blessings included in that term. It is the belief of something out of yourself. The object of faith is the work of Christ for you, not the work of the Spirit in you. It is, to rest upon the word and work of Christ for salvation; to depend on his atonement and righteousness, and upon nothing else, for acceptance with God; and, really, to *expect* salvation because he has promised it.' I then perceived that I had doubted the power of Christ, and the willingnesss of God. I fell down on my knees before him, and rose a believer that my sins were pardoned through the blood of the Lamb."

This is not a narrative of fancies, but of deep convictions and solemn realities. To the end of life Ebenezer Birrell never saw reason to doubt that Divine love on that occasion obtained its blessed victory over the ungodliness of his heart. His character, thenceforward, was adorned with the evidences of genuine piety. His conduct in the warehouse, and especially among his associates, exhibited with decision, but without ostentation, the change which he had undergone. On his natural gentleness there was engrafted the boldness which religious convictions produce. Within three years from the time of his conversion he was removed from the world. Throughout a protracted illness his christian character shone with a mild and engaging loveliness. The principles which gave him peace when he was awakened to a sense of personal sinfulness, supported him in death, and his confidence never forsook him that he was in the hands of a "most loving Father."

For our FOURTH EXAMPLE we select a lady whose name is well-known in the world of letters—CAROLINE FRY, the author of "The Listener," and of "Christ our Example."*

Caroline Fry; born at Tunbridge Wells, December 31st, 1787; died at the same place, September 17th, 1846.

As a child, Caroline Fry was intensely sensitive. "Back to seven or eight years, she could remember an intense, unreasonable, almost maddening anguish, which was produced by a sense of unkindness, or injustice, or discouragement, often imaginary, always exaggerated." And the discipline of a too indulgent father was not much fitted to correct these morbid sensibilities. She enjoyed a home education of a high order, so far as education is comprehended in mere instruction; and literary tastes were cultivated from childhood. "The exact morality of her father's house was such, that she did not remember to have ever heard a free expression, or an indelicate allusion, or a profane or immoral word in jest or earnest. The very name of vices and follies was strange to her ear—and all her knowledge of the living world, its positions and pursuits, was no more than she learned from those parts of the newspapers which her father desired to hear, and which were generally read aloud." "Her earliest remembered pleasure was the first-blown flower of the spring, or the new-born lamb in her father's meadow; she knows distinctly—and never returns to her native place without a vivid recurrence of the impression—where she used to go with her nurse to see if the wild snowdrop was budding, to gather the first primroses, to hunt the sweet violets from

* Our information respecting Caroline Fry is derived from her "Autobiography."

among the nettles, where they were yearly to be found."

Of such an one, trained amid the finest influences of nature, it will be said by some that she needed no conversion, and that a divine life must have been natural to her. We shall see how far she formed this judgment of herself. Her religious position in early life she describes thus:—"Caroline never learned to fear sin, as sin—least of all as measured against the law of God. Her first notions of right and wrong were such as she gathered from her reading; a purely heathen code, in which heroism and high-mindedness stood as the first of virtues, weakness and pusillanimity as the worst of vices. To be faultless, to be perfect, were her early and long-continued desire and determination; and much of the suffering of the first part of her life arose from her conscious ill success in the government of herself. No one ever told her where she might have help, or why she could not be perfect. The only thing, of which she never thought, for which she never asked, never felt, never cared, was religion. True, it was never brought under her observation; but that was true of many other things about which her curiosity and consideration was insatiable. The religion of her father's house will seem almost a caricature in these bestirring days; but it was common enough then. Caroline does not remember an individual in the family ever omitting to go to church twice on the Sunday, except from illness—it would have been thought absolutely wicked; neither does she remember any instance of the Sabbath being profaned by week-day occupations and pleasures; certainly she never heard in jest or earnest the holy Name profaned, or his word and power disputed, or irreverently treated. But, except on Sunday, the Bible never left its shelf, and religion was not anybody's business in the week. During the Sunday, religious books, if they may be so called, came forth out of their hiding-places, and all others disappeared. The children learned and repeated the collects and the church catechism, the only lesson which to Caroline appeared a hardship, and with good reason, for no one ever told her what it meant, and how she was interested in it."

"No nurse nor mother ever talked to her of Jesus' love, nor told her stories of his sufferings; nor ever warned her of God's displeasure. Her infant mind was never stored with sacred words, nor her memory exercised with holy writ. When she listens now to the exercises of the infant or the Sunday school, deeply can she estimate, while they cannot, the value of the instructions thus received in preparation for the day of grace. Her reading of the Scriptures was confined to a chapter read every Sunday evening by each of the four younger children to their parents and the family assembled; but as they always chose what they would read, it seldom varied beyond the stories of the Old Testament: David and Goliath, Joseph and his brethren, Daniel in the lions' den, etc. Never applied, never remarked upon by any one, this was followed by one of Blair's, or other similar lectures, read aloud by some one of the elders, and then religion was dismissed till the next Sabbath. The only unseen world that occupied little Caroline's attention, was that of the classic poets." These statements are her own.

Young's "Night Thoughts" fell into her hands at a time when she was prepared to take the poetry of life, of time, and of eternity, in the stead of its realities. She was enraptured with Young's poetry, and acquired from it, at the least, a quickened sensibility to the follies of life: viewed however only as follies, not as sin; weighed by reason and philosophy, not by the word of God. Of the period between fourteen and seventeen years of age she remembered nothing afterwards "but happiness, freedom, mirth, hilarity, good humour with every one, and delight in everything." By consent of her family, she was "its wit, its life, its plaything, its spoiled child, from first to last." And more than twenty years from this period were given to her to try that world of fashion and gaiety after which she now began to long, before she found her rest in God.

We now find her in London, under the roof of a relative of polished manners and brilliant wit. In her father's house she had never heard a profane or licentious expression; nothing came amiss here to point a jest, provided it was not coarse nor low. "Caroline does not remember to have been shocked." The drive in the park was more frequent than the visit to church. On occasion of her relative's absence from home, his wife and Caroline Fry, wanting something to do, would go to church on the Sunday morning to pass the time. In one of these freaks "she heard, for the only time, that eminent man of God, Mr. Cecil, but it was with absolute offence and disgust." She had heard the same doctrines before in lady Huntingdon's chapel at Tunbridge Wells, whither she went occasionally after her father's death, and she understood them, but her heart rejected them. In the midst of the gaiety of London she "ceased to perform the ceremony of prayer in her chamber night and morning, (she has no reason to believe that she had ever really prayed,) from that time never more to bend the knee in private, or her heart anywhere, before the God of heaven, until of his sovereign mercy she was born anew."

Before this great event took place, Caroline Fry descended into a still lower depth of irreligion than we have indicated. At her relative's table there was a frequent guest, of literary reputation, of venerable age, courtly and high bred, whose "wit spared nothing human or Divine; friends, life, mortality, religion, nothing barred the jest." "As was most natural, Caroline attached herself entirely to this fascinating old man." Her own account of his influence over her is most instructive. If his insidious flattery "failed to make any impression on her delicacy, artlessness, and purity of thought and feeling, there was that in which the influence of his corrupt companionship did not fail; she was too innocent for his immorality, she was just ready for his irreligion. Never, perhaps, at the early age of nineteen and twenty, in a heart of such simplicity and uncorruptness, and real ignorance of evil, was the enmity of the fallen nature so developed. We wish to call attention to it (she wrote many years after); and if we have been writing what seems useless to detail, we have done so on purpose to give the full value to this particular point. It is written that the natural heart is 'enmity' against God. Who believes this as a universal truth? When vice has indurated the heart, when habit has vitiated and the world corrupted it, it may be so; but what virtuous, happy, young, and unspoiled nature ever thought of hatred towards the God that made us? Fearlessness, indifference, forgetfulness, are natural; but not, surely not, 'enmity.' Perhaps there are very few believers looking back upon their days of gay and joyous godlessness, that can at all verify the Scripture statement in themselves—how should they have hated the Being they never thought about and cared for, who never crossed their path with present ills, nor marred their pleasures with fear of retribution? But here, in the bosom of a simple girl, brought up in all the virtuous regularity and real religious observance of a secluded country life; a stranger to all that is morally evil, to a degree that would not be credited if it were fully explained; with a mind solidly instructed, and unused to any manner of evil influence by books or company, hitherto a stranger to sorrows, wrongs, and fears, that tend to harden the ungracious heart—in this unvitiated, unworldly bosom was manifested at that early age, clear and strong to her memory as if it was of yesterday, a living, active hatred to the very name of God. She persuaded herself there was no God, and thought she believed her own heart's lie; but if she did, why did she hate him? Why did she feel such renovated delight when his name was the subject of the profane old poet's wit? 'No God' was probably with her, as it probably is with every other infidel, the determination of the heart, and not of the judgment. Thus, while she thought herself above all religious doubts, she seized delightedly on every manifestation of infidelity in those around her, and laughed with the very utmost zest of gratified aversion at every profanation of the holy Name."

After three years of London life, Caroline Fry found another home in the country. But now she was "an atheist in heart, and only not quite one in understanding." She was no longer, however, uninformed upon religion. "She had read books, heard preachers, known saints—several of her own family were already under the influence of Divine grace—she knew and hated all, and most intensely Him of whom is all. . . . . To the few who would speak to her upon religion she listened with silent amenity, or studied philosophical indifference. They had a right to their opinions; she would not have disturbed them on any account; since they liked to think so there was no harm in doing it." . . . . . "She had no dislike to hear the truth preached, or to the conversations of those who believed it, or to their persons. She would as soon have thought of disliking the Copernican system or its advocates, or any other scientific controversy. Her eldest brother was at this time a distinguished minister and writer in the church of Christ—a man of acknowledged talent and learning. Caroline had heard him preach, and read his works, and held him in very high esteem and much affection; but his religious opinions had not the smallest influence. He considered Caroline as the most hopeless of his family, several of whom were beginning to be spiritually affected.

"She did not dislike to hear the truth, but there was that which she did dislike, which she hated—the word that taught it. Neither the poetic beauties, nor the historic interest of the Bible, could give it any charm. She could not endure it, she would not read it, and when read before her, she deliberately determined not to listen." How was a mind to be reached that was thus trenched and fortified?

At this momentous period Caroline Fry was residing in a family where everything was against the probability of her receiving religious impressions, "except the restless, unsatisfied, unhappy state of her own mind, displeased with everything around her and within her; weary and disgusted with the present, and gloomy and hopeless of the future, without a single sorrow but the absence of all joy." Living in the utter neglect of prayer, there were times when, not upon her knees but on her bed, she would give mental expression to her feelings thus: "God, if thou art a God, I do not love thee, I do not want thee, I do not believe in any happiness in thee; but I am miserable as I am; give me what I do not seek, do not like, do not want, if thou canst make me happy; I am tired of this world, if there is anything better, give it me."

"In the destitution of her affections at this moment, Caroline fixed them with vehement partiality on the daughter of a clergyman in an adjoining parish." This young lady was beautiful and fascinating, but disappointments of a painful character had made her moody and melancholy. She denounced the world, she wished to leave it, she talked much of its vanity; she was, or thought she was, of a consumptive habit, and not likely to live many years; she talked much of death, and much of eternity, and much of God. "I do not remember," says Miss Fry, "that she ever spoke of Christ, of atoning merit, or redeeming love; I believe she knew them not. She talked of the world's emptiness, levity, and injustice. I do not remember that she ever spoke of her own sin. I believe her religion was purely sentimental."

To this friend Caroline never spoke of her unbelief, nor confessed the total absence of religious feeling in her bosom. But she continually bewailed her impetuosity and want of self-control, compared with the composure and philosophy manifested by her friend on all occasions. Friendship, however, looked through the cover of silence that slightly concealed Caroline's infidelity. And her friend addressed a letter to her, to tell her that religion was the source of all the advantage over her which Caroline had so often noticed and so often envied—all that she called philosophy. The truth, the bare, bald truth—that religion was the one thing needful that she had not—struck conviction to Miss Fry's soul; it pierced to the very depths of her moral being. Her first emotion on perusal of the letter was a paroxysm of grief and indignation—grief that the idol of her affections should condemn her, and indignation that she should presume to teach her; the next was a determined resolution that her friend should not influence or persuade her. On three successive days she attempted to answer the letter, but could not. "Before the third night arrived, the struggle was over; the battle had been fought and won; the strong man armed was vanquished; the banner of Jesus waved peacefully over the subdued and prostrate spirit of the infidel despiser of his word, the conscious hater of his most precious name."

"'Lord, save me, or I perish,' has been, and is, from first to last, the sum of her religion, dated from that most wondrous night, the first in which she knelt before the cross; in which she prayed; in which she slept in Jesus."

"The most immediate result of this change of heart was, the happiness, to which it had at once restored her; at peace with God, she made up her quarrel with all things. The zest of life returned; she no longer quarrelled with her destiny, or felt distaste of all her pursuits, or grew weary of her existence without any reason. The void was filled;

she never after wanted something to do, or something to love, or something to look forward to; the less there was of earth, the more there was of heaven in her vision; whenever man failed her, Christ took her up. She had no more stagnant waters, long as her voyage was through troubled ones; she was, with all the leaven of the older nature that remained, essentially a new creature to herself."

This great revolution was as entire as it was sudden. It was no mere paroxysm or convulsion of soul. It was a change which brought with it new principles of life. And what may seem most strange, these principles were very different from those of the friend who was the unconscious instrument of Miss Fry's conversion. It was not to a mere religiousness, earnest and pharisaic, that she emerged out of her heart-chosen infidelity; it was to a faith in our Lord Jesus Christ as the one Mediator and High Priest, and to a simple-hearted trust in him as all her salvation. The bare truth that religion is the one thing needful, stung her to the quick; but the seeds of other truths were in her mind, though hated and disbelieved. And these sprang up, now that the fallow ground was broken, and produced those fruits of humble trust in the Saviour of sinners, devout love to his holy name, and an earnest zeal to consecrate to his praise a life that had been redeemed by his mercy. The believer in Holy Scripture will not hesitate to see in all this the operation of a power that is more than human, and it would not be difficult to maintain that no other *rational* solution can be given of the change.

Colonel Gardiner, John Urquhart, Ebenezer Birrell,

and Caroline Fry may be regarded as representative cases; and we may infer from them the moral condition of mankind in relation to God. If we had no other means of judgment, it would not, indeed, be safe to stake a general conclusion on so small a number of instances. But it is sustained by Bible testimony, and by our knowledge of human society in general.

What, then, is man, morally, in relation to God? Is there one moral attribute characteristic in common of all the individuals we have named?

We have maintained that man is a religious being in this sense, that the most distinctive character of his nature is his faculty of knowing, loving, and serving God. But it is equally true, that wherever this faculty is in actual exercise apart from the teachings of revelation, its exercise is fearfully defective or perverse. We shall find the religious susceptibility of our nature exercised nowhere intelligently and rightly without the guidance of God's own Book. Most nations still derive some advantage from the surviving fragments of a primeval knowledge which was carried by their ancestors from the plains of Shinar, the second birthplace of the human family; and all nations have the benefit of daily and ceaseless instruction from the works of God; for "The heavens declare his glory, and the firmament showeth his handywork: day unto day uttereth speech, and night unto night showeth knowledge."—"The invisible things of God from the creation of the world are clearly seen, being understood by the things that are made, even his eternal power and Godhead." But such is man's moral inaptitude to receive lessons of God, that he does not hear the voice which nature utters so loudly, or see the truths which are engraven in light over the entire surface of the universe. The apostolic explanation is the only sufficient one, of the universal blindness which has fallen upon the nations, whether refined or barbarous, in reference to the character and worship of the true God: "When they knew God, they glorified him not as God. . . . They did not like to retain God in their knowledge."

This estrangement of the heart from God, which displays itself on so large a scale in the varied idolatries and sensualities of the world, is the characteristic of our moral nature—that which unites into an evil oneness such opposites as James Gardiner and John Urquhart. The practised rake and the youth of unsullied virtue had this in common before their conversion, that they were "without God" as an object of filial reverence and love. And in this they were only in fellowship with the whole race of mankind. The sublime and affecting words of John Howe are not the less true that they are based on a figure—the very natural figure which represents man as a temple of God: "The stately ruins are visible to every eye, that bear in their front (yet extant) this doleful inscription:—'HERE GOD ONCE DWELT.' Enough appears of the admirable frame and structure of the soul of man, to show the Divine presence did sometime reside in it; more than enough of vicious deformity to proclaim he is now retired and gone. The lamps are extinct, the altar overturned; the light and love are now vanished, which did the one shine with so heavenly brightness, the other burn with so pious fervour; the golden candlestick is defaced, and thrown away as a useless thing, to make room for the throne of the prince of darkness; the sacred incense, which sent rolling up in clouds its rich perfumes, is exchanged for a poisonous, hellish vapour. The comely order of this house is turned all into confusion; the beauties of holiness into noisome impurities; the house of prayer into a den of thieves. The noble powers which were designed and dedicated to divine contemplation and delight, are alienated to the service of the most despicable idols, and employed unto vilest intentions and embraces; to behold and admire lying vanities, to indulge and cherish lust and wickedness. What! have not 'the enemies done wickedly in the sanctuary?' How have 'they broken down the carved work thereof!' Look upon the fragments of that curious sculpture which once adorned the palace of the great King; the relics of common notions; the lively points of some undefaced truth; the fair ideas of things; the yet legible precepts that relate to practice. Behold with what accuracy the broken pieces show these to have been engraven by the finger of God, and how they now lie torn and scattered, one in this dark corner, another in that. . . . You come amidst all this confusion as into the ruined palace of some great prince, in which you see here the fragments of a noble pillar, there the shattered pieces of some curious imagery, and all lying neglected and useless among heaps of dirt. He that invites you to take a view of the soul of man, gives you but such another prospect, and doth but say to you,—'Behold the desolation;' all things rude and waste. So that, should there be any pretence to the Divine presence, it might be said, 'If God be here, why is it thus?' The faded glory, the darkness, the disorder, the impurity, the decayed state in all respects of this temple, too plainly show the great Inhabitant is gone."

Hence the repentance on which the Bible insists as

universally necessary is "repentance *toward God.*" "The most flagrant wickedness of our unconverted condition, is the *ungodliness* of that condition. Most expressive, in its proper and full sense, is our term 'godliness,'as denoting what ought ever to be deemed the natural bent of the soul towards God; its creaturely, its filial temper of dependence, veneration, love, and duty. The loss of this most precious disposition is 'human nature's broadest, foulest blot.' But the 'carnal mind' is pronounced to be, and by the most deeply thoughtful is ever painfully felt to be, 'enmity against God,' and the bitter source of all evil. Nor is this unnatural, uncreaturely, unfilial temper ever removed, except by a true change of heart. So that true repentance is emphatically repentance 'toward God,' leading to conduct not only 'sober and righteous,' but 'godly,' also; and bringing those on whom it operates, not only to 'do justly and to love mercy,' but 'to walk humbly with God.' The heart thus wrought upon may still be a very imperfect heart; but it is no longer, in the sense in which it had previously been so, an ungodly heart."

Another opportunity will occur of showing the inseparable connection there is between "repentance toward God" and "faith toward our Lord Jesus Christ." At present we wish to mark with emphasis that no degree of human virtuousness renders unnecessary that great change which introduces into the soul the principles and affections of the divine life—filial love and reverence to our God and Father in heaven. Actions uninspired by these motives "may vary in beauty or in value, from the most repulsive forms of human depravity to the fairest impulses of social affection; but they are all equally remote from the preparatory life of heaven, in so far as they are apart from God, and would equally exist were God conceived to exist no more."

The ground and substance of the charge which religion brings against the world, is not that it does not abound in manifestations of moral as well as of physical beauty. "What it does assert is this,—that all which is excellent in the natural man is excellent irrespectively of his God; that he loves, hates, prefers, rejects—and often rightly too—but without any thought of God's laws of preference and rejection; that thus all—and there is much—that is beautiful in his best impulses, is beautiful only as the flower or the landscape is beautiful; his heart as little moving through its circle of social kindness from a desire to approve itself to the God who has commanded them, as the flower expands its petals and sheds its fragrance in voluntary obedience to Him who created it—the one beauty being as much and as little *religious* as the other." "I deal not," says professor Butler, from whom we quote these just and striking observations—"I deal not now with open and avowed vice. My object is to prevent misconception, obscurity, self-deceit; and no subtlety of self-hypocrisy can reconcile with the law and love of God, vices which the world itself professes to discountenance. I come among the amiabilities, the noblenesses, the stern and lofty virtues, of our social life. It is *there* that the warfare against man's fancied perfection must be prosecuted, and the true nature of that one principle of Christian excellence, which is yet to be the light and blessedness of heaven, vindicated against all its counterfeits. It is these virtues which the man of the world and the philosopher equally declare themselves unable to conciliate with the uncompromising denunciations of the gospel. It is these in which I find them the most amply justified. The depravity of the world is just its forgetfulness, impatience, contempt of its God; the godless excellences, the unsanctified noblenesses of man, are the truest, the most awful proofs of the fact. That the murderer, the adulterer, the thief, should disclaim subjection to his God is sad, but scarcely surprising; the depth, the universality of the rebellion, is seen in the independence of our very virtues upon God; in the vast sphere of human excellence into which God never once enters; in the amiability that loves all but God; in the self-devotion that never surrendered one gratification for the sake of God; in the indomitable energy that never wrought one persevering work for God; in the enduring patience that faints under no weight of toil except the labour of adoring and praising God. This it is which really demonstrates the alienation of the world from its Maker, that its *best* affections should thus be affections to all but him; that not the worst alone, or the most degraded, but the best and loftiest natures among us should be banded in this conspiracy to exile him from the world he has made; that when he thus 'comes to his own,' 'his own' should 'receive him not;' that he should have to behold the fairest things he has formed—kindness, gratitude, and love—embracing every object but himself; the loveliest feelings he has implanted taking root, and growing and blossoming through the world, to bear fruit for all but him."

By this evil characteristic of our nature—its ungodliness—the rake and the man of virtue, the most savage and the most refined, are joined, as we have said, in an evil oneness. Hence may be inferred, by contrast, the primary and most obvious feature of the divine life, the recognition of God in all things; not, however, the mere earnest recognition of him, as we have seen sufficiently in the example of Saul of Tarsus, but that loving recognition which is characteristic of the humbled, penitent, and pardoned child.

But a few years ago an Indian Brahmin became a Christian. By the operation of an unjust law, he was deprived of his property, separated from his wife and children, and cast on the tender mercies of a cruel world. Loathed as a leper by those who were dearest to his heart, the question was put to him, What have you gained by becoming a Christian? "Much," he replied, "much—I have learned to say, 'Our Father which art in heaven.'" He had acquired a knowledge of the one true God as his FATHER in Christ. By this the troubled sea of his heart was quieted, the earnest longings of his soul were satisfied, and he could endure to be an outcast for Christ's sake.

In this same filial recognition of God as our Father, the foremost characteristic of the Divine Life, we have the mightiest and happiest stimulus to our conscience. The Divine authority does not become less binding because it is the authority of our Father, but a new class of feelings comes into play, powerfully and yet sweetly persuasive. They who are thus "alive unto God" do their work not as under the eye of a great taskmaster, but as under the eye of their loved and loving Father.

PART THE SECOND.

THE DIVINE LIFE: ITS ORIGINATION.

FACTS.

CONTENTS.—Diversity and Unity—Remarks of Wilberforce, Chalmers, and Fletcher—Miracles of Christ—Changes in Nature —First class of Instances; John Foster, R. Morrison, Knibb —Second class; Bengel, Blackader, J. J. Gurney, J. Fletcher, Mrs. Graham—Third class; Paul, Philippian Jailor, C. Anderson—Fourth class; Bilney, Archer Butler, M. Boos—Fifth class; Lyttleton, West, Dykern, Rochester, Wilson, H. K. White—Sixth class; Inspiration and Constitutional Peculiarities, Jonathan Edwards, Mrs. Phelps—Remarks.

"There are diversities of operation, but it is the same God which worketh all in all." THE APOSTLE PAUL (1 Cor. xii. 6.)

"The appearance of a new personality sanctified by the divine principle of life necessarily forms a great era in life, but the commencement of this era is not (always) marked with perfect precision and distinctness; the new creation manifests itself more or less gradually by its effects: 'The wind bloweth where it listeth.'"—NEANDER.

"These things happened unto them for ensamples."—THE APOSTLE PAUL (1 Cor. x. 11.)

"Scott's Force of Truth is an example: Doddridge's Rise and Progress of Religion in the Soul, another: and last, though not the least, The Pilgrim's Progress. I pronounce them all to be excellent, and that there are many exemplifications as they describe. But the process (described in these books) is not authoritative, nor is it universal. The Spirit taketh its own way with each individual, and you know it only by its fruits."—DR. CHALMERS.

"This change is discovered in people of all temperaments, in the phlegmatic as well as the ardent, in the slow and cautious as well as the impetuous and sanguine, in minds wholly subject to the understanding as well as those that submit more to the dominion of the imagination. It takes place in people of all ranks and conditions, in the wise and learned as well as the simple and ignorant; in persons insulated by society of a different cast, and strongly prejudiced against the belief of such a change."—DR. EDWARD D. GRIFFIN.

THE DIVINE LIFE:

ITS ORIGINATION.

THE grand characteristics of the process of conversion are diversity and unity. Dr. Chalmers could not say of himself "that he ever felt a state of mind corresponding to John Bunyan's Slough of Despond." Wilberforce, on the other hand, speaking of the "strong convictions of guilt" which accompanied his conversion, said that "nothing which he had ever read of in the accounts of others exceeded what he then felt." And yet no two men could exhibit a stronger spiritual likeness than these. In their convictions of personal demerit before God, in their views of the mediation through which sin is pardoned and the sinner reconciled to his Maker, in their filial love and confidence towards their Father in heaven, and in their practical love to all mankind, they were one.

This diversity and unity become the more striking when on the one hand the spiritual relationship of Chalmers and Wilberforce is remembered, and on the other their constitutional differences are remarked. Wilberforce's "Practical View" was put into Chalmers's hand at a time when his soul was struggling earnestly but pharisaically to attain conformity to the Divine law, and was the means of "a great revolution in all his opinions about christianity." But not in his opinions merely. "The deep views which Mr. Wilberforce gives of the depravity of our nature, of our need of an atonement, of the great doctrine of acceptance through that atonement, of the sanctifying influences of the Spirit—these all (said Dr. Chalmers) give a new aspect to a man's religion; and I am sure (he continues) that in as far as they are really and honestly proceeded upon, they will give a new direction to his habits and his history." It was so in his own case. The "revolution" which he underwent, left him a "new man." And yet between these illustrious men, spiritual father and son, there were the widest constitutional differences. Describing them as he saw them in 1830, Joseph John Gurney says:—

"I have seldom observed a more amusing and pleasing contrast between two great men than between Wilberforce and Chalmers. Chalmers is stout and erect, with a broad countenance; Wilberforce minute and singularly twisted;—Chalmers, both in body and in mind, moves with a deliberate step; Wilberforce, infirm as he is in his advanced years, flies about with astonishing activity; and while with nimble finger, he seizes on everything that adorns or diversifies his path, his mind flits from object to object with unceasing versatility. Chalmers can say a pleasant thing now and then, and laugh when he has said it; and he has a strong touch of humour in his countenance; but in general he is grave—his thoughts grow to a great size before they are uttered: Wilberforce sparkles with life and wit, and the characteristic of his mind is 'rapid productiveness.' A man might be in Chalmers's company for an hour, especially in a party, without knowing who or what he was, though in the end he would be sure to be detected by some unexpected display of powerful originality; Wilberforce, except when fairly asleep, is never latent. Chalmers knows how to veil himself in a decent cloud; Wilberforce is always in sunshine—seldom, I believe, has any mind been more strung to a perpetual tune of love and praise. Yet these persons, distinguished as they are from the world at large, and from each other, present some admirable points of resemblance. Both of them are broad thinkers and liberal feelers; both of them are arrayed in humility, meekness, and charity; both appear to hold self in little reputation; above all, both love the Lord Jesus Christ, and reverently acknowledge him to be their only Saviour."

The absence of uniformity in the process of conversion, and the essential sameness of the divine life which follows, have been remarked by many. "It has often been a cause of much distress to me," said Dr. Joseph Fletcher, of Stepney, when a young man, and in reference to his early experience, "that I could not particularize the place, the time, the means of my conversion." But in maturer years he remarked with wise discrimination: "In some cases, the means by which this renovation is effected may be so distinctly traced, as to enable the subject of it to develope all the process by which he is 'turned from darkness to light;' and, in such circumstances, to use the words of Dr. Paley, 'a man may as easily forget his escape from shipwreck,' as forget the manner, time, and means of his conversion. In other cases, the operation of various causes may be so complicated, so gradual, so interwoven with a series of events and influences, that a distinct remembrance and disclosure may be difficult, if not impossible. Still, in both the origin of the change is Divine, the medium of effecting it is the same holy truth, however diversified the manner and circumstances of its communication; and the results in the excitement of holy affection, and the working of practical consequences, will prove that it is 'the same Spirit' whose power is the source of this new creation."

The diversities which are observed in the process of spiritual conversion may be illustrated by the miracles of our Lord.

The records of these miracles are usually of this character:—"There came a leper to him, beseeching him, and kneeling down to him, and saying unto him, If thou wilt, thou canst make me clean. And Jesus, moved with compassion, put forth his hand, and touched him, and saith unto him, I will; be thou clean. And as soon as he had spoken, immediately the leprosy departed from him, and he was cleansed."* To a paralytic Jesus said, "Arise, and take up thy bed, and go thy way into thine house. And immediately he arose, took up the bed, and went forth before them all."† To the daughter of Jairus, lying in her shroud, he said, "Damsel, I say unto thee, arise. And straightway the damsel arose and walked."‡ And to Lazarus, who had been dead four days, Jesus "cried with a loud voice, Lazarus, come forth. And he that was dead came forth."§ Shall we be surprised, then, if a spiritual resurrection, and the work of spiritual healing which Jesus performs, be accomplished in the same manner, and become apparent both to the consciousness of those that are cured and to the observation of others with the rapidity of lightning?

In a few instances the miracles of Christ were performed by degrees, or at least the result of them was developed gradually, although even in these cases it

* Mark i. 40—42. † Mark ii. 11, 12.
‡ Mark v. 41, 42. § John xi. 43, 44.

was in a manner to show the Divinity of the power which wrought them. At Bethsaida, Jesus took a blind man that was brought to him, " and led him out of the town; and when he had spit on his eyes, and put his hands upon him, he asked him if he saw aught. And he looked up, and said, I see men as trees, walking. After that he put his hand again upon his eyes, and made him look up: and he was restored, and saw every man clearly."* In this case the first operation is not to be regarded as a failure; it accomplished all that it was designed to accomplish—a partial restoration. And the vision of the man thus partially healed resembles that of many in the process of conversion; they are no longer blind, but see; they see spiritual objects, but they do not see them as they are, but through a haze which produces distortion and confusion. On another occasion Jesus made clay of spittle, and anointed the eyes of a man who had been born blind, with the clay, "and said unto him, Go, wash in the pool of Siloam." The man " went his way and washed, and came seeing."† In this case the cure was a work of time and of degrees. The radical change in the condition of the blind man's eyes was effected no doubt by the word of Jesus Christ; the waters of Siloam possessed no curative efficacy, but the washing which our Lord commanded was essential to the man's enjoyment of sight. The Divine operation by which the spiritual eye is made to see may be instantaneous; but the soul's conscious enjoyment of vision may be a work of arduous progress and of many degrees.

The most familiar changes in nature furnish us with other analogies wherewith to illustrate the diversities

* Mark viii. 22—26. † John ix. 6, 7.

which are seen in the manner of the soul's conversion to God.

In some latitudes the dawn of day is almost instantaneous. The transition from darkness to light is clearly defined. So is it often with the soul. Up to a given hour or day the spiritual darkness is complete, the soul loves it and endures all its misery without one prayer for light; when suddenly, by some unseen agency, which Holy Scripture teaches us to recognize as the Spirit of God, the dark night passes away, and the true light shines. In other latitudes the dawn of day is more gradual, and the night is separated from the day by a considerable twilight. The first rays that reach our horizon are so faint, that even if we watch for them, we cannot distinguish them or determine the moment when they penetrate the darkness. And, if we continue to watch the progress of sunrise, so gradually does the darkness disappear before the approach of light, that we cannot mark its departure, except by the comparison of considerable intervals. The emergence of the soul from spiritual darkness is often similarly imperceptible, and its reality is to be seen only by the comparison of the antecedent night with the brightness of the day to which it has happily given place.

Again, the sun rises sometimes in a cloudless sky, and rejoices as a strong man to run a race, his progress not only unimpeded, but unobscured by cloud or storm. But it is often otherwise. Though risen, it is concealed from us by dark and tempestuous clouds, and pursues a course which to mortal eyes is uncertain, and which bears the aspect of a long and doubtful conflict between the light of heaven and the vapours of a turbid atmosphere. Even so is it with human spirits. One man emerges from the night of ignorance and sin, and, as it were, shakes from him at once all signs of its darkness, and his light shines more and more, without fluctuation or hindrance, unto the perfect day. Another comes forth from the deep night of his impenitency and unbelief feebly and uncertainly; now seems to be "light in the Lord," and then seems covered by a cloud of thick darkness; and not until many days or months, or even years, of conflict, have been endured, does it become evident, either in his soul's experience or in his life's practice, that he has really passed from death unto life.

The diversities which characterize the spring of our English climate likewise illustrate the variety which distinguishes the process of conversion. Our ideal of spring is very beautiful: "The earlier dawn of day—a certain cheerful cast in the light; even though still shining over an expanse of desolation, it has the appearance of a smile—a softer breathing of the air at intervals—the bursting of the buds—the vivacity of the animal tribes—the first flowers of the season —and, by degrees, a delicate, dubious tint of green. It needs not that a man should be a poet, or a sentimental worshipper of nature, to be delighted with all this." It is in this gentle and gradual manner that the divine life often appears, especially in the young. We see its first indications in "serious thoughts and emotions—growing sensibility of conscience—distaste for vanity and folly—deep solicitude for the welfare of the soul—a disposition to exercises of piety—a progressively clearer, more grateful, and more believing apprehension of the necessity and sufficiency of the work and sacrifice of Christ for human redemption. To a pious friend or parent this is more delightful than if he could have a vision of Eden, as it bloomed on the first day that Adam beheld it."

But the progress of spring is not always according to our ideal. "How reluctantly the worse (often) gives place to the better! While the winter is forced to retire it is yet very tenacious of its reign; it seems to hate the beauty and fertility that are supplanting it. For months we are liable to cold, chilling, pestilential blasts, and sometimes biting frosts. A portion of the malignant power lingers, or returns to lurk, as it were, under the most cheerful sunshine; so that the vegetable beauty remains in hazard, and the luxury of enjoying the spring is attended with danger to persons not in firm health. It is too obvious to need pointing out how much resembling this there is in the moral state of things—in the hopeful advance and improvement of the youthful mind, in the early and indeed more advanced stages of the Christian character, and in all the commencing improvements of human society."

First Class.

Our first illustrations of the process of conversion will be taken from the histories of John Foster, Robert Morrison, and William Knibb; the first, one of the greatest of thinkers, the other two among the greatest of workers for God and mankind. The experience of the three was of the most common order.

John Foster; born near Halifax, Sept. 17, 1770; died at Stapleton, Oct. 15, 1843.

The peculiarities of JOHN FOSTER's great mind, desirable and undesirable, were distinctly marked while yet in early youth he helped his father at the loom. When not twelve years old he had a painful sense of an awkward but entire individuality. Thoughtful and silent, he shunned the companionship of boys whose vivacity was merely physical and uninspired by sentiment. His constitutional pensiveness at times induced a recoil from human beings into a cold interior retirement, where he felt as if dissociated from the whole creation. His imagination was imperious and tyrannical, and would often haunt him with scenes which disturbed his nights' repose. He was full of restless thoughts, wishes, and passions, on subjects that interested none of his acquaintance.

With much that was uncongenial and disadvantageous in Foster's circumstances, their moral and religious influences were for the most part highly salutary. In his parents he had constantly before him examples of fervent piety, combined with great sobriety of judgment and undeviating integrity. A meeting was held in their house every Tuesday evening, which was always closed with a prayer by Mr. Foster, who never omitted one petition—"O Lord, bless the lads!" meaning his son John and a young companion. The earnestness with which these words were uttered made a deep impression on the two youths. To trace the progress of Foster's piety in its earliest stages, "mingled," as it was, "almost insensibly with his feelings," would be impracticable; its genuineness, happily, was proved by its shining more and more unto the perfect day. When about fourteen years old, he communicated to the associate just referred to, the poignant anxiety he had suffered from comparing his character with the requirements of the Divine law, and added, that he had found relief only by placing a simple reliance on the sacrifice of Jesus Christ for acceptance before God.

This is all that his biographer tells us of John Foster's conversion; and for general instruction it is enough. John Foster has been happily described as "a great man, with many peculiarities, but no littlenesses." The march of thought in his writings is felt to be the tread of a giant. Especially impressible by all that is grand and awful, he was equally sensitive to all that is tender and beautiful. Mountains filled him with emotions of sublimity and majesty; flowers the most delicate, retiring, and minute, inspired him with delight. Much given to profound and searching thought, and often restlessly desirous to penetrate the veil that separates the seen from the unseen, it is instructive to find that his personal religious consciousness was of a character common to that of the most ordinary minds.

Evangelical Christianity contains—to use his own words—"a humiliating estimate of the moral condition of man as a being radically corrupt; the doctrine of redemption from that condition by the merit and sufferings of Christ; the doctrine of a Divine influence being necessary to transform the character of the human mind, in order to prepare it for a higher station in the universe; and a grand moral peculiarity by which it insists on humility, penitence, and a separation from the spirit and habits of the world." These principles constituted no mere creed or theory, but actuated John Foster's whole spiritual nature. "It seemed to him not less preposterous than impious to assume any other posture than that of deep abasement before Him whom the heaven of heavens cannot contain, and in whose sight the heavens are not clean." But while he stood in awe from conscious sin, he did not tremble like a slave. He found peace and hope in Christ. "What would become of a poor sinful soul (he said, a few days before his death), but for that blessed, all comprehensive sacrifice, and that intercession at the right hand of the Majesty on high?" Still nearer his last hour, and while speaking of his weakness, he said, "But I can pray—and that is a glorious thing." "Trust in Christ, trust in Christ," he said to his attendant. And with almost his dying breath, he was overheard to repeat the song of triumph—"O death, where is thy sting? O grave, where is thy victory? Thanks be to God, which giveth us the victory through our Lord Jesus Christ."

Dr. Morrison; born at Morpeth, Jan. 5, 1782: died at Canton, Aug. 1, 1834.

The following is in substance the account which ROBERT MORRISON gave of himself in 1802. He had enjoyed the inestimable advantage of a godly parentage, and was habituated to a constant and regular attendance on the preaching of the gospel. His father was careful to maintain the worship of God in his family, and to train his children in the way of holiness. When further advanced in life, young Morrison received much advantage from the public catechetical instructions of the Rev. John Hutton. By these means his conscience was informed and enlightened, and he was kept from running to any "excess of riot," though as yet he lived without Christ, without God, and without hope in the world. He was a stranger, he testified, to the plague of his own heart; and, notwithstanding that he often felt remorse, and the upbraidings of conscience, yet he flattered himself that somehow he should have peace, though he walked "in the ways of his own heart."

When about fifteen or sixteen years of age, he was "much awakened to a sense of sin." He could recall no particular circumstance which led to this, unless it were that at that time he grew somewhat loose and profane, and was oftener than once led into intoxication by wicked company. He was startled by his own conduct, and reflection led him to serious concern about his soul. The fear of death compassed him about, and he was led to cry mightily to God, that he would pardon his sin, and that he would renew him in the spirit of his mind. Sin became a burden. His life and his heart were now changed. He broke off from his wicked companions, and gave himself to reading, meditation, and prayer. "Since that time," he wrote five years after, "the Lord has been gradually pleased to humble and prove me; and though I have often enjoyed much peace and joy in believing, I have likewise experienced much opposition from the working of in-dwelling sin—'the flesh lusting against the spirit, and the spirit against the flesh; and these being contrary the one to the other, I could not do the things that I would.' I have gradually discovered more of the holiness, spirituality, and extent of the Divine law; and more of my own vileness and unworthiness in the sight of God; and the freeness and richness of sovereign grace. I have sinned as I could; it is 'by the grace of God I am what I am.'"

When Robert Morrison consecrated his life to missionary service, it was his prayer that God would station him in that part of the missionary field where the difficulties were the greatest, and to all human appearance the most insurmountable. His prayer was answered in his appointment to China; and from the day of his appointment to the day of his death, he had but one ruling object—the conversion of that great empire to Christ. Everything he thought, and said, and did, henceforward, tended directly or indirectly to this end; and to this every personal gratification and advantage was cheerfully subordinated. His name will throughout all time be associated with one of the greatest triumphs at once of Christian zeal and of high scholarship in the translation of the Holy Scriptures into the Chinese language, and the preparation of a Chinese dictionary. His moral and spiritual character harmonized with the rank which he must ever take among the servants of Christ as the first apostle of the Protestant church to China. And in the conversion of the Northumbrian last-maker's son to God, common-place as the manner of it may be said to have been, there was laid the foundation of great personal excellence, and there was opened a fountain of blessing to the long estranged and benighted land of Sinim.

William Knibb; born at Kettering, Sept. 7, 1803; died in Jamaica, Nov. 16, 1845.

It was the privilege of WILLIAM KNIBB to enjoy in childhood the care and instruction of the best of mothers. "There was that about her," says one who knew her well, "which would at once excite love and reverence. Her piety was not only above the common rate, but it was highly intelligent and attractive. She passed most of her life in most trying circumstances, under which she uniformly displayed a magnanimity and pious cheerfulness that could not fail to be observed and admired by hei children, even at an early age. With much calmness of temper she combined great energy in all her undertakings; and there was a strength of intellect, a breadth and depth in her views on all subjects, religious and others, and a certain mild eloquence and felicity of language and benignity of manner, which at the same time inspired respect for her understanding and affection to her person."

It would be strange if the children of such a mother were not the subjects of religious impressions from their childhood. But it was not till William Knibb was a youth of eighteen or nineteen that these impressions ripened into decision. The Sunday school connected with the Baptist church at Broadmead, Bristol, in which he was not a scholar but a junior teacher, was always regarded by him as the birthplace of his soul. And the account which his own words contain of his transition from darkness to light may be regarded as the reflection of the experience of thousands who have been placed in similar circumstances:—

"Having enjoyed the unspeakable advantages of a religious education, and of being trained under the care of a pious and affectionate mother, I was early taught my state as a sinner, and the necessity of flying to Jesus Christ as the only hope of escape from that punishment which my sins had deserved, and I was at an early age subject to many convictions; and, though separated from under the immediate care of my parents at a very early age, yet the pious letters which I received from my mother from time to time, together with being placed in a serious family, were continual restraints upon my conduct, and tended continually to revive those convictions which I had received under the parental roof. Under these convictions the state of my mind was various. Often did I treat them as intruders upon my peace and comfort, and foolishly envied the condition of those of my associates who, as I thought, could continue in their sins without being so often disturbed by those cutting reflections which I so frequently felt. At other times I endeavoured to lull my conscience asleep, under the delusion that I was willing to return to God if he would be pleased to change my heart, and that therefore it was not my fault. I impiously dared to charge it on my Maker. And not unfrequently did I make many resolutions of amendment, and many promises that, if the Lord would be pleased to pardon my sins, I would devote my future life to his service, and attend to those things which concerned my everlasting welfare. But these resolutions and promises were formed in my own strength, and I soon found, by sad experience, that they were of no avail in the hour of temptation; for no sooner did Satan present his allurements than I fell an easy prey to them, and returned to my old courses with as great an eagerness as ever. Indeed, under these convictions, I have reason to believe that it was not sin as committed against a holy, just, and good God that affected me, so much as the consequences which I knew would inevitably result from continuing in it. I did not wish to be saved *from* my sins, but *in* them; and if I could have continued in sin and escaped the consequences, I am afraid that I should still have been willing to have rolled it as a sweet morsel under my tongue." Those who know what true conviction of sin is, will not infer from these self-criminations that

William Knibb was a youth of immoral life. On the contrary, he was virtuous and upright. But he writes in the light of that law which requires inward purity and godliness. The narrative of his conversion proceeds thus :—

"A little less than a year ago (in 1821) I was invited to take one of the junior classes in the Broadmead Sunday school. Before I had continued any length of time in the school, the thought struck my mind that I could not properly discharge the duties of my office if I did not devote a portion of my time to preparation for religious instruction. When I made the trial, such thoughts as these entered my mind, and almost induced me to abandon the attempt— Have you attended to these things which you recommend to the children? You tell them they are of infinite importance, but do you really value them? If not, are you not, while instructing them, pronouncing your own condemnation? And how can you expect any blessing to result from your instructions? Some time after this, a most earnest and affectionate address, which was delivered to the children by the superintendent, from the character of young Abijah, under the Divine blessing, made a deep, and I trust lasting impression on my mind, and I hope that I was enabled to cast myself at the foot of the cross as a perishing sinner, pleading for mercy for the alone sake of Jesus Christ."

Young Knibb was now on the Lord's side, resting in the peace and hope of the gospel, and filled with zeal to make others partakers of the same blessings. Within two years and a half from this period he was appointed to missionary service in the West Indies. And there, after twenty-three years of faithful labour and successful conflict, he was called away from earthly toil in November, 1845, not building his hopes of heaven on what he had done, but on what Christ had done for him. "I am not afraid to die," he said; "the blood of Christ cleanseth from all sin, both of omission and commission, and that blood is my only trust."

The commonness, if the expression may be used, of Knibb's early experience, and the commonness of the elements of his character, render his example all the more useful. "He was not a man of original genius," says his biographer. "He was not a man of lofty intellect. He was not a man of literary taste. He was not a man of finished education. He was not a man of scientific attainments. He was not a metaphysician, not a poet, not even a theologian. . . . . He was kind, just, firm, active, and fearless. He had good sense, strong nerves, simple speech, a warm heart, and lively piety. What commonplace qualities are these! Yet they made an extraordinary man."

Second Class.

"The light and insinuations of the Divine Spirit," to use the words of Robert Hall, "so often accompany the conduct of a strictly religious education, that some of the most eminent Christians have acknowledged themselves at a loss to assign the precise era of their conversion." Instances of this order are found in every condition of life, and in every variety of mental character. We shall use for illustration the histories of Bengel the Student, Blackader the Soldier, Joseph John Gurney the Philanthropist, Joseph Fletcher the Preacher, and Mrs. Graham, a woman of gentle and tender spirit.

It has been maintained, and perhaps correctly, that

in all cases regeneration is instantaneous—that the impartation of spiritual life to the soul by the Holy Spirit is effected at once—that the "stony heart" is not softened by degrees into flesh, but by one decisive effort removed, and a heart of flesh substituted in its room. And the fact that the consciousness of the spiritual life within a man's soul, and its development before the observation of others, is not always instantaneous, has been explained thus:—"Conceive of a man sitting in a dungeon, so occupied in thought as not to notice the change gradually produced by a light approaching at a distance. Turning his eye, at length he discerns objects, and perceives that there is a light in the room; but when it began to enter he cannot tell; yet there was a moment when the first ray passed the window." Be the truth on this point what it may, the *conscious* turning of the heart to God is often not the work of a moment, but of years, and is to be compared, not to the rapidity of the lightning flash, but to the silent and imperceptible dawn of a spring morning.

Bengel; born 1687; died 1752.

Of those who have been partakers of the divine life from childhood, and in whom it has seemed to grow with their growth, it would be difficult to find a more illustrious example than that of ALBERT BENGEL, the German commentator. We preface his history by words of his own, which will show that his views of human nature, and of the great change which it needs, were not superficial and inadequate. "What is conversion, and what properly belongs to it? It is the turning and submission of the soul, hitherto sunk in self-ignorance, self-love, and idolatry to the creature, consequently something hitherto alienated from God; it is the returning and submission of such a soul to him, and to his good and holy will, for the sake of his honour and glory, and for the sake of its own health and salvation." "May a fixed time ever be referred to as the commencement of true conversion? Yes; when a state of open sin has been exchanged for decided obedience to the grace of Christ, the very day of such a change, or even the hour, or perhaps moment, may be referred to. But when the transition has proceeded by slow degrees, and many false steps and backslidings have intervened, a person finds it very difficult with respect to himself, and still more difficult with respect to others, to point out the time when evil or good gained the ascendant." Then, in answer to the question, "How may we most scripturally express ourselves upon our own state of grace?" he replied, "All that we can possibly utter upon this subject is contained in one sentence of St. Paul, 'Nevertheless I obtained mercy;' or, 'The Lord hath called me out of darkness into marvellous light;' or, 'Though such and such was I, yet I am washed, I am sanctified, I am justified in the name of the Lord Jesus, and by the Spirit of our God.'"

Albert Bengel said of himself, that "in his childhood he experienced grace a hundredfold more than sufficient to have destroyed the very life of sin within him." This was not the language of spiritual pride, but of humble and adoring gratitude. He appears to have been baptized of the Holy Ghost from infancy, and to have possessed the devout consciousness of being a child of God from the first dawning of reason. "In his earliest years he had many clear, pure, tender feelings and stirring in his heart concerning God;

and the texts inscribed on the church walls of his native town, from the Epistle to the Romans, concerning sin, righteousness, the crucifixion, and other subjects, produced in him as a mere child emotions of great joy and peace." "With childlike simplicity he followed his heavenly Father's guidance, and submitted to God's inward and outward discipline; and though he did not yet fully understand what a high and rare privilege he enjoyed, the power of the Divine word took such possession of his heart, that he had confidence in God like that of a little child in its parent; took great delight in prayer, longed for the better life to come, loved the Scriptures, enjoyed the church hymns, and the simplest books of devotion; had a tender conscience, dreaded doing wrong, and showed complacency in everything that was excellent."

This truly christian child enjoyed a large share of the love of his schoolfellows and of older persons. For a time his piety grew "like the grass, that tarrieth not for man," eluding observation, but continually advancing under the blessing of God. As he grew up into boyhood, he was no stranger to the stirrings of our common corruption. Speaking of blasphemous and bad thoughts, he said in after life, "Oh, how many such darts have heretofore gone through my soul! They have occasioned me such distress and dejection in my younger days, as quite to alter my manner of behaviour to others, and I knew not how to prevent it." The distress which he thus suffered was evidence of the repugnance of his heart to these evil intruders. Sudden and injurious suggestions, and sallies of thoughtless, foolish levity, assailed him likewise, but he was preserved from their power without losing the character of a boy and becoming a recluse. At the same time, the very early and gradual character of his Christian experience was itself the occasion of certain difficulties which only increased knowledge could remove. Speaking of the seven psalms which are called *penitential*, and which young persons at school were specially taught to commit to memory, he says, "Such passages occasioned me much perplexity in my younger days; for, wishing to measure myself by the measure I found in these psalms, I endeavoured to realize the same strong experience, and could not."

In youth he endured temptation and trials of another order, more severe and perilous. These came from the study of philosophy. "My will was compliant (he says), but many a doubt assailed my understanding." Too timid to communicate his difficulties to any one, he brooded over them in secret, and disquieted himself in vain. But at the very time he was thus suffering, the goodness of God afforded him, he tells us, such affecting discoveries, and such experiences of inward peace, that he felt encouraged to persevere in childlike prayer. His spiritual condition at this time is easily understood. His affections found their enjoyment and repose in the gospel of Christ, but his reason put in its claim, right or wrong, to demonstration and certainty upon truths which had already taken possession of his heart. "A raw, unconverted man," he said afterwards, "living after the course and fashion of this world, and therefore indifferent to the truth altogether, meets with no difficulty in subscribing to any form of doctrine. He takes a thing for granted, just as he finds it, and cares not for the trouble of proof. But a really converted man feels truth to be a precious thing; is disposed to inquiry after it; preserves it when found;

and handles it as he would an invaluable jewel, with great care and circumspection. Finding it impossible to go on in a careless, trifling spirit, he is obliged to prove all things, whatever trouble it may give him. Now, as truth upon every point is not attainable without many a hard struggle, his progress is often very slow." But it was well for Bengel that "his heart was established with grace." While earnestness, operating as he describes, may be the *occasion* of error, indifference is usually its *cause* and parent. And young Bengel grew up into an enlightened and steadfast faith in the doctrine of the cross and all the truths which cluster around it. His life was one great exposition of their power. And in death they lighted his spirit through the dark valley.

Col. Blackader; born in Dumfrieshire, Sept. 14, 1664; died at Stirling, Aug. 31, 1729.

The name of Colonel Blackader is associated with memories of military courage and Christian piety. The father of this good and brave man was a minister of the church of Scotland, in dark and troublous times. He was the fellow labourer of Welsh, Peden, Cargill, and other undaunted Covenanters, who maintained the rights and the freedom of their national worship in the face of peril and sword. In 1674, he was proclaimed rebel and fugitive, and a premium of a thousand marks was offered to any that should kill or apprehend him. But a good Providence preserved him from the violence of barbarous edicts. On his return from Holland, where he spent a short time after the defeat of Bothwell Bridge, he was apprehended at Edinburgh, in his own house, and sent a prisoner to the Bass Rock. In this bleak and solitary isle, he lingered several years in rigorous captivity, till the harshness of his treatment and the ungenial air of the place terminated his days in 1685.

In the midst of confusion and distraction, this worthy man had carefully trained his family for God. And he had his reward. In his son, John, "we have not an example which we sometimes find in the histories of good men, of the subduing power of regenerating grace over a reprobate and unrenewed heart—of the mysterious efficacy with which it operates in awakening and transforming sinners, to all appearance irrecoverably lost, who, after having given in to every lawless excess, have been suddenly recovered, as by miracle, from the most daring profanity, or the grossest licentiousness." The heart of John Blackader was impressed with religion from his infancy. At twelve years of age he was admitted a communicant to the Lord's supper. He frequently attended conventicles and communions, which were celebrated in the open fields, and which had begun, about 1677, to attract immense crowds of hearers from all parts of the country. In the Diary of later years, he speaks with rapture of those quickening and refreshing ordinances, and complains that he felt not on Sabbaths, in the army abroad, the same ardent desires and tender meltings of soul that he used to have in Scotland. Amidst the confusion of battles, and the licentiousness of camps, he reverts, with a mixture of delight and regret, to the days of old, when he went with the multitude that kept solemn feast and took sweet counsel together.

Blackader's piety, though early, proved uniform and abiding. He went steadily forward in the paths of righteousness, without straying from his course—his life advancing to perfect day like the morning light, and shining to the last with increasing brightness. It was his happiness to maintain his integrity and his godly simplicity in a station replete with dangers and temptations, and where exemption from flagrant vice may be regarded as virtue of rare and difficult attainment.

As in the case of Bengel, there is abundant evidence that the piety of Blackader, which grew silently and without observation, like the grass of the field, was not of a superficial character. In his views of doctrinal truth he distinctly recognized the corruption of our nature, the atonement of our Lord Jesus Christ as the only ground of the sinner's hope before God, and the inworking of the Holy Spirit as the only source of spiritual good in man. And in every page of his Diary there is evidence of those spiritual conflicts, and consolations, and longings, which are experienced by those whose conversion to God is more marked, both in the consciousness of the Christian himself, and in the outward changes with which it is accompanied.

It will excite surprise that a youth like John Blackader should have embraced a military life. But this may have been from necessity rather than from choice. And, so far as it was of choice, the circumstances of the times may account for it. The revolution of 1688 was achieved, but not yet completed. The country, emerging from oppression, made an appeal to the patriotism of every citizen to take arms in the common cause—an appeal which must have been doubly enforced by the remembrance of past injuries and the hope of a glorious deliverance. To such considerations the history of his family sufferings would render young Blackader tenderly sensitive. And a sense of duty, at such a juncture, might overcome the scrupulous reluctance with which his Christian heart must have contemplated scenes of war and bloodshed.

Joseph John Gurney; born at Earlham Hall, 1788; died in 1847.

The name of JOSEPH JOHN GURNEY stands side by side with that of his honoured sister, Mrs. Elizabeth Fry, among the greatest philanthropists of his age. And his philanthropy was not the fruit of mere humanity, but of the divine life that was in him.

His mother is described as a woman "of very superior mind, as well as personal charms, who in her latter years became a serious Christian and a decided Friend." When removed by death, the maternal mantle fell upon the eldest sister, who, though scarcely seventeen years of age, ripened with an early maturity which admirably fitted her for the necessities of the occasion. The father was a generous, ardent, and warmhearted man, with an acute intellect and extensive information.

Of the state of mind and feeling which prevailed in this young and interesting family after the death of their mother, the biographer of Joseph John says, that the naturally grave and practical disposition of their elder sister Catherine hardly formed an exception to the general liveliness and gaiety which pervaded the circle, and which rendered the members of it peculiarly liable to be led away by the various temptations to which they were exposed. Their earlier years were, in fact, distinguished by much which they afterwards felt to have partaken largely of the vanity of youth, but which was yet singularly mingled with not a little of an opposite character. The evening dance, with its whirl of mirth and merriment, the excitement of the youthful day-dream, gave place, in their turns, to days of industry and study, to concern for the poor, and at times to religious seriousness. The contrast was striking, and not without promise.

Joseph John was the tenth child in this family in the order of age, and is described by his sisters as full of tender feeling, of love and gentleness, and possessing a temper that nothing could irritate or render fretful. He was studious and fond of reading, and whether at home or at school he maintained the character of a boy of unsullied conduct, of fine disposition, and excellent talents.

Speaking of the year 1806, when Joseph John Gurney was in his eighteenth year, his biographer says—"Happy in his family circle, the world around seemed to him to partake of its loveliness. His fondness for music and dancing gave an additional fascination to some of the more specious allurements of pleasure; and whilst the duties of business were not neglected, and his studies were pursued with unremitting eagerness, he became at this period a frequent visitor at balls and other similar entertainments, where his engaging manners and person, and varied accomplishments, rendered him an object of general attraction. It is plain, however, from his private memoranda, that Divine grace was through all secretly working in his heart."

Of his own spiritual progress his autobiography contains the following account:—"I was by no means insensible, in very early life, to religious considerations; being no stranger, from the first opening of my mental faculties, to those precious visitations of Divine love which often draw the young mind to its Creator and melt it into tenderness. If religion has indeed grown in me (as I humbly believe it has, though amidst innumerable backslidings), it has pretty much kept pace with the growth of my natural faculties, for I cannot now recall any decided turning point in this matter, except that which afterwards brought me to plain 'Quakerism.' Cases of this description are, in my opinion, in no degree at variance with the cardinal Christian doctrine of conversion, and of the new birth unto righteousness. The work which effects the vital change from a state of nature to a state of grace, is doubtless often begun in very early childhood—nay, it may open on the soul with the earliest opening of its rational faculties; and that its progress may sometimes be so gradual as to preclude our perceiving any very distinct steps in it, we may learn from our blessed Lord's parable—'So is the kingdom of God, as if a man should cast seed into the ground; and should sleep and rise, night and day, and the seed should spring and grow up, he knoweth not how. For the earth bringeth forth fruit of herself; first the blade, then the ear, after that the full corn in the ear.' I have no doubt that some seed was sown in my heart when I was little more than an infant, through the agency of my watchful mother; and afterwards that seed was sedulously watched and cultivated by my dearest sister Catherine. Yet I believe that much of the feeling into which my young mind was at times brought, on the subject of religion, was the simple result of those gracious visitations which are independent of all human agency, and like the wind which 'bloweth where it listeth.'"

We have said that the philanthropic labours of Joseph John Gurney were the fruit of the divine life within him. He was not impelled to them by the mere tenderness of humanity, nor by the hope of thus working out his own salvation. No one could have clearer views of "the contrast between legal and gospel obedience." In 1833 he thus wrote to a young friend: "When we call to mind that we are by nature corrupt and sinful, and have actually sinned (alas, how much and how often!) in thought, word, and deed, our hearts ought to overflow with gratitude to Him who hath redeemed us with his precious blood. Under this feeling of gratitude to our Lord Jesus Christ, and of ardent love for God, we shall be constrained, by the most heart-cheering of motives, to take up our daily cross, to walk in the paths of Christian self-denial, and to 'follow the Lamb whithersoever he goeth.' *Our motive, then, is love, and the effect is obedience.* . . . The law of God is emphatically called the 'law of liberty;' for while it binds down every unruly passion, and leads into true 'simplicity and godly sincerity in all things,' it encourages a noble freedom of action in the service of our Lord. The spirit of Christ within us is a 'spirit of power, of love, and of a sound mind.'"

In the same year we find Joseph John Gurney giving an account of a visit to an aged patriarch in the Society of Friends, and of an address in which this patriarch called on his children to "press after the salvation of their immortal souls, and recommended to them their various social and religious duties." "One thing, however, above all others," he says, "struck me in this address. It was the clear and oft-repeated declaration of this servant of Christ that he had no trust whatever in his own righteousness, but that all his confidence was in the Lord; all his hopes of future happiness in the availing mediation and perfect righteousness of the Redeemer of men. His address, like the letters of Paul, was full of 'Jesus Christ and him crucified.' All boasting was excluded. Deep humiliation was the distinguishing mark of every passing sentence. Mercy, mercy, was the theme; and God in Christ was exalted over all. Thus, out of the mouth of two experienced witnesses [the other, his dying mother-in-law] has the gospel of life and salvation been confessed and confirmed in our hearing; and in both cases has the eye as well as the ear perceived its delightful efficacy, its gladdening, quickening influence. What, indeed, can be more lovely than the spectacle of advancing age softened, and ripened, and mellowed into sweetness, under the sunshine of genuine Christianity?"

Dr. Joseph Fletcher; born at Chester, Dec. 3, 1784; died at Stepney, June 8, 1843.

From his childhood, JOSEPH FLETCHER was trained up in the nurture and admonition of the Lord, and the instruction of his parents, enforced by their uniformly consistent example, laid the foundation of his piety. In the tenth year of his age he was the subject of strong religious impressions under the preaching of the word. And other circumstances contributed to render them deep and permanent. "At a very early age," he says, "serious impressions were made upon my mind, which were particularly effected by the reading of Janeway's 'Token for Children.' The author's very pathetic address in the preface of that work tended much to convince me of the importance and necessity of religion. This address was often read and prayed over with considerable interest and delight. But levity and folly, the usual characteristics of childhood, succeeded these first impressions.

I cannot recollect any particular circumstance till my eleventh or twelfth year, when convictions which had been forgotten were revived and deepened. It has often been the cause of much distress that I could not particularize the place, the time, the means of my conversion. The Lord's work was gradually effected: I cannot better describe it at its commencement than by the words of the blind man in the gospel, who at first only saw 'men as trees, walking.' As I was constantly in the way of learning something, having from my earliest years a predilection for reading, and being furnished with the necessary means of instruction, I did, indeed, acquire a theoretical knowledge of some of the distinguishing doctrines of the gospel. But, I fear, that knowledge was merely speculative. I saw not so much of the evil of sin, nor of the beauty and inestimable worth of the Friend of sinners as afterwards. Though orthodox in my notions of some things, my dependence was centred in myself. But by a constant attendance on the means of grace, the Lord was graciously pleased to remove the veil of spiritual ignorance from the eyes of my understanding, and afford me more scriptural views of the way of salvation through a Mediator."

This gradual change and growing light issued in no doubtful character. "His personal religion," said the Rev. J. A. James, after many years of the closest intimacy, "was not only free from every shadow of a shade of suspicion arising from external blemishes and actual inconsistencies, but was of that experimental kind which manifests itself in watching the heart with all diligence, in maintaining habitual communion with God through Christ, in bowing with deep submission to the will of God, and in a growing meetness for the heavenly world. His beautiful tract on Spirituality of Mind, was with him no theory. He copied from his heart, as well as set a model for it. . . . . . Perhaps the most appropriate term, if one only were selected, to set forth his character, would be *completeness*. There was more of symmetry in it than in that of any other man I am acquainted with. It would be possible to find some in whom detached and separate excellences rose to a higher eminence; but it would not be easy to point to one in whom so many were combined, and combined in such nice proportions as to form extraordinary beauty."

Mrs. Graham; born in Lanarkshire, 1742; died in New York, 1814.

In Mrs. Isabella Graham we have a beautiful specimen of true religion, at once feminine and practical. And its origin was peaceful, imperceptible, and early, like that of Albert Bengel. Her childhood and youth were spent among all the traditional associations of Elderslie, once the habitation of the Scottish hero, Sir William Wallace. Of the period at which her heart first tasted that the Lord is gracious, her biographer tells us she had no precise recollection. As far back as she could remember, she took delight in pouring out her soul to God. In the woods of Elderslie she selected a bush to which she resorted in seasons of devotion; and under this bush she was enabled to devote herself to God through faith in her Redeemer, before she attained her tenth year. To this favourite, and to her sacred spot, she would repair, when exposed to temptation, or perplexed with youthful troubles. From thence she caused her prayers to ascend, and always found peace and consolation.

That this was more than mere girlish sentiment was proved by its growing and practical character. While only twenty-four years of age we find her married, and with her husband, a regimental surgeon, resident at Fort Niagara, on Lake Ontario. The want of religious ordinances was here, no doubt, the occasion of injury to the life of God in her soul. But a conscientious observance of the Sabbath was the means of her preservation. She wandered, on those sacred days, into the woods around Niagara, searched her Bible, communed with God and herself, and poured out her soul in prayer to her covenant Lord.

A few years after, we find her returning from America, a sorrowful widow with three infants to care for. After a stormy and trying voyage she arrived in safety at Belfast, and thence embarked for Scotland on board a packet on which, as she afterwards learned, there was not even a compass. There arose a great storm, and they were tossed to and fro for nine hours in imminent danger. The rudder and the masts were carried away; everything on deck was thrown overboard; and, at length, the vessel struck in the night upon a rock on the coast of Ayr. The greatest confusion pervaded the passengers and the crew. Of a number of young students going to the university of Edinburgh, some were swearing, some were praying, and all were in despair. The widow only remained composed. The faith which was implanted in her, while in girlhood she rambled amongst the woods of Elderslie, was her support. With her babe in her arms, she hushed her weeping family, and told them that in a few moments they should all go to join their father in a better world. The passengers wrote their names in their pocket-books that their bodies might be recognized. One young man came into the cabin, asking, "Is there any peace here?" He was surprised to find a female so tranquil, and a short conversation showed that religion was the source of comfort and hope to them both in this perilous hour.

That her early piety, though of a quiet, imperceptible growth, was not superficial, nor merely emotional, will appear likewise from the language in which she described it many years after. Writing from New York to a friend in Edinburgh, she said, "It is now, I think, thirty-five years since I simply, but solemnly accepted of the Lord's Christ, as God's gift to a lost world. I rolled my condemned, perishing, corrupted soul upon this Jesus, exhibited in the gospel as a Saviour from sin. My views then were dark compared with what they now are; but this I remember, that, at the time, I felt a heart-satisfying trust in the mercy of God as the purchase of Christ; and, for a time, rejoiced with joy scarcely supportable, singing almost continually the 103rd Psalm." Of the many times and ways in which she was conscious that her heart had departed from God during her Christian life, she speaks with natural pathos and deep humility. "Never," she says, "did the children of Israel's conduct in the wilderness depict any Christian's heart and conduct in gospel times better than mine." But she adds, "In general the Lord had some affliction for me which laid me afresh at his feet, and made me take a fresh grasp of Christ, and a fresh view of his covenant; then again I felt safety, joy, peace, and happiness: thus by line upon line, by precept upon precept, and by stripe upon stripe, he taught me that I could not walk a moment alone. This is now my fixed faith; and in proportion as I keep it in sight, I walk safely; but I still forget, and still stumble, and still fall; but I am lifted up, and taught lesson after lesson; and I shall stumble and fall while sin is in me; but I am as sure that I shall be lifted up, and be restored, as I am sure I now breathe, and write these things; and the last stumble shall come, and the last stripe shall be laid on, and the last lesson taught, and that which concerns me shall be perfected. Then shall I look back, and see all the way by which he has led me, to prove me, and try me, and show me what was in my heart, that he might do me good in my latter end." The Atlantic rolled between the scene of her death and the scene of her birth, but in her dying hours she was sustained by the very hopes which she had first acquired and sung in the woods of Elderslie.

Third Class.

In these cases the work of conversion was developed gradually. But there are others in which it is wrought with a rapidity which may be characterized as instantaneous. The apostle Paul is an illustrious example. Full of wrath against the followers of Christ as he hastens towards Damascus, a few moments suffice to prostrate his spirit before that Jesus whom he had bitterly hated, crying, "Lord, what wilt thou have me to do?" And in three days, as we have seen, he is an established Christian, prepared to go forth in the face of all danger to preach Jesus as the Saviour of the world.

The Philippian Jailor.

Among the converts of Paul's ministry in after years, the jailor at Philippi may be cited as an example of the same order.

With rigorous cruelty, he thrusts Paul and Silas into the inner prison, and forces their limbs, lacerated as they are by the scourge, into the stocks, an instrument employed to torture the bodies of the worst malefactors. He is awakened in the night by an earthquake, and seeing the doors of the prison open, and preferring death to disgrace, he draws his sword with the desperate hardihood of a Roman officer. The prisoners, however, are not fled, and Paul exclaims, "Do thyself no harm; for we are all here." "But now a fear of a higher kind took possession of his soul. The recollection of all that he had heard before concerning these prisoners, and all that he had observed of their demeanour when he brought them into the dungeon, the shuddering thought of the earthquake, the burst of his gratitude towards them as the preservers of his life, and the consciousness that even in the darkness of midnight they had seen his intention of suicide—all these mingling and conflicting emotions made him feel that he was in the presence of a higher power. He fell down before them, and brought them out, as men whom he had deeply injured and insulted, to a place of greater freedom and comfort; and then he asked them, with earnest anxiety, what he must do to be saved. . . . The awakening of his conscience, the presence of the unseen world, the miraculous visitation, the nearness of death, coupled, perhaps, with some confused recollection of the 'way of salvation' which these strangers were said to have been proclaiming, were enough to suggest that inquiry which is the most momentous that any human soul can make—'What must I do to be saved?' Their answer was that of faithful apostles. They preached not themselves, but Christ Jesus the Lord. 'Believe not in us, but in the Lord Jesus, and thou shalt be saved; and not only thou, but the like faith shall bring salvation to all thy house.' From this last expression, and from the words which follow, we infer that the members of the jailor's family had crowded round him and the apostles. No time was lost in making known to them 'the word of the Lord.' All thought of bodily comfort and repose was postponed to the work of saving the soul. The meaning of faith in Jesus was explained, and the gospel was preached to the jailor's family at midnight, while the prisoners were silent around, and the light was thrown on anxious faces and the dungeon wall." The jailor received the truth and was baptized. His cruelty was immediately changed into hospitality and love. The sun had set upon him a hardened heathen, it arose upon him a humble and rejoicing Christian. "From being the ignorant slave of a heathen magistracy, he had become the religious head of a Christian family."

The miracles which accompanied the conversion of Paul and of the Philippian jailor, and which contributed to produce them, are easily separable from the conversion itself. So are the extraordinary circumstances which accompanied the conversion of colonel Gardiner. Without any such circumstances, we have seen conversion effected with equal suddenness in Latimer and Caroline Fry. Many other instances will occur as we proceed. At present we give only one. The subject of it became a minister of Christ's gospel, and spent a long lifetime in honourably and usefully "serving his generation by the will of God."

Christopher Anderson; born in Edinburgh, 1782; died in Edinburgh, 1852.

Christopher Anderson was, we are told, naturally of an impulsive and fearless disposition, with a strong dislike to whatever was deceptive, and impatient of anything that was doubtful. With a more than usual aversion to hypocrisy of every kind, he never made the smallest pretence to religious feeling as long as he was conscious he had none. Till he could *enjoy religion*, he was determined to *enjoy the world*, and went as far in gratifying his taste for the gaieties of life as his place in a well-ordered religious family would permit. While his walk was after the course of this world, he needed no prompter to its pleasures. He was then, as afterwards in a better cause, ever the *leader*, never the *led*. The early conversion of all his brothers had left him companionless in that course. One after another, and in the very order of their age, they had been called by Divine grace to the possession of that truth which weaned them from the pursuits which continued for some years longer to charm their youngest brother. "My delight in folly," he says, "was my own choice." In the country, where many of his earlier years were spent, in consequence of the delicacy of his constitution, he was a devotee to the music and dancing of rural fêtes. In town, where the accompaniments are less harmless, these gratifications were no less keenly sought after and indulged in.

It was scarcely possible that, surrounded as he was with all the circumstances favourable to early piety, he could be altogether free from convictions of sin. And when he began to attend the Tabernacle in Edinburgh, where Mr. James Haldane ministered, and where such men as Mr. Rowland Hill often preached, Divine truth laid hold of him more closely.

Ever in earnest himself in all his pursuits, he saw that these men were in earnest too, and about matters of infinitely more importance than those to which he had given himself. In the early part of 1799, when about seventeen years of age, he was sometimes alarmed at the course he was pursuing, and shuddered at the thought of where it must end; but would not allow himself to think long enough on the subject, lest it should cost him those pleasures which he knew to be inconsistent with a godly life. Returning late one evening of the following summer from a concert of music, he was suddenly and strangely impressed with a sense of the vanity of the world and all its pleasures. From that hour he resolved to "seek after God," nor was it long till he found him. He had soon occasion to praise that "Redeemer who had recalled him from his former stupidity, and made him see the riches of his grace, his will and power to save, as well as his own hardness of heart and rebellion against the kindest of Saviours and the most loving Lord." His prayer, within a few weeks of the hour when he was first arrested on his way from the concert room, was, "O Lord, keep me! O Lord, guide me! I am happy in thy communion. I have no pleasure in this world of vexation and vanity when thou art with me. Oh, then, do thou in mercy keep me from offending thee, and afterwards receive me to thyself and glory, for Jesus Christ's sake." Repeatedly has he stated to Christian friends, that in his case the transition from darkness to God's marvellous light, from the spirit of bondage to the Spirit of adoption, was nearly instantaneous. In less than one hour he was conscious of the change, and was seldom afterwards troubled with doubts respecting its reality.

Let it not be supposed that in cases like that of Mr. Anderson there is no intelligent process of thought and feeling, no succession of mental reasonings and emotions. The truth seems to be that the whole is so rapid, that a man's consciousness cannot trace them, or his memory cannot retain them. Even in ordinary circumstances, and without any special impulse, the mind can, in almost an instant, effect a process of reasoning, the steps and links of which it might require hours to trace and describe. And this power of rapid thinking is greatly increased by peculiar impulses and circumstances. It is told by a distinguished English officer, that having fallen into the sea, during the few moments of consciousness which he had while under the waves, the whole events of his life, from childhood, seemed to repass with lightning-like rapidity and brightness before his eyes. "A narration," it has been aptly remarked, "which shows on what accurate knowledge the old oriental framed his story of the sultan who dipped his head into a basin of water, and had, as it were, gone through all the adventures of a crowded life before he lifted it out again." The rapidity of thought in dreaming is well known. "A friend of mine (says Dr. Abercrombie) dreamed that he crossed the Atlantic and spent a fortnight in America. In embarking on his return he fell into the sea, and having awoke with the fright, discovered that he had not been asleep above ten minutes." And this is no uncommon case. There are few whose own experience will not supply illustrations of the same kind. But it may be questioned whether the rapidity of thought is greater in sleep than while we are awake. "For," to use the words of professor

Dugald Stewart, "the rapidity of thought is at all times such, that, in the twinkling of an eye, a crowd of ideas may pass before us to which it would require a long discourse to give utterance, and transactions may be conceived which it would require days to realize."

Even on these common principles, then, the instantaneousness of conversion is quite compatible with the exercise of intelligent reason and deliberate choice. In one moment the mind may exercise its judgment on the claims of God, on the demerit and wretchedness of sin, and on the sufficiency and suitableness of the mediation of our Lord Jesus Christ. Great as these themes are, they are simple likewise. And in the awakening and renewing of the mind by an influence which the Bible teaches us to regard as from God, they often flash upon the soul with a light in which it may be said there "is no darkness at all."

Fourth Class.

We now proceed to illustrate the fact that in the spiritual world, as in the natural, the winter often yields to the spring only after a long and severe conflict. The histories of John Bunyan and of Major-General Andrew Burn will be sufficient for the purpose.

John Bunyan; born at Elstow in 1628: died in London, Aug. 31, 1688.

JOHN BUNYAN was brought up by his father in his own craft of brazier or tinker. As to his early character, he never was a drunkard, a libertine, or a lover of sanguinary sports; his special sins were profanity, Sabbath-breaking, and heart atheism. "The thing which gave Bunyan any notoriety in the days of his ungodliness, and which made him afterwards appear to himself such a monster of iniquity, was the energy which he put into all his doings. He had a zeal for idle play and enthusiasm in mischief which were the perverse manifestations of a forceful character."* "He walked according to the course of this world, fulfilling the desires of the flesh and of the mind; and, conscious of his own rebellion, he said unto God, 'Depart from me for I desire not the knowledge of thy ways.' The only restraining influence of which he then felt the power was terror. His days were often gloomy through forebodings of the wrath to come; and his nights were scared with visions, which the boisterous diversions and the adventures of his waking day could not always dispel. He would dream that the last day had come, and that the quaking earth was opening its mouth to let him down to hell; or he would find himself in the grasp of fiends who were dragging him powerless away."

These were the fears of childhood. As he grew older he grew harder. He experienced some remark-

* "The reader need not go far to see young Bunyan. Perhaps there is near your dwelling an Elstow—a quiet hamlet of some fifty houses sprinkled about in the picturesque confusion, and with the easy amplitude of space, which gives an old English village its look of leisure and longevity. And it is now verging to the close of a long summer's day. The daws are taking short excursions from the steeple, and tamer fowls have gone home from the darkening and dewy green. But old Bunyan's donkey is still browsing there, and yonder is old Bunyan's self—the brawny tramper dispread on the settle, retailing to the more clownish residents tap-room wit and road-side news. However, it is young Bunyan you wish to see. Yonder he is, the noisiest of the party, playing pitch-and-toss—that one with the shaggy eyebrows, whose entire soul is ascending in the twirling penny—grim enough to be the blacksmith's apprentice, but his singed garments hanging round him with a lank and idle freedom which scorns indentures; his energetic movements and authoritative vociferations at once bespeaking the ragamuffin ringleader. The penny has come down with the wrong side uppermost, and the loud execration at once bewrays young Badman. You have only to remember that it is Sabbath evening, and you witness a scene often enacted on Elstow green two hundred years ago."—DR. JAMES HAMILTON—*to whose life of John Bunyan our sketch is considerably indebted.*

able escapes from death, but these providences neither startled nor melted him. He married very early, and his wife was the daughter of a godly man. Her whole property consisted of two small books, "The Plain Man's Pathway to Heaven," and the "Practice of Piety," which her father had left her on his deathbed. Young Bunyan read these books, and was often told by his wife what a good man her father had been. The consequence was that he felt some desire to reform his vicious life, and went to church twice a-day, and said and sang as others did. He became at the same time so overrun with the spirit of superstition, that "had he but seen a priest, though never so sordid and debauched in his life, his spirit would fall under him, and he could have lain down at the feet of such and been trampled upon by them; their name, their garb, and work, did so intoxicate and bewitch him." But whilst adorning the altar, and worshipping the surplice, and deifying the individual who wore it, Bunyan continued to curse and blaspheme and spend his Sabbaths in the same riots as before.

One day, however, he heard a sermon on the sin of Sabbath-breaking, and it haunted his conscience throughout the day. When in the midst of the excitement of that afternoon's diversions, a voice seemed to dart from heaven into his soul, "Wilt thou leave thy sins and go to heaven, or have thy sins and go to hell?" His arm, which was about to strike a ball, was arrested, and looking up to heaven, it seemed as if the Lord Jesus was looking down upon him in remonstrance and deep displeasure, and at the same time the conviction flashed across him that he had sinned so long that repentance was now too late. "My state is surely miserable," he thought; "miserable if I leave my sins, and but miserable if I follow them. I can but be damned; and if I must be so, I had as good be damned for many sins as few." In the desperation of this awful conclusion he resumed the game; and so persuaded was he that heaven was for ever forfeited, that for some time after he made it his deliberate policy to enjoy the pleasures of sin as rapidly and intensely as possible. "For a month or more he went on in resolute sinning, only grudging that he could not get such scope as the madness of despair solicited. When one day standing at a neighbour's window, cursing and swearing, and 'playing the madman after his wonted manner,' the woman of the house protested that he made her tremble, and that truly he was the ungodliest fellow for swearing that she ever heard in all her life, and quite enough to ruin the youth of the whole town. The woman was herself a notoriously worthless character; and so severe a reproof from so strange a quarter had a singular effect on Bunyan's mind. He was silenced in a moment. He blushed before the God of heaven; and as he there stood with hanging head, he wished with all his heart that he were a little child again, that his father might teach him to speak without profanity; for he thought his bad habit so inveterate now, that reformation was out of the question."

So it was, however, that from that instant onward Bunyan ceased to swear, and people wondered at the change. Immediately after this circumstance, interested by the conversation of a poor man who seemed religious, he betook himself to his Bible, and began to take pleasure in reading the historical parts of it. His outward life underwent much reformation, and onlookers might conclude that the winter was at length past and gone, and that spring was truly come. But he wanted the soul-emancipating and sin-subduing knowledge of Jesus Christ. The Son had not made him free. His own account of himself is very instructive :—" I did set the commandments before me for my way to heaven ; which commandments I also did strive to keep, and, as I thought, did keep them pretty well sometimes, and then I should have comfort; yet now and then should break one, and so afflict my conscience ; but then I should repent, and say I was sorry for it, and promise God to do better next time, and there got help again ; for then I thought I pleased God as well as any man in England. Thus I continued about a year ; all which time our neighbours did take me to be a very godly man, a new and religious man, and did marvel much to see such great and famous alteration in my life and manners ; and, indeed, so it was, though I knew not Christ, nor grace, nor faith, nor hope ; for, as I have well since seen, had I then died, my state had been most fearful. But, I say, my neighbours were amazed at this my great conversion from prodigious profaneness to something like a moral life ; and so they well might, for this my conversion was as great as for Tom of Bedlam to become a sober man. Now I was, as they said, become godly ; now I was become a right honest man. But, oh ! when I understood these were their words and opinions of me, it pleased me mighty well. For though, as yet, I was nothing but a poor painted hypocrite, yet I loved to be talked of as one that was truly godly." A " poor painted hypocrite " he calls himself—not that he was a conscious deceiver, but that all his goodness lay on the surface, being as yet ignorant, he says, both of the corruption of his nature and of the want and worth of Jesus Christ to save him.

The lips of other women, but persons of a very different character from her who had reproved him for his profane oaths, were the means of another step greatly in advance.

He had gone to Bedford in prosecution of his calling; when passing along the street, he noticed a few poor women sitting in a doorway, and talking together. He listened to their conversation. It surprised him; for though he had by this time become a great talker on sacred subjects, their themes were far beyond his reach. God's work in their souls, the views they had obtained of their natural misery and of God's love in Christ Jesus, what words and promises had particularly refreshed them and strengthened them against the temptations of Satan—it was of matters so personal and vital that they spoke to one another. They seemed to Bunyan as if they had found a new world. Their conversation made a deep impression on his mind. He saw that there was something in real religion into which he had not yet penetrated.

What John Bunyan heard in the society of these humble instructors suggested to him a sort of waking vision. "I saw as if they were on the sunny side of some high mountain, there refreshing themselves with the pleasant beams of the sun, while I was shivering and shrinking in the cold, afflicted with frost, snow, and dark clouds. Methought also, betwixt me and them I saw a wall that did compass about this mountain; now through this wall my soul did greatly desire to pass, concluding that, if I could, I would even go into the very midst of them, and there also comfort myself with the heat of their sun. About this wall I thought myself to go again and again, still prying as I went, to see if I could find some gap or passage to enter therein. But none could I find for some time. At the last, I saw, as it were, a narrow gap, like a little doorway in the wall, through which I attempted to pass. Now, the passage being very strait and narrow, I made many offers to get in, but all in vain, even till I was well right beat out in striving to get in. At last, with great striving, methought I at first did get in my head, and after that, by a sideling striving, my shoulders and my whole body. Then I was exceeding glad; went and sat down in the midst of them, and so was comforted with the light and heat of their sun. Now this mountain and wall were thus made out to me. The mountain signified the church of the living God; the sun that shone thereon, the comfortable shining of his merciful face on them that were therein; the wall, I thought, was the word, that did make separation between the Christian and the world; and the gap which was in the wall, I thought was Jesus Christ, who is the way to God the Father. But forasmuch as the passage was wonderful narrow, even so narrow that I could not, but with great difficulty, enter in thereat, it showed me that none could enter into life but those who were in downright earnest, and unless they left that wicked world behind them; for here was only room for body and soul, but not for body and soul and sin."

This waking dream did Bunyan good. He began to read the Bible with new eagerness; and that portion of it which had formerly been distasteful to him, the Epistles of Paul, now became the subject of his special study. But he fell into a very common error. The object to which the eye of an inquiring sinner should be directed is CHRIST, the finished work, and the sufficient Saviour. But, in point of fact, many go in quest of that act of the mind which unites the soul to the Saviour, and makes salvation personal; and it is only by studying faith that they come at last to an indirect and circuitous acquaintance with Christ. By some such misdirection Bunyan was misled. In quest of faith he went a long and joyless journey, and was wearied with the greatness of his way. There is scarcely a fear which can assail an inquiring spirit which did not at some stage of his progress arrest his mind. He was no longer a proud Pharisee, but a deeply humbled sinner. "My original and inward pollution—that was my plague and affliction. *That* I saw at a dreadful rate, always putting forth itself within me,—*that* I had the guilt of to amazement; by reason of *that* I was more loathsome in my own eyes than a toad; and I thought I was so in God's eyes, too."

Years of despondency passed over him before he came to the enjoyment of the peace of the gospel.

The light which first stole in upon his soul, and in which his darkness finally melted away, was a clear discovery of the person of Christ, more especially a distinct perception of the dispositions which he manifested while here on earth. And one thing greatly helped him; he alighted on a congenial mind, and an experience in many respects like his own. Providence threw in his way an old copy of Luther's Commentary on Galatians, "so old (he says), that it was ready to fall piece from piece if I did but turn it over. When I had but a little way perused the book, I found my condition in his experience so largely and profoundly handled, as if his book had been written out of my heart." And such were the benefits he derived from this book, that he preferred it ever after before all the books he had ever seen, excepting the Holy Bible, "as most fit for a wounded conscience." His happiness was now as intense as his misery had been. He wished he were fourscore years old, that he might die quickly, that he might go to be with Him who had made his soul an offering for his sins. "I felt love to Him as hot as fire; and now, as Job said, I thought I should die in my nest." But another period of fearful agony awaited him, and like the last, it continued for a year. It arose from a temptation which took this strange and dreadful form—to sell and part with his Saviour, to exchange him for the things of this life—for anything. This horrid thought he could not shake out of his mind, day nor night, for many months together. It intermixed itself with every occupation, however sacred, or however trivial. The only case he could compare to his own was that of Judas. At last, after many alternations of feeling, he so far emerged from his misery that "he seemed to stand upon the same ground with other sinners, and to have as good a right to the word and prayer as any of them." This was a great step in advance. His misery had hitherto been occasioned by an error which keeps many anxious souls from comfort. He regarded his own case as a special exception to which a gospel, otherwise general, did not apply; but his snare was now broken, and, though with halting pace, he was on the way to settled rest and joy. Relief came slowly but steadily, and was the more abiding because he had learned by experience to distrust any comfort which did not come from the word of God. Such passages as these, "My grace is sufficient for thee," and "Him that cometh to me I will in no wise cast out," greatly lightened his burden; but he derived still stronger encouragement from considering that the gospel, with its benignity, is much more expressive of the mind and disposition of God than the law with its severity. Mercy rejoiceth over judgment. "How shall not the ministration of the Spirit be rather glorious? For if the ministration of condemnation be glory, much more doth the ministration of righteousness exceed in glory. For even that which was made glorious had no glory in this respect, by reason of the glory that excelleth."* The same truth was presented to him by the narrative of the Transfiguration, when the voice came out of the cloud, saying, "This is my beloved Son: hear him." "Then I saw (says Bunyan) that Moses and Elias must both vanish, and leave Christ and his saints alone."

One day, as he was passing into the field, these words fell upon his soul, "Thy righteousness is in heaven." The eyes of his soul saw at the same time Jesus Christ at God's right hand, and there, he said, is my righteousness. "I saw, moreover, that it was not my good frame of heart that made my righteousness better, nor my bad frame that made my righteousness worse; for my righteousness was Jesus Christ himself, 'the same yesterday, to day, and for ever.'" Now was he loosed from his afflictions and his irons; his temptations also fled away; and he went home rejoicing for the grace and love of God. The words, "Thy righteousness is in heaven," were not to be found in the Bible, but then there were these, "He is made of God unto us wisdom, and righteousness, and sanc-

*2 Cor. iii. 8—10.

tification, and redemption."* This blessed truth was his peace with God. He was complete in Christ Jesus; and though sometimes interrupted by disquieting thoughts and strong temptations, his subsequent career was one of growing comfort and prevailing peace.

The occasion of the protracted conflict through which John Bunyan passed into the kingdom of God, is not to be found in the gospel, but in himself. His ignorance, his love of sin, his strong passions, his overmastering imagination, are distinctly traceable in various combinations, in the bitter struggles by which his progress to life was impeded.

Major-General Andrew Burn; born at Dundee, Sept. 8th, 1742; died, Sept. 18, 1814.

ANDREW BURN was the child of Christian parents, and it is his own testimony that infant reason no sooner dawned, than they began to use every possible means to give that reason a right bias towards its proper object. The history of his youth and early manhood reads more like a romance than a true tale, so full is it of singular combinations of circumstances and hairbreadth escapes by sea and land. But amid his wanderings, and all the miseries in which they involved him, he seldom thought of the God to whose providence he owed so much. Speaking of his residence in Jamaica, he says, "By this time the serious impressions of childhood had lost great part of their influence, and as that diminished, the darling inclinations of a corrupt heart gradually prevailed, and so far gained the ascendency, that some of the most glaring sins, which at first appearance struck me with horror, imperceptibly lost their deformity in my eyes, and,

* 1 Cor. i. 30.

Proteus-like, transformed themselves into innocent enjoyments. Thus advancing, step by step, in the dangerous road of sin, I soon arrived at dreadful lengths; drank in the deadly poison with as much eagerness as the thirsty ox drinks in water, and rushed on rapidly with the wicked multitude in the broad road to eternal ruin." From this time the most imminent perils and the most unexpected deliverances failed alike to impress his heart. Brought low by a fever on one occasion, when at sea, he expected every hour to be thrown overboard with others who had died around him, but he "had not the least painful conviction of his accumulated guilt." "I was dying," he says, "and that in every respect like the brute that perisheth, though endued with all the faculties of a rational being, and these in full exercise, unimpaired by bodily pain." On another occasion his ship struck on a sand bank, and the scene of dismay which followed was enough to make the stoutest sinner tremble. One of his messmates, who had acquired considerable property in Jamaica, cursed God that he had made him spend so many toilsome years in a scorching and unhealthy climate to procure a little wealth; and when with pain and trouble he had heaped it together, had tantalized him with a sight of the happy shore where he expected peacefully to enjoy it, but now with one cruel sudden stroke had defeated all his hopes. The conduct of this blasphemer, whose despair seemed like that of a fiend of the bottomless pit, was in striking contrast with that of the captain, who, "fearless, with composure smiled at danger's threatening form." The captain was a Christian, and with a presence of mind and a wisdom which seemed almost inspired, gave instructions which were the means of saving his ship. But neither the despair of the blasphemer, nor the calmness of the Christian, produced any salutary impression on young Burn's mind, and he landed on the shores of England as godless as ever.

After a time we find him stationed at Chatham, as an officer in the Marines. The review of the past three years of folly and adventure led him to return to the externally religious habits in which he had been trained, and to observe the ordinances of public worship. In the esteem of many he was now a good Christian, but his own confession is, that he remained the willing slave to various sinful lusts and passions, and felt no remorse in daily doing many things which he could not think of in after life without shuddering. He was only a Pharisee. Yet by degrees he cut off many sins which were as dear to him as a right hand or a right eye. His struggles with his love of gambling were protracted and painful. First he vowed—and that very solemnly—that he would devote only a certain time to cards, and no more; but this resolution failing, he vowed to play only for a certain sum, and never to exceed it. When that would not do, he vowed still more resolutely to play only for recreation. But all proved ineffectual. The more he resolved, the stronger grew the sin. A multitude of broken vows heaped guilt upon guilt, and brought an accumulated load of sorrow upon his soul. One Lord's day, when he was to take his place at the table of the Lord, his conscience so condemned him, that he tried in vain to pacify it by a renewal of his vows. "There is an Achan in the camp," said conscience; "approach the table of the Lord, if you dare." Scared by these monitions, and yet unwilling to part with his darling lust, he became like one possessed. Restless and uneasy, he fled to the fields to vent his misery under the wide canopy of heaven. Thoughts of future judgment filled him with indignation against the "accursed thing" which was corrupting and tormenting his soul, and, crying to God for help, he knelt down under a hedge, and taking heaven and earth to witness, wrote on a piece of paper with his pencil a solemn vow that he never would play at cards on any pretence whatsoever, so long as he lived. This was no sooner done than his burden was gone and he was at peace. But, alas! the reformation was all on the surface. While endeavouring to heal his soul in one place, ere he was aware, sin broke out in another. At the same time there was much about him that fostered the delusion that he was now a Christian, and that it was impossible for him to fall into gross sins again.

After enjoying his commission in the Marines for some two years, the restoration of peace reduced him to half pay, and circumstances took him into France, where he was left to plunge again into all manner of wickedness. It was by slow degrees, and after many hard fought battles with his conscience, that he succeeded in persuading himself that his vow to abstain from card-playing was rash, and need not be kept. The bondage of sin in which he was now held was strengthened by the inroads of scepticism. But the doubts which he gradually entertained as to the immortality of his soul, instead of relieving him from anxiety respecting the future, became as a quenchless fire of torment within him. The grossest sins assumed a very different aspect under the teaching of infidelity, and appeared to him nothing more than lawful gratifications, so that they awakened no fear. But the idea of annihilation was unbearable. "If death is to destroy in me this part which thinks, which reasons and with so much ardour breathes after an assuranc of its existence in a future state, what a despicable being do I appear in my own eyes! Beyond all expression miserable! How much reason have I to curse the day wherein I was born!"

When the poor miserable man would return to England he had not the means, and he betook himself to the writing of plays to provide them, but in vain. That unseen Hand which had protected him, even amid his sins, at length opened a way. But he saw not its leading. On his way home he spent six weeks in Paris, and indulged without remorse in every forbidden pleasure which that city could present. And after an absence of six years, Andrew Burn finds himself once more in England—not now a proud Pharisee as when he left it, but a proud sceptic. He was not a little self-complacent that he had shaken off the prejudices of education, and could look down with pity on well-meaning people who knew no better. His religion was, he thought, of a most refined description, though he confessed it would puzzle an abler judgment than his to define what it was. At the same time, amid the confused crowd of philosophical notions with which his brain teemed, he frequently heard the murmuring of two distinct voices which sometimes forced him to listen to them alternately. One, an importunate visitor, very roughly told him he was wrong; and when he endeavoured to convince him to the contrary, would grow so bold and clamorous, that, for the sake of a little peace, he was obliged to stifle the voice in the pursuit of some worldly pleasure, but never could silence it altogether. To the other voice he listened with pleasure. It whispered to him, in the language of hope, that a day would come when he should alter his present way of thinking, and adopt one far better. At the same time, while this hope was secretly cherished, the whole bent of his mind was opposed to a practical reception of the truths of the gospel.

Soon after his return to England, the sudden death of a beloved brother made him feel the worthlessness of those notions to which he had clung tenaciously for years. "They now stood dressed in their proper colours, and loudly proclaimed their diabolical origin. A strong and restless desire to be savingly united to God and his people, drove them from their place in his heart, and evidently prevailed in their room. I saw (he says) the absolute necessity there was of such a Saviour as Jesus Christ, and was convinced there was no possibility of being saved any other way than by him." While in this state of mind he dreamed a dream, which produced results that made him regard it ever after as the principal means of his conversion. He dreamed that he was sitting, a little before daylight, with his deceased brother, on the wall of the parish churchyard with which they had been familiar in boyhood. His brother asked him if he would not go with him into the church. Immediately rising, they walked together towards the porch, and when they reached the inner door, the brother somehow or other passed in before him, and when he attempted to follow, the door, which slid down from above, like those in ancient fortifications, was instantly let down more than half way, so that he now found it requisite to bend himself almost double before he could possibly enter. But as he stooped to try, the door continued falling lower and lower, till the passage became so narrow that he found it impracticable in that posture. Grieved to be left behind, and determined to get in if possible, he fell down on his hands and tried to squeeze his head and shoulders through; but, finding himself still too high, he kneeled down, crept, wrestled, and pushed eagerly, but all to no purpose. He now threw off all his clothes, and crawled like a worm; but being very desirous to preserve a fine silk embroidered waistcoat which he had brought from France, he kept that on in the hope of being able to carry it with him; then laying himself flat on his face, he pushed, and strove, and soiled the precious waistcoat, but could not get in after all. At last, driven almost to despair, he stripped himself entirely, and forced his body between the door and the ground, till the rough stones and gravel tore all the skin and flesh off his breast, and, as he thought, covered him with blood. Perceiving, however, that he advanced a little, he continued to press in with more violence than ever, till at last he got safely through. As soon as he stood on his feet inside, an invisible hand clothed him in a long white robe; and as he looked round to view the place, he saw a goodly company of saints—among whom was his brother—all dressed in the same manner, partaking of the Lord's supper. He sat down in the midst of them, and the bread and wine being administered to him, he felt a seraphic ecstasy which no mortal could express. He heard a voice call him three times by name, and tell him he was wanted at home. And so great was the joy of his soul that it awoke him out of his slumbers, and "made him start up in bed singing the high praises of God."

Now what shall we make of this dream? It is easy to trace in it the natural workings of the particular state of mind in which he was at the time. Sick of the sinful courses he had followed, and sick of that infidelity which had persuaded him that sin was no evil, he had now a "strong and restless desire" to be found in Christ. And the struggle to which this desire prompted him became, in his dream, a physical struggle to effect an entrance into a material building. But admitting the dream to have had this natural origin, it exhibits the intensity of the mental conflicts in which it originated, and became, through the mercy of God, the means of increasing the desires from which it sprang, and of encouraging him to hope for victory. That the hand of God was in it was soon apparent. Mr. Burn, from the day of that dream, began to live a life as different from that which went before as any two opposites can be. "Old things were now done away, and all things became new. Not (he says) that I obtained a complete victory over my domineering sins all at once, or renounced all my false opinions in one day; but a bitter and eternal war was instantly declared against the one, and as God made the discovery to me, I let go the other. My mind was gradually enlightened to comprehend the glorious and important truths of the everlasting gospel, and the eyes of my understanding were so opened to discern spiritual things, that I now read my Bible with wonder and astonishment." And as he read he grew in grace and in the knowledge of God. "Surely nothing less than Divine power," he wrote many years afterwards, "could in the space of a few months have thus effectually overthrown the massive bulwarks of infidelity, which Satan had been continually strengthening for the space of six years in my corrupt heart, or have bent my vicious and stubborn will to embrace the self-abasing doctrines of the gospel. That such a change has been wrought I am as certain as of my own existence; so likewise am I confident that it was not in the smallest degree attributable to any inherent strength of my own. God alone must have been the author of it; to him therefore be all the glory." At the time of his conversion, Andrew Burn was twenty-six years of age, and his future life was one both of exemplary virtue and of enlightened piety. "Forty-three years," to use the words engraved on his tomb, "he served his God as a faithful soldier of Jesus Christ."

To the question whether personal conversion is not to be understood somewhat differently now from what it was among the primitive Christians, Albert Bengel replied:—"The mark, the object, the end of conversion, must ever be the same; though the point where conversion begins, or from which it sets out, must vary with different classes of men, as idolaters, Jews, and nominal Christians." The mental positions of the superstitious man and of the sceptic, for example, are opposites. The point from which, to use the words of Bengel, conversion sets out in these cases is very different, and the process will be very different. But still, as Bengel has it, "the mark, the object, the end," will be found to be the same.

Fifth Class.

The histories of Luther and Latimer, as already narrated for another purpose, may be cited as illustrations of the conversion of men under the baneful influence of superstition; and those of Caroline Fry and Andrew Burn as illustrations of the conversion of sceptics. We now add

Thomas Bilney, professor Butler, and Martin Boos, as belonging to the former class; and captain James Wilson and Henry Kirke White as belonging to the latter.

Thomas Bilney; suffered martyrdom at Cambridge in 1531.

THOMAS BILNEY was distinguished in Trinity Hall, Cambridge, as a young doctor of canon law, of earnest mind, and modest disposition. His tender conscience strove to fulfil the commandments of God, but ineffectually; and he applied to the priests, whom he looked upon as physicians of the soul. Kneeling before his confessor, with humble look and pale face, he told him all his sins, and even those of which he doubted. The priest prescribed at one time fasting, at another, prolonged vigils, and then masses and indulgences, which cost him dearly. The poor doctor went through all these practices with great devotion, but found no consolation in them. Being weak and slender, his body wasted away by degrees, his understanding grew weaker, his imagination faded, and his purse became empty. "Alas," said he, with anguish, "my last state is worse than my first." From time to time an idea crossed his mind: "May not the priests be seeking their own interests, and not the salvation of my soul?" But immediately rejecting the rash doubt, he fell back under the iron hand of the clergy.

One day Bilney heard his friends talking about a new book: it was the Greek Testament of Erasmus, printed with a translation, which was highly praised for its Latinity. Attracted by the beauty of the style, rather than the divinity of the subject, he stretched out his hand; but just as he was going to take the volume, fear came upon him, and he withdrew it hastily. In fact, the confessors strictly prohibited Greek and Hebrew books, "the sources of all heresies;" and Erasmus's Testament was particularly forbidden. Yet Bilney regretted so great a sacrifice. Was it not the Testament of Jesus Christ? Might not God have placed therein some word which perhaps might heal his soul? He stepped forward, and then again shrank back. At last he took courage. Urged, as he believed, by the hand of God, he walked out of the college, slipped into the house where the volume was sold in secret, bought it with fear and trembling, and then hastened back and shut himself up in in his room.*

He opened it—his eyes caught these words: "This is a faithful saying, and worthy of all acceptation, that Christ Jesus came into the world to save sinners; of whom I am chief." He laid down the book and meditated on the astonishing declaration. "What? St. Paul the chief of sinners, and yet St. Paul sure of being saved?" He read the verse again and again. "Oh, assertion of St. Paul, how sweet art thou to my soul!" he exclaimed. This declaration continually haunted him, and in this manner God instructed him in the secret of his heart. He could not tell what had happened to him; it seemed as if a refreshing wind were blowing over his soul, or as if a rich treasure had been placed in his hands. The Holy Spirit took what was Christ's and announced it to him. "I also am like Paul," exclaimed he with great emotion, "and more than Paul, the greatest of sinners. But Christ saves sinners. At last I have heard of Christ." There followed a wonderful transformation. An un-

* We take our narrative mainly from D'Aubigné.

known joy pervaded him; his conscience, until then sore with the wounds of sin, was healed; instead of despair, he felt an inward peace, passing all understanding. "Jesus Christ," exclaimed he, "yes, Jesus Christ saves." "I see it all," said Bilney; "my vigils, my fasts, my pilgrimages, my purchase of masses and indulgences, were destroying, instead of saving me. All these efforts were, as St. Augustine says, a hasty running out of the right way."

Bilney's experience of the power of Christ's gospel directed his teaching of others. Neither priestly absolution nor any other rite could give remission of sins, he and his fellow converts declared: the assurance of pardon is obtained by faith alone; and that faith purifies the heart. With these convictions they said to all men, "Repent and be converted." But this new mode of teaching produced a great clamour. A famous orator undertook one day at Cambridge to show that it was useless to preach conversion to a sinner. "Thou, who for sixty years past," said he, "hast wallowed in thy lusts, like a sow in her mire, dost thou think that thou canst in one year take as many steps towards heaven, and that in thine age, as thou hast done towards hell?" Bilney left the church with indignation. "Is that preaching repentance in the name of Jesus?" he asked. "Does not this priest tell us, Christ will not save thee? Alas for so many years that this deadly doctrine has been taught in Christendom!" The young convert had evidence in himself, that the true doctrine of Christ's gospel is the power of God to the conversion of the chief of sinners.

Professor ARCHER BUTLER, of Dublin, has become known since his decease to multitudes who had not heard of his name while living. His "remains" fully justify the esteem in which he was held by his friends, as a brilliant ornament of Irish literature, and still more as a "vessel unto honour, sanctified, and meet for the Master's use, and prepared unto every good work." "His master-mind could charm by the playfulness of its fancy, while it astonished by the vastness of its intellectual resources." "His multifarious knowledge was communicated on the most trivial suggestion, yet without effort or display. The profound reflection, the subtle analysis, the most pungent wit, dropped from him in brilliant succession, while he appeared entirely unconscious that he was speaking more than household words." The spiritual history of such a man must be full of interest. But it has been given to the world only in a brief and general statement—a statement, however, which, though lacking in minute detail, is suggestive and instructive.

Wm. Archer Butler; born near Clonmel in 1814; died July 5, 1848.

Professor Butler's father was a member of the Established Church of Ireland; his mother was a zealous Roman Catholic, and by her solicitude he was baptized and educated in the Romish faith. His early childhood was spent amidst scenery which made an ineffaceable impression upon a susceptible temperament. He was never a proficient in the noisy games of his co-evals, but his playful wit and amiable manners made him universally popular. His leisure hours were devoted to poetry and music, in which he became greatly skilled. And while yet a schoolboy, we are told that he had penetrated deep into the profound depths of metaphysics.

"It was about two years before his entrance into college that the important change took place in Butler's religious views, by which he passed from the straitest sect of Roman Catholicism into a faithful son and champion of the church of Ireland. He had from the cradle been deeply impressed with a sense of religion, and conscientious in the observance of the rites and ceremonies of his creed. His moral feelings were extraordinarily sensitive. For long hours of night he would lie prostrate on the ground, filled with remorse for offences, which would not for one moment have disturbed the self-complacency of even well-conducted youths. Upon one occasion, when his heart was oppressed with a sense of sinfulness, he attended confession, and hoped to find relief for his burdened spirit. The unsympathizing confessor received these secrets of his soul as if they were but morbid and distempered imaginations, and threw all his poignant emotions back upon himself. A shock was given to the moral nature of the ardent, earnest youth; he that day began to doubt; he examined the controversy for himself, and his powerful mind was not long before it found and rested in the truth."

Could we fill up the outline which his biographer has thus given us, we should doubtless have a record of mental conflict as thrilling and instructive as that of Luther, and Bilney, and Latimer. Butler was burdened with the same sense of sin, tried the same means of deliverance, and discovered their inefficacy, and at last, like them, found at once peace to his conscience and holiness to his heart by faith in the all-sufficient atonement of the Son of God. His brief life was, as man would say, terminated too soon, but not before he had ample time to prove in his own experience the Divinity of the truths in which his soul found both rest and purity. The last sermon he preached was founded on Matthew xxviii. 18—20, and one who heard it informs us, that in reference to the Godhead of our Lord he maintained that it might be proved by internal evidence to any mind which could be brought to feel what sin was, for such a mind could never feel sure of an adequate atonement without an infinite sacrifice. Christ's servants, he said, had to preach the cross of Christ: on the one hand its efficacy to save; on the other, its sharpness and its sternness, its contradictoriness to luxury and ease, and its daily self-denials. Within a few days from the delivery of this sermon he was prostrated by sudden fever, and during the few days which preceded his departure to a sinless world, one ejaculation was constantly upon his tongue, "Christ my righteousness."

Martin Boos; born on the confines of Upper Bavaria, Dec. 25, 1762; died Aug. 29, 1825.

MARTIN BOOS entered on the duties of the priest's office in the Roman Catholic church with an unspotted character. From his earliest years his conduct had been irreproachable; his application to his literary and theological studies had been close and successful, and he was habitually conscientious and devout. Yet his heart was not at rest; nor could he say with the apostle Paul, "The life which I now live in the flesh I live by the faith of the Son of God, who loved me, and gave himself for me." He was trying to be his own saviour, and to find for himself a path to heaven. His good works, mortifications, and fasts, were the sacrifices he offered to God for expiating his sins, and obtaining everlasting life. Twenty years afterwards (1811) he wrote of the "immense pains" which he took to be a very pious man, in these terms: "For years together, even in winter, I lay on the cold floor. I scourged myself till I bled again. I fasted and gave my bread to the poor. I spent every hour I could spare in the church or the cemetery. I confessed and took the sacrament almost every week. In short, I gained such a character for piety that I was appointed prefect of the congregation by the ex-Jesuits. But what a life I led! The prefect, with all his sanctity, became more and more absorbed in self, melancholy, anxious, and formal. The saint was evermore exclaiming in his heart, 'Oh wretched man that I am! who shall deliver me?' And no one replied, 'The grace of God through Jesus Christ our Lord.' No one gave the sick man that spiritual specific, 'The just shall live by faith;' and when I had obtained it, and found the benefit of it, the whole world, with all its learning and spiritual authority, would have persuaded me that I had swallowed poison, and was poisoning all around me; that I deserved to be hung, drowned, immured, banished, or burned. . . . . . I tried as long as other people the notion that a man can be saved and justified by his own doings; but I have found in an ancient document that we are to be justified and saved for Christ's sake, without our merits, and in this faith I shall die. If others will not make use of this bridge, they must wade through the stream; but let them see to it that they are not drowned."*

The history of the change which the young priest

* See the Life of Martin Boos; Monthly volume of the London Religious Tract Society.

Boos underwent is deeply interesting. His own account of it is very simple: "In 1788 or 1789 I visited a sick person, who was respected for her deep humility and exemplary piety. I said to her, 'You will die very peacefully and happily.' 'Why so?' she asked. 'Because you have led,' I replied, 'such a pious and holy life.' The good woman smiled at my words, and said, 'If I leave the world relying on my own piety, I am sure I shall be lost. But relying on Jesus my Saviour, I can die in comfort. What a clergyman you are! What an admirable comforter! If I listened to you, what would become of me? How could I stand before the Divine tribunal, where every one must give an account, even of her idle words? Which of our actions and virtues would not be found wanting if laid in the Divine balances? No; if Christ had not died for me, if he had not made satisfaction for me, I should have been lost for ever, notwithstanding all my good works and pious conduct. He is my hope, my salvation, and my eternal happiness.'"

Martin Boos found instruction where he sought it not. He entered the house of affliction to console, without knowing the true consolation. At first he was astounded and ashamed, that what he, after all his studies, was ignorant of, should be taught him by a simple-hearted woman on her death-bed. Happily for him, he was humble enough not to reject the truth when conveyed to him by so mean an instrument. It made an indelible impression on his mind, and formed the foundation of his future faith and life.

The spiritual results of the doctrines which Boos now taught, both in public and in private, may be understood from one example. Among the Roman Catholics in Wiggensbach, of which he was curate for a time, were many persons, who, failing to find comfort, either by attending the confessional, or by receiving absolution from the priests, retired into convents, where they hoped to obtain relief for their spiritual wants. Of this class was a female, who, having been disgusted with the world, formed the design of entering a nunnery, imagining that in such a retreat she would lead a holy and happy life. Accordingly, she withdrew to a nunnery, with a feeling of ecstasy, as if entering heaven itself. But she found there no spiritual life—no Saint Theresa—and told her associates that they were no nuns, but mere hood-wearers. She soon left them, and then tried what pilgrimages could do for her. She travelled twice to Maria Einsiedel in Switzerland, but the second time came back more uneasy and dissatisfied than before. She entreated her parish priest to tell her some other method of appeasing the inexpressible longings of her heart; but to no purpose. He only taxed her with pride and folly, and asked her whether she was not learned enough, or whether she wanted to be wiser than himself. At last she consulted Boos, and found what her soul had been seeking; he led her to Christ, and in him she found the rest and comfort which he offers to the weary and heavy laden. From that time she felt no delight in her rosary and other formal devotions. This disturbed her, and she almost suspected herself of heresy. She laid the matter before Boos. He asked her what so occupied her time and thoughts, that she could no longer use her rosary. "I do nothing and think of nothing," she replied, "but to love Jesus because he is in me and with me." "You can do nothing better than that," said Boos; "it is no heresy to love Jesus and think of him. To do everything out of love to him is of more worth than many rosaries." This satisfied her for a while; but soon after the thought struck her, "This clergyman makes so little account of rosaries, perhaps he is not of much worth himself." She went and told him, with fear and trembling, what had passed through her mind. Boos laughed heartily, and said, "Yes, you are in the right; in myself I am of no worth, but what I have taught you is of worth, for it was taught by Jesus Christ and his apostles; that remains true; continue then in faith; do good and shun evil."

Not long after, a feast of indulgences was held in her neighbourhood; but instead of attending it she went to Boos, fifteen miles off. On his asking her the reason, she said, "Jesus is my absolution, since he died for me. His blood, simply and alone, is the absolution for all my sins." "But who teaches you this?" said Boos. "No one," she replied, "the thought comes of itself into my mind; Jesus takes away my sins, and those things, too, on which I have depended so much, but have found them to afford neither rest nor peace. I am now convinced that all is of no avail, unless Jesus takes away our sin, and dwells in our hearts."

The gospel which Boos now loved and preached produced fruits which those who saw them witnessed with astonishment. Men were at a loss to account for that "faith which worketh by love," that meekness and humility, which were so conspicuous in his converts. Their surprise was soon exchanged for hatred, and they actually accused these pious people of having intercourse with the devil, an accusation which will not surprise us when we remember that virtually the same charge was brought against their Lord and

Master, although in him there was no sin. Many were dragged before the magistrates, and their houses ransacked. But when the magistrates found that no charge could be substantiated against them, except the ardour of their devotion, they dismissed them as silly pietists, but without promising them any protection. This lenity of their judges only stimulated the fury of the persecutors, who raised an outcry against them everywhere, in the pulpits, streets, and taverns. Some were obliged to remain in obscure retreats for five or six months. Others were tracked like wild beasts to their hiding-places, and forced to leave their kindred and native country for ever. And the only crime of these victims of fanaticism was that they received Jesus Christ as their only Saviour, and lived according to the holy commandments of God. It was the divine life which the gospel produced in them that made them hateful to the world. The future ministry of Martin Boos was a perpetual martyrdom. Bonds and imprisonment and exile, were his lot. But he was faithful unto death.

Sixth Class.

Many histories of conversion from infidelity do not furnish us with sufficient information to enable us to judge how far the intellectual conviction of the Divinity of Christianity has been accompanied with heart-faith in Christ as the sinner's Saviour. But even of these many are deeply interesting and instructive.

Lord Lyttleton and Gilbert West.

It is told of LORD LYTTLETON and his friend GILBERT WEST that they agreed together to write something in support of their unbelief. The former chose the conversion of

St. Paul as his theme, and the latter the resurrection of Jesus Christ. But the result of their studies was the reverse of their anticipations. Lyttleton found in the history of the conversion of St. Paul an irrefragable argument in support of the entire Christian scheme, and West found a like argument in the history of our Lord's resurrection. And to this circumstance we owe the valuable works of these authors on these special topics in defence of the Christian faith.

It is not, however, in all cases by the simple process of inquiry and reasoning that the bonds of infidelity are loosed. The infidelity of John Newton, as we shall see, gave way amid the terrors of the storm. The infidelity of Richard Cecil gave way, as we shall see, through the wretchedness of soul to which it reduced him. Soame Jenyns, who was member of parliament for Cambridge, could find no rest for his spirit, and was thus impelled to examine the grounds of his unbelief. The result was that he discovered his error, believed in the Saviour of mankind, and wrote a small treatise in defence of the gospel, entitled, "A view of the internal evidences of Christianity." General Dykern was a professed deist till he received his mortal wound at the battle of Bergen, in 1759. During his illness, however, a great change was wrought upon his mind, and he died in the full assurance of faith, glorying in the salvation of Jesus, and wondering at the happy change that had taken place in his soul. The case of the earl of Rochester is well known—"a great wit, a great scholar, a great poet, a great sinner, and a great penitent." He had sunk and wallowed in the very slough of wickedness, but when "he came

Soame Jenyns.

General Dykern.

The Earl of Rochester.

to himself," he regarded himself as the greatest sinner the sun had ever shone upon, and wished he had been a crawling leper in a ditch, rather than have offended God as he had done. "One day, at an atheistical meeting in the house of a person of quality (he told a friend afterwards), I undertook to manage the cause, and was the principal disputant against God and religion; and for my performances received the applause of the whole company. Upon this my mind was terribly struck, and I immediately replied thus to myself: 'Good God! that a man who walks upright, who sees the wonderful works of God, and has the use of his senses and reason, should use them to the defying of his Creator!'" But there was no genuine conversion till the fifty-third chapter of Isaiah was read to him, together with some other parts of the Sacred Scriptures, "when it pleased God to fill his mind with such peace and joy in believing, that it was remarkable to all about him. Afterwards he frequently desired those who were with him to read the same chapter to him; upon which he used to enlarge in a very familiar and affectionate manner, applying the whole to his own humiliation and encouragement. 'O blessed God,' he would say, 'can such a horrid creature as I am be accepted by thee, who have denied thy being, and contemned thy power? Can there be mercy and pardon for me? Shall the unspeakable joys of heaven be conferred on me? O mighty Saviour, never but through thine infinite love and satisfaction! Oh! never but by the purchase of thy blood!' adding, that with all abhorrence he reflected upon his former life—that from his heart he repented of all that folly and madness of which he had been guilty."

Even in those cases in which men are led to embrace the gospel through a slow and painstaking process of reasoning, it is found that the paths they travel in search of truth, and the arguments which affect them most, are very different. The author of a small work called the "Philosophy of the Plan of Salvation," says of himself—

"The Philosophy of the Plan of Salvation."

"During some of the first years of the writer's active life, he was a sceptic; he had a friend who has since been well known as a lawyer and a legislator, who was also sceptical in his opinions. We were both conversant with the common evidences of Christianity. None of them convinced our minds of the Divine origin of the Christian religion, although we both thought ourselves willing to be convinced by sufficient evidence. Circumstances which need not be named led the writer to examine the Bible, and to search for other evidence which had been commended to his attention by a much esteemed clerical friend, who presided in one of our (American) colleges. The result of the examination was a thorough conviction in the author's mind of the truth and Divine authority of Christianity. . . . Coleridge has somewhere said that the Levitical economy is an enigma yet to be solved. To thousands of intelligent minds it is not only an enigma, but an absolute barrier to their belief in the Divine origin of the Bible. The solution of the enigma was the clue which aided the writer to escape from the labyrinth of doubt; and now, standing upon the rock of unshaken faith, he offers the clue that guided him to others."

In the histories of captain Wilson and Henry Kirke White, which we narrate more minutely, there will be found a marked contrast between the manner of conversion of the hardy and hardened adventurer, and of the gentle-hearted poet. But in the end both will be found to have been brought to a living and trustful faith in the same Divine Saviour.

Captain James Wilson; born in 1760; died 1814.

Captain JAMES WILSON is well known as the commander of the ship Duff, which carried the first Christian Missionaries to the islands of the Pacific Ocean in 1796. His earlier life had been spent in battle and adventure in America and India, and its incidents read more like the wonders of fiction, than a literal detail of truth and fact. The history of his attempt to escape from one of the prisons of Hyder Ali, and the sufferings to which he was subjected for two-and-twenty months after, would form the basis of a startling tale of romance. In 1794 he returned to England, made rich by one fortunate enterprise, and bought an estate in Hampshire, where he hoped to repair his shattered health, and to enjoy happiness in the sports of the country and the fashionable society of the neighbourhood. On his return voyage he had frequent discussions on religious subjects with a missionary who was on board, and who was greatly scandalized at his infidel principles. He had come out of the furnace of suffering, insensible as the millstone to any feelings of gratitude or devotion, and his mercies had no better effect than his afflictions. He saw no Divine hand in the providence which had preserved him in deaths oft—in hunger, and thirst, and nakedness—in journeying and in prisons—in perils of waters, in perils in the wilderness, in perils by the heathen; and which, after all these dangers, had crowned his mercantile pursuits with wealth by means which appeared almost miraculous.

Captain Wilson's infidelity, his biographer says, may be ascribed mainly to two causes: the want of an early and scriptural acquaintance with religion; and his residence for so many years in India, "a country which has proved fatal to the principles of Europeans, who, making wealth the sole object of their worship, prostrate their hearts before the shrine of this golden image, with a more unhallowed devotion than if they bent the knee in the chambers of Asiatic idolatry. His mind had been rendered completely callous by the events and occupations of his life; and this baneful influence had darkened down upon his faculties, so as to obliterate any remains of religion and all sense of God's moral government among men. Like all other disciples of deism, he entertained lofty conceptions of human nature, and was deeply imbued with a self-complacent admiration of his own goodness. He considered that he had so conducted himself as to merit the congratulations of the world, and had done nothing he could reproach himself with, as unjust to his neighbour or offensive in the eye of God. He had even in some instances behaved with a generosity that he thought could not fail to secure for him the Divine approbation, and when compared with others of his countrymen in that part of the world, he flattered himself he ought rather to be celebrated as a man of exalted virtue, than regarded as an unbeliever or a sinner. Besides, his many wonderful escapes, his singular preservations, and, above all, his success in his mercantile engagements, which had raised him to affluence, after being stripped of all he possessed, led him proudly to imagine that he was not only a child of fortune, but in special favour with the Deity."

"It is difficult indeed to imagine (says his biographer) almost anything more unlikely than that the subjects of revelation should engage or interest a mind so wrapped up in the flattering opinions of superior worth, and the romantic schemes of earthly happiness. The objections must have appeared to him numerous and formidable against receiving a book as a revelation from God, the design of which was to teach him that his heart was deeply depraved—that he had been a rebel through life against his Maker—that he had incurred his displeasure, and must expect pardon and happiness solely through the unmerited mercy of Him he had offended."

Captain Wilson had a pious niece who superintended his household affairs, and though he regarded her religion as a weakness, her character was not without some influence on his mind. One of his neighbours, an old sea-captain, often invited his attention to religion; but, though this man knew his Bible well, he was not sufficiently acquainted with the general evidences of Christianity to meet the reasonings of his sceptical friend. The Indian captain proudly defied the artillery of his denunciations against unbelievers, and smiled at his entreaties to abandon the ranks of scepticism. Occasionally, however, and at intervals, transient convictions would strike his conscience, like the flashes of lightning that cross the path of the benighted traveller. He would sometimes indulge the reflection, that if Christianity were from God, his plan of life was altogether wrong, his estimate of himself erroneous, and his hopes of future happiness fallacious.

At the table of the old sea-captain, Mr. Wilson

met the Rev. J. Griffin, of Portsea, and the authenticity of the Sacred Scriptures became the topic of conversation. The host pleasantly remarked that he had already been foiled on that subject, and referred the cause to his young friend the minister, who was better able to maintain the contest than he was. But the minister politely declined what might seem an obtrusion of his sentiments on the company, and added, that he thought the matter too serious and important for the occasion, although he was ready at all times to defend the truth, according to the best of his abilities. Captain Wilson smiled at the gravity of the clergyman, and observed, that it would be no obtrusion. "I assure you, sir," he continued, with a dogmatical air, "I am glad of the opportunity to converse on it; for I have never met with a clergyman yet, and I have conversed with several, that I could not foil in a quarter of an hour." This challenge could not be declined, and when the party broke up, the two combatants, embracing the delightful opportunity which a fine evening in July afforded, adjourned to a shady bower in the garden to debate the point, whether Christianity was a revelation from God.

In that shady bower Mr. Griffin met all the objections of his new acquaintance to the religion of Christ, for hours, in a calm, intelligent, and earnest spirit. Step by step they advanced, till the whole field of the Christian evidence was surveyed. The approach of night brought the discussion to a close, and the minister recommended to Captain Wilson such books as treated on the subjects they had been discussing. "From these," he said, "your mind, I am persuaded, will receive such a refulgency of evidence, that you will as readily admit the Divine authenticity of the

Scriptures as you do that light is the medium of vision, or that life is the cause of sensibility."

The impression produced on captain Wilson's mind by this conversation did not amount to entire conviction, but he was thoroughly aroused to consider a question which he was now prepared to admit was the most important of all. For days he read the Scriptures carefully, and when the Lord's day arrived, he offered to drive his niece to her place of worship, a distance of ten miles; but his chief object was to hear the minister who had interested him so deeply by his defence of Christianity. The simplicity of the worship, and the solemnity of the congregation impressed him much. "But," says his biographer, "the text was rather unfavourable for disarming the prejudices of one who had objected to the mysterious doctrines of Christianity. It was taken from the 8th of Romans, and treated of the subject of predestination—a subject which, in whatever view it is taken, is not unattended with difficulties. The preacher, who naturally felt anxious when, on entering the pulpit, he perceived an unexpected hearer in his late adversary, and would gladly have changed the subject, not only steered wide of anything like offensive or obnoxious sentiments, but illustrated his knotty text in such a manner that the captain ever after regarded it as highly instrumental in his conversion to God. Notwithstanding the dark and unpromising theme, the doctrine was presented to him in such a light as roused his soul to a sense of his danger, and constrained him to seek in earnest for pardoning mercy and Divine teaching. He listened to it with fixed attention. It seemed to produce a conflict of feelings in his breast, like what we may conceive to have been the conflict of the primary elements of nature, when blended in chaos; each striving to obtain its situation and influence in the universe. His memory, reason, conscience, imagination, and passions, were all in agitation. His prejudices for and against the doctrine, his hopes and fears, his love and hatred, raised a storm in his soul which he could not subdue; for while his heart rose in rebellion against the sovereignty of God, the events of his whole life appeared before him as incontestable evidences of its truth. The silent tears which he endeavoured to suppress, and which he was afraid to wipe off lest he should attract notice, excited in the bosom of his friend feelings of benevolent and sympathetic joy."

On their way home, captain Wilson said to his niece, "If what I have heard to-day be true, I am a lost man." Reason and conscience urged him to investigate the matter patiently, but the fear of enthusiasm, and the dread of becoming an object of ridicule, determined him to resist the current. The painful remembrance of former sins, and the fearful apprehensions of futurity, aggravated this internal conflict. He now became pensive and thoughtful; the Bible and religious books formed his constant and almost his only companions. He attended regularly the place of worship, joined with fervour in the service, and seemed wholly absorbed in the inquiry, "What must I do to be saved?" The change which he was undergoing attracted the notice of the gay society with which he mingled, and the artillery of wit which he had often poured on others now returned upon himself. He frequently tried to stem the torrent by argument; at other times he attempted to go with it, by joining in the laugh, till it had spent itself, but all in vain. They were resolved either to rout him out of his strange notions, or to laugh him out of their society; but as they could not do the former, they gradually accomplished the other by breaking off the connection.

Captain Wilson gradually "obtained such a firm persuasion of the truth of revelation, as to declare that nothing in the world, not even Satan, with all his principalities and powers, could persuade him that the Bible was not the word of the Most High; neither could anything have weaned him from his errors so completely as that precious volume had done." "He perceived that the sanctification of the Spirit forms the evidence of our meetness for heaven, and is as essentially necessary to salvation as an interest in the justifying righteousness of Christ; he likewise saw that the atonement of the Redeemer, and the promises of God, constitute the foundation of our hopes of acceptance with him. On this basis he was enabled to build the superstructure of his faith, hope, and practice."

The retirement of Horndean and the luxuries of wealth could not now satisfy the mind or heart of captain Wilson. He was in all the vigour of manhood—what could he do for the honour of his Saviour and the good of his fellow-creatures? The devotedness and self-denial of the worthies recorded in the Epistle to the Hebrews filled him with admiration. Was his faith like theirs? Could he suffer and serve like them, and give up all for Christ, and go forth at the Divine bidding? Circumstances occurred speedily which brought these questions to a practical issue. The London Missionary Society was formed, and it was proposed to send the gospel to the lately discovered islands of the Southern Pacific. If called upon to take the command of the expedition, could he embark once more upon the deep, not in quest of worldly substance, but to carry to heathen lands treasures more valuable than the gold of nations? He felt that he could do it with pleasure; his faith was equal to the sacrifice; he could quit his home, encounter the perils of the ocean, and brave all the dangers and difficulties to which such an enterprise must necessarily expose him. And he did it. On the 10th of August, 1796, the ship Duff sailed from the river Thames, having for her flag three doves argent, on a purple field, bearing olive branches in their bills. And after a voyage of five months the missionaries landed at Tahiti on the 4th of March, 1797. Thus auspiciously began the glorious enterprise through which fifty or sixty islands of these southern seas have already cast away their idols and returned to the living and true God.

"Who would have looked," as Dr. Haweis says, "for a convert in a haughty, unprincipled Indian merchant; or for a commander of a Christian mission in an infidel sailor, chained in a prison at Seringapatam? Who could expect the deist, who returned from India contradicting the faith of Christ, and blaspheming the cause of the cross, within five years afterwards on the quarter-deck, in the midst of prayer and praise, carrying the everlasting gospel to the isles of the Pacific Ocean? Yet such are the mysterious ways of Providence, such the irresistible influence of truth, and such the power and efficacy of Christian principles."

Henry Kirke White; born March 21, 1785; died Oct. 19, 1806.

Henry Kirke White, whose name is associated with all that is beautiful and tender, was the son of a Nottingham butcher. His mother was endowed with the best qualities of a pure and exalted feminine character. At a very early age Henry's love of reading was a passion to which everything else gave way. He was only in the fifteenth year of his age when he was chosen to deliver lectures on general literature to a literary society of which he was a member. And he soon began to have higher aspirations, and to cast a wistful eye towards the universities. But, at this time, his opinions on the most important of all subjects were sceptical—they inclined towards deism. "It needs not be said on what slight grounds the opinions of a youth must needs be founded." The doubts of Henry Kirke White were, perhaps, nothing more than the natural questionings of an active and restless mind that has not been chastened by discipline nor matured by reflection and knowledge. Our information respecting them is very scanty. But in the history of his deliverance from them we see less into his mind than into his heart; less of the process by which his understanding was satisfied than of the awakening and quickening of his soul. The statement of his biographer is, in substance, the following:—

At the time when Henry doubted the truth of Christianity, it so happened that one of his earliest and most intimate friends, Mr. Almond, was accidentally present at a deathbed, and was so struck with what he then saw of the power and influence and inestimable value of religion, that he formed a firm determination to renounce all such pursuits as were not strictly compatible with it. That he might not be shaken in this resolution, he withdrew from the society of all those persons whose ridicule or censure he feared; and was particularly careful to avoid Henry, of whose raillery he stood most in dread. He anxiously shunned him, therefore, till Henry, who would not suffer an intimacy of long standing to be broken off he knew not why, called upon his friend, and desired to know the cause of this unaccountable conduct towards himself and their common acquaintance.

Mr. Almond, who had received him with trembling and reluctance, replied to this expostulation, that a total change had been effected in his religious views, and that he was prepared to defend his opinions and conduct, if Henry would allow the Bible to be the word of truth and the standard of appeal. Upon this, Henry exclaimed in a tone of strong emotion, "Good God! you surely regard me in a worse light than I deserve!" His friend proceeded to say, that what he had said was from a conviction that they had no common ground on which to contend, Henry having more than once suggested, that the book of Isaiah was an *epic*, and that of Job a *dramatic*, poem. He then stated what the change was which had taken place in his own views and intentions, and the motives for his present conduct. From the manner in which Henry listened, it became evident that his mind was ill at ease, and that he was no way satisfied with himself. His friend, therefore, who had expected to be assailed in a tone of triumphant superiority by one in the pride and youthful confidence of great intellectual powers, and, as yet, ignorant of his own ignorance, found himself unexpectedly called upon to act the monitor; and, putting into his hands Scott's "Force of Truth," which was lying on the table, entreated him to take it with him and peruse it at his leisure.

That which first made Henry dissatisfied with the creed he had adopted, and the standard of practice which he had set up for himself, was, he informed a friend afterwards, the *purity of mind* which he perceived was everywhere inculcated in the Holy Scriptures, and required of every one "who would become a successful candidate for future blessedness." "He had supposed that morality of conduct was all the purity required; but when he observed that purity of the very *thoughts* and *intentions* of the soul also was requisite, he was convinced of his deficiencies." These are the words of his friend. His own would, no doubt, have been stronger, and would have breathed more of the spirit of Him who said, "The law is holy, and the commandment holy, and just, and good. . . . But I am carnal, sold under sin. . . . O wretched man that I am! who shall deliver me from the body of this death?"

Southey says that Scott's "Force of Truth" produced little effect on Henry's mind, and was returned with disapprobation. "Men differ," he adds, "as much in mind as in countenance: some are to be awakened by passionate exhortation, or vehement reproof, appealing to their fears, and exciting their imagination; others yield to force of argument, or, upon slow inquiry, to the accumulation of historical testimony and moral proofs; there are others in whom the innate principle of our nature retains more of its original strength, and these are led by their inward monitor into the way of peace. Henry was of this class." Which, being interpreted, must mean that Henry Kirke White was constitutionally more likely to be delivered from scepticism by an appeal to his heart and conscience than by the slow process of argument and historical proof. "His intellect might have been on the watch to detect a flaw in evidence, a defective argument, or an illogical inference; but in his heart, he felt that there is no happiness, no rest without religion; and in him who becomes willing to believe, the root of infidelity is destroyed."

At the same time this youthful inquirer derived benefit from books which appealed to his intellect rather than to his heart, and which helped to remove speculative difficulties. We find him writing to a friend in August, 1801, in acknowledgment of a book on the Trinity, from which he "received much gratification and edification." "Religious polemics," he wrote, "have seldom formed a part of my studies, though whenever I happened accidentally to turn my thoughts to the subject of the Protestant doctrine of the Godhead, and compared it with the Arian and Socinian, many doubts interfered, and I even began to think that the more widely the subject was investigated, the more perplexed it would appear, and was on the point of forming a resolution to go to heaven in my own way, without meddling or involving myself in the inextricable labyrinth of controversial dispute, when I received and perused this excellent treatise, which finally cleared up the mists which my ignorance had conjured around me, and clearly pointed out the real truth."

The date of Henry Kirke White's salutary intercourse with his friend Almond has not been recorded, but it was probably later than the date of his letter. His breast was, to use his own words, "the chaos of all contradiction"—now religious, now deistic, "now moody and sad, now unthinking and gay." But Mr. Almond's conversion was the means of a spiritual crisis in young White, which issued, happily, in his conversion likewise. Mr. Almond was about to enter Cambridge. On the evening before his departure for the university, Henry requested that he would accompany him to the little room, which was called his study. "We had no sooner entered," says Mr. Almond, "than he burst into tears, and declared that his anguish of mind was insupportable. He entreated that I would kneel down and pray for him; and most cordially were our tears and supplications mingled at that interesting moment. When I took my leave, he exclaimed, 'What must I do? You are the only friend to whom I can apply in this agonizing state, and you are about to leave me. My literary associates are all inclined to deism; I have no one with whom I can communicate.'"

The history of his heart's progress, after the departure of his friend, has not been written. But we know the spiritual condition in which it issued. Piety "was in him a living and quickening principle of goodness, which sanctified all his hopes and all his affections. . . . There never existed a more dutiful son, a more affectionate brother, a warmer friend, nor a devouter Christian." In his statement of reasons for wishing to enter into the ministry, we see what those views of truth were which produced this beautiful character. "Since the time I was awakened to a true sense of religion, I have always felt a strong desire to become useful in the church of Christ; a desire which has increased daily, and which it has been my supplication might be from God. It is true, before I began to be solicitous about spiritual things, I had a wish to become a clergyman, but that was very different. I trust I may now say, that I would be a minister, that I may do good; and although I am sensible of the awful importance of the pastoral charge, I would sacrifice everything for it, in the hope that I should be strengthened faithfully to discharge the duties of that sacred office. I think I have no other reason to offer but this—the hope of being an instrument in the hands of God for the promotion of his glory is my chief motive. With regard to the doctrines of the church contained in the articles, I conceive them to be strictly formed upon the gospel, as setting forth salvation through the blood of Jesus Christ alone; the original depravity of man, whereby he is rendered utterly unfit for every good thing, and dead to the light of truth, until he is renewed and born again in the Holy Spirit by the free grace of God; and as teaching that no man can claim acceptance on account of his works, because, being ourselves incapable of doing good, they spring from the grace of God, and to *him*, therefore, must be assigned; but that they are the fruits and testimony of sound faith."

The mental conflicts through which the youthful poet passed in his transition from scepticism to a living faith in Christ, have been recorded in his well-known "Star of Bethlehem."

"Once on the raging seas I rode,
The storm was loud—the night was dark—

* * * * * * *

Deep horror then my vitals froze,
Death-struck, I ceased the tide to stem;
When suddenly a star arose,
It was the Star of Bethlehem.

It was my guide, my light, my all,
It bade my dark foreboding cease;
And through the storm and danger's thrall,
It led me to the port of peace.

Now safely moored—my perils o'er,
I'll sing, first in night's diadem,
For ever and for evermore,
The Star, the Star of Bethlehem."

Seventh Class. Constitutional differences.

Constitutional mental differences diversify the process of conversion, and stamp themselves on the permanent character of individuals. So likewise do national characteristics.

The imaginative oriental and the matter-of-fact western, the strong-minded Saxon and the sensitive negro, do not lose their individuality, but have it sanctified and ennobled. A popular writer, after describing her hero as "enjoying (slave though he was) with a quiet joy, the birds, the flowers, the fountains, the light and beauty" of the scene amidst which he dwelt, remarks—"If ever Africa shall show an elevated and cultivated race—and come it must, some time, her turn to figure in the great drama of human improvement—life will awake there with a gorgeousness and splendour of which our cold western (or northern) tribes faintly have conceived. In that far-off mystic land of gold, and gems, and spices, and waving palms, and wondrous flowers, and miraculous fertility, will awake new forms of art, new styles of splendour; and the negro race, no longer despised and trodden down, will, perhaps, show forth some of the latest and most magnificent revelations of human life. Certainly they will, in their gentleness, their lowly docility of heart, their aptitude to repose on a superior mind and rest on a higher power, their child-like simplicity of affection, and facility of forgiveness—in all these they will exhibit the highest form of the peculiarly *Christian life*, and perhaps, as God chasteneth whom he loveth, he has chosen poor Africa in the furnace of affliction, to make her the highest and noblest in that kingdom which he will set up when every other kingdom has been tried and failed; for the first shall be last, and the last first."

We shall not be surprised to find that individual and national peculiarities show themselves amid the operations of Divine truth, modifying the manner of its action on the human soul, and ultimately modifying the character which it produces, when we remember that even the inspiration which pervades Holy Scripture does not override the original differences of the writers, and either bring down or elevate them all to a common standard. We cannot read their books without observing how much their modes of reasoning and their style have been influenced by their habits, their condition in life, their genius, their education, their recollections—all the circumstances, in short, that have acted upon their outer and inner man. "They tell us what they saw, and just as they saw it," says Gaussen. "Their memory is put into requisition, their imagination is called into exercise, their affections are drawn out, and their moral physiognomy is clearly delineated." We are sensible that the composition of each has greatly depended on its author's circumstances and peculiar habits of mind. "Here is the phraseology, the tone, the accent of a Moses; there of a John; here of an Isaiah; there of an Amos; here of a Daniel or of a Peter; there of a Nehemiah; there, again, of a Paul." But, with all their diversities, they all spoke as they were moved by the Holy Ghost, and the entire body of their writings is declared to have been given by inspiration of God.

If, in inspiration, individual varieties were not overborne by the mighty afflatus of the Holy Ghost, much less may we expect to find it so in the soul's conversion from sin to holiness. "There is in the constitution of men," says Dr. Tholuck, "either great power of feeling and power of action; or a predominant power of feeling, with but little power of action; or a predominant power of action, with but little power of feeling; or an equally small degree of both." There is thus a foundation in nature for the classification of human temperaments into the choleric, the melancholic, the sanguine, the phlegmatic. "The choleric temperament inclines its possessor to outward activity, the melancholic to inward, the sanguine to enjoyment, the phlegmatic to rest." These varieties are greatly increased by combination and mixture. And it is the glory of the gospel not to destroy but to sanctify them. It adapts itself to the man of a cold, mathematical understanding, and to the man of a warm, poetic heart; to the man of feeble intellect, who, like "poor Joseph," can just understand that Christ died for sinners, and draw the inference, "Why not, then, for poor Joseph?" and the man of mighty intellect, who, like Jonathan Edwards, can seize the greatest problems with a giant's grasp. The diversity of its action in such dissimilar cases as those of Saul of Tarsus and Caroline Fry, John Urquhart and John Bunyan, captain James Wilson and Henry Kirke White, cannot have escaped the reader's attention. Two additional examples will now be given; the one that of a man whose writings have long held a first place among the loftiest products of the human mind; the other that of a lady whose writings have only recently become known in England, and whose biography reveals a heart of the most delicate sensitiveness. The gospel met the wants of the great mind of the one and of the tender heart of the other, and in its operation we can trace the constitutional differences which it does not overbear, but hallow to the glory of God.

Jonathan Edwards; born 1703, in Connecticut; died in 1758.

The name of JONATHAN EDWARDS occupies one of the first, if not the very first, place among the masters of human reason. And this position he has attained in spite of great disadvantages. He was "born in an obscure colony, in the midst of a wilderness, and passed the better part of his life as the pastor of a frontier village, and the residue as a missionary in a still humbler hamlet." His writings were not addressed to the learned and philosophic, but to the narrow circle of a few colonial congregations; and their style, instead of being adorned with the graces of imagination, is usually most bald and repulsive. "Under such circumstances," says a distinguished essayist, "nothing but transcendent greatness could have subdued the disgust which the pride of philosophy would necessarily feel at the peculiarities of his religious opinions, or with which a sensitive taste would recoil from the hideous deformities of his style. Yet his gigantic force of intellect, and that alone, has not merely redeemed his writings from obscurity, but attracted the attention not only of many of the wisest, but the most polished of mankind. Like Paul at Athens, he has compelled even the Stoics and Epicureans to listen to him by the depth and originality of his speculations." It will be interesting to observe how this great mind, at once profoundly intellectual and deeply emotional, was affected by the entrance of divine truth, and in what manner his mental constitution moulded his experience of its power.

The parents of Jonathan Edwards possessed the virtues of the Puritans in a high degree. In the martyr spirit of the pilgrim fathers, their highest ambition was to train their only son for God. And their devotion reaped its reward while he was yet a child. Deep and frequent, and of long continuance, were his impressions of religion.

He was only seven or eight years old when, with two companions of his own age, he erected a booth for an oratory in a retired spot in a swamp. And amidst the solemn majesty of the primeval forest did the three children address their prayers and praises to the Great Spirit, their Father in heaven. But, not oppressed by the gloomy grandeur of the scene around them, their devotions were cheerful and happy. How far they were enlightened and imbued with the evangelical elements of contrition and simple-hearted reliance on the Saviour of sinners, it is perhaps impossible to say. His own later judgment on his state at this time may have been correct. "I experienced I know not what kind of delight in religion. My mind was much engaged in it, and had much self-righteous pleasure, and it was my delight to abound in religious duties. . . . . My affections seemed to be lively and easily moved, and I seemed to be in my element when I engaged in religious duties. And I am ready to think many are deceived with such affections, and such a kind of delight as I then had in religion, and mistake it for grace."

In progress of time, he tells us, his convictions and affections wore off, and he "went on in the ways of sin." A purer and lovelier life, externally, it would be difficult to find than was his. But he judged rightly in characterizing a course of life of which God is not the Alpha and Omega, as "the way of sin."

The decay of interest in religion during the earlier part of his college life is easily accounted for. He was only twelve years of age when he entered Yale college, and before he was fourteen the strength and the peculiar bias of his mind were developed, and he revelled in the study of mental philosophy as in the richest luxury. In the perusal of "Locke on the Human Understanding," he enjoyed "a far higher pleasure than the most greedy miser finds when gathering up handfuls of silver and gold from some newly discovered treasure." Between these studies and the fresh and living power of religion in the heart, there is no natural or necessary contrariety. But, through human infirmity, the most lawful pursuit, especially if it be of an intensely engrossing nature, possesses an "expulsive power," by which more important concerns are for a time driven from the soul. Jonathan Edwards was awakened from his spiritual slumber by severe illness. And now he gave himself afresh, with all the earnestness of his great mind, to "seek salvation," but without that kind of affection and delight which he had formerly experienced. His "inward struggles were many and varied. The idea of the sovereignty of God in the exercise of mercy had been repulsive to him from childhood, and now his soul rose in rebellion against it. By degrees, however, he learned to regard it not with submission merely, but with delight. "The first instance of inward sweet delight in God and in divine things" was in reading the doxology—"Now unto the King eternal, immortal, invisible, the only wise God, be honour and glory for ever and ever." "As I read the words," he says, "there came into my soul, and was as it were diffused through it, a sense of the glory of the Divine King—a new sense, quite different from anything I ever experienced before. From about that time I began to have a new kind of apprehension and idea of Christ and the work of redemption, and the glorious way of salvation by him. An inward sweet sense of these things at times came into my heart, and my soul was led away in pleasant views and contemplations of them. And my mind was greatly engaged to spend my time in reading and meditating on Christ, on the beauty and excellency of his person, and the lovely way of salvation by free grace in him." If the child's delight in God was "self-righteous," if it was self-complacent, or consisted in mere pleasurable emotions, the young man's delight was of a different order. He now knew himself, and was humbled before God, and contemplated with "a joy that was unspeakable" the glory of God as revealed in the mediatorial work of his Son. Here his whole nature found rest; and the result was characteristic of the constitutional grandeur of his intellect. Walking abroad alone in a solitary place, "and looking upon the sky and clouds, there came into my mind," he says, "so sweet a sense of the glorious majesty and grace of God, as I know not how to express. I seemed to see them both in a sweet conjunction, majesty and meekness joined together: it was a sweet, and gentle, and holy majesty; and also a majestic meekness; an awful sweetness; a high, and great, and holy gentleness. After this the appearance of everything was altered; there seemed to be, as it were, a calm, sweet cast, or appearance, of Divine glory in almost everything. God's excellency, his wisdom, his purity and love, seemed to appear in everything; in the sun, moon, and stars; in the clouds and blue sky; in the grass, flowers, trees; in the water, and all nature; which used greatly to fix my mind."

The very thunders and lightnings of heaven seemed to change their character. Formerly nothing had been so full of terror to him. The approach of a thunder-storm used to fill him with dread; now he saw it with joy, and went forth into the fields to watch the thunder-cloud and the lightning's flash, which only led him to "sweet contemplations of the great and glorious God." "While thus engaged," he says, "it always seemed natural for me to sing or chant forth my meditations, or to speak my thoughts in soliloquies with a singing voice."

These statements will recall to many readers a fact in the early history of Dr. Chalmers. "I remember," we find him saying in a letter, "when a student of divinity, and long ere I could relish evangelical sentiments, I spent nearly a twelvemonth in a sort of mental elysium; and the one idea which ministered to my soul all its rapture, was the magnificence of the Godhead, and the universal subordination of all things to the one great purpose for which he evolved, and was supporting creation."

The profound work of Jonathan Edwards on the Will, was, in part, the occasion of this elevation of soul. By its perusal, young Chalmers "rose to the sublime conception of the Godhead, as that eternal, all-pervading energy by which the vast and firmly-knit succession of events in both the spiritual and material universe was originated and sustained; and into a very rapture of admiration and delight his spirit was upborne." Not a single hour elapsed, during this singular period of Dr. Chalmers's mental history, in which the overpoweringly impressive imagination did not stand bright before the inward eye. And his custom was to wander early in the morning into the country, that, amid the quiet scenes of nature, he might luxuriate in the glorious conception.

In some respects similar, yet essentially dissimilar, were these states of mind of Chalmers and Edwards. The one idea which filled Chalmers's soul with emotion was intellectual—the magnificence of the Godhead. The idea which filled the soul of Edwards was moral—the glorious holiness of the Godhead. And the difference had its root in essentially different states of heart. Chalmers, at the period referred to, was entirely destitute of anything distinctively Christian. His system of religion did not go beyond sublime ideas of the Divine omnipresence, omnipotence, omniscience, and goodness, and the grandeur, extent, and variety of God's works, combined with some lively conceptions of the character, the teaching, and the example of the Author of Christianity. And, looking back to this period twenty-four years after, he said, "Oh that God possessed me with a sense of his holiness and love, as he at one time possessed me with a sense of his greatness and his power, and his pervading energy!" The religion of Chalmers in his youth was the religion of the imagination alone. It had no elements of permanence, no power to renew the heart. And the magnificent vision that so enraptured the young philosopher soon vanished away. Edwards, on the contrary, had so learned Christ, as to regard him as the one Mediator, the way, the truth, and the life. He was deeply contrite and humbled before God, and was enlightened to see the gloriousness of the way of justification through the righteousness of Christ. In reference to the very period when, year after year, he sought the solitude of the woods for the utterance of his overflowing emotion, he said, "I had vehement longings of soul after God and Christ, and after more holiness, wherewith my heart seemed to be full and ready to break; which often brought to mind the words of the psalmist, 'My soul breaketh for the longing it hath.' I often felt a mourning and lamenting in my heart that I had not turned to God sooner, that I might have had more time to grow in grace."

Elizabeth Stuart Phelps; born Aug. 13, 1815; died Nov. 30, 1852.

MRS. STUART PHELPS* inherited the natural temperament, and many other peculiarities of her father, professor Moses Stuart. The predominance of her nervous system over every other part of her physical nature gave an early and positive development to all her natural tastes. The movements of her mind were rapid and strongly marked, and yet accompanied with great, and often excessive delicacy of sensibility. Her temperament favoured the formation of a vigorous yet feminine character.

Elizabeth Stuart possessed in early life a taste for music, and through life was often dependent on its power to soothe her agitated mind, or to elevate her depressed spirits. Her imagination often disturbed her sleep with dreams of harmony, from which she would awake in tears, and which she could not describe but in terms of rapture. She was passionately fond of painting and statuary; and her taste for the fine arts had mellowed and refined her character before she seemed to herself to possess any religious principle. Very nearly allied with it in her nature

* Well known as a writer under the assumed cognomen of "H. Trusta." In this sketch of her Christian experience, we make free use of the exquisite memorial of her by her husband.

was her nice sense of honour. She manifested this early and always. By nature her conscience found its most frequent, if not its strongest development, in a regard for the honourable and magnanimous. And it was often fascinating to observe the childlike artlessness with which she would attribute to others honourable motives of actions, the interpretation of which, as the world would give it, she seemed unable to understand.

Her natural temperament was not well fitted to produce a life of equable enjoyment. Even in childhood she seems to have been subject to fluctuations of hope and despondency. She lived in a world of emotion. She describes herself as having been by nature wild and wayward, and impetuous in her feelings, yet too sensitive to utter them to any human being. An instinct which she could not resist impelled her to hold herself in reserve from her nearest friends. And so far as concerns the expression of her inner life, she passed the early periods of her youth in a solitude which is not very common even to sensitive natures. This she afterwards regarded as a great misfortune, especially in its effects upon her subsequent religious experience; it seemed to her the occasion of irreparable evils. As might have been expected, her early habits of religious feeling became morbid, and tended strongly to bind her thoughts to some one narrow circle. The central object in that circle was death. On a stray leaf found among her papers she has written as follows: "All my early religious emotions were concentrated on the one thought of death. I used to think much about it. It gave a melancholy direction to all my childish feelings. It was a naked sword ever hanging over me by a hair. My nurse took me to almost all the funerals that took place in the village, and at last I was fond of going to them; not because death had become any the less terrible, but because there was something in the exciting stir of so strong an emotion as deep grief which suited my nature. . . . . I can remember, as far back as when I was but three years old, and from that time onward, having again and again cried myself to sleep because I must some time or other see my mother die." The morbid association of her childish feelings with death was never wholly broken up. Long after she had learned to think and speak of her own death with a calm hopefulness, she could not meet with composure the death of friends.

At the age of sixteen Elizabeth Stuart left her father's house to enter the Mount Vernon school at Boston, under the care of the Rev. Jacob Abbott, in whose family she resided for the greater part of two years. This period was exceedingly fruitful of events which affected her whole character. The secluded life she had previously led rendered her transition to a large city a great event. New scenes, the formation of new acquaintances, and subjection to a new discipline, could not but impress a nature so susceptible as hers. Her mind now unfolded itself rapidly, and her tastes matured, and it was now especially she became a partaker of the divine life.

Up to this time her religious opinions do not appear to have been the subject of much reflection, nor does she seem to have experienced anything unusual to children who have been religiously educated; indeed the fidelity of Christian parents appears not to have produced in her case so great a distinctness of religious convictions as that which commonly results from such fidelity. The exclusiveness with which the idea of death possessed her childhood on the subject of religion, shut out, apparently, much of the more valuable reflection which the children of Christian parents often have in early life. In the fragmentary record she has left of the fascination with which funerals affected her, she thus speaks: "The deep solemnity which such seasons left upon my mind was the result of fear and of indefinable awe with which a child looks over beyond the grave. I used at such times to go often to meetings. I would pray much that I might be forgiven, and accepted for Christ's sake; but I had no definite ideas of what it was for which I must be forgiven. I read a great deal about dying, and about the soothing presence of Christ with his followers in their dying hour. When my fears were wide awake, as they used most often to be at night, I used to repeat before going to sleep—

"Jesus can make a dying bed
Feel soft as downy pillows are."

She elsewhere speaks of having been often anxiously interested in the salvation of her soul; and she adds, respecting these occasions, "They were mostly at times of unusual excitement, caused by some sudden death, or by a protracted meeting. I particularly remember a visit of Dr. Nettleton's at Andover, and his 'inquiry meetings,' all of which I faithfully attended. None of these impressions, however, were lasting; they died away with the exciting cause," at least so far as the immediate event of her conversion is concerned.

Her narrative of the way in which her mind was again engaged in religious inquiries is interesting as an illustration of the diversity of God's ways. It shows how he adapts his grace to individual peculiarities of temperament. Silence is often made more eloquent than speech.

The history of "the great change" is thus continued: "The course which Mr. Abbott adopted was entirely the reverse of that to which I had been accustomed, and which I expected. Instead of urging God's claims upon me, as others had often done, he preserved an unbroken silence on the subject of personal religion. This surprised me, and after a while made me uneasy. I brought myself at length to ask him for the cause of his silence towards me on that subject. He told me that he considered the circumstances under which I had been brought up to have been such, that every motive which could influence me had been already urged, and that I had deliberately made my choice, and, therefore, that it remained for him only to fit me for happiness as far as it could be had in this world. This startled me, and led me to look more earnestly into my heart. From this beginning I was led on gradually, and to myself almost imperceptibly, until I began to dare to hope that I had become a child of God, and to wish to take upon myself the name of Christ. I was conscious of a great change in me. Thoughts of God no longer filled me with horror; but a view of his holiness and purity was granted to me, which filled me with inexpressible joy. I felt that life was an 'unspeakable gift,' because there was a God. I desired most earnestly to approach as near to his holiness as I was able; but many struggles taught me how strong a hold sin had in this heart. Here the atonement of Christ first met me with power. I felt driven to it; and, in view of it, even such a sinning heart still dared to look up and struggle on, feeling that its heaviest burden Christ himself bore.

I began to desire to give myself wholly to God in Christ; I wished to live and die for him; I longed to lose myself in him; I wished to indulge no plans, nor purposes, nor feelings, nor thoughts, of which love to him was not the guiding spring. To live for his glory seemed all that rendered life worth possessing. If I must cease to do this, I would also cease to live. This was a great change from my former self, and I have dared to hope that it was God's own work."

The "gradual," and to herself "almost imperceptible" process of which she speaks, as having preceded the dawn of Christian hope in her heart, was protracted, we are told, through a period of nearly two years. Her susceptible nature could not but be stirred to its very depths by earnest religious inquiry. Her experience was rendered the more tumultuous in its character by the fact that this inquiry was awakened just at the time when her whole intellectual being was opening itself to new influences, and approaching the maturity of womanhood. The great thoughts of life, and death, and destiny, and God, swayed her feelings impetuously to and fro; often, for long periods, her soul was too powerfully agitated to admit of her resting in calm hope.

Even at this early period, however, her strength of character prevented any tumultuous exhibition of her feelings to others. The impression which they received of the workings of her mind may be best inferred from the judgment expressed by Mr. Abbott. "My impression is, decidedly," he writes, "that her religious experience, in all its stages, though connected with deep feeling within, was very calm, quiet, and gentle, in all the external manifestations of it. There always seemed to me to be a certain principle of *momentum*, so to speak, in Elizabeth's mind, which gave great steadiness to all its action."

It was with the utmost difficulty that this young convert brought herself to communicate her feelings on the subject of religion, even to those who possessed her entire confidence. Yet this very delicacy of her too sensitive heart gave a depth of tenderness to her first love to her Saviour. That love was mingled with a feeling of self-reproach, as if she wronged him by being a mute friend. But before she could speak for him, she would write for him. And many of her letters, written at the time when she first indulged Christian hope, breathe the most importunate desires for the salvation of her companions

---

Amidst constitutional, circumstantial, social, and even moral diversities, we find in these histories, the gospel producing in all cases substantially the same effects. Speaking of Loskiel's account of the Moravian Missions among the North American Indians, Cecil said, "I have found in it a striking illustration of the uniformity with which the grace of God operates on man. Crantz, in his account of the Missions in Greenland, had shown the grace of God working on a 'man-fish:' on a stupid, sottish, senseless creature, scarcely a remove from the fish on which he lived. Loskiel shows the same grace working on a 'man-devil:' a fierce, bloody, revengeful warrior, dancing his infernal war-dance with the mind of a fury. Divine grace brings these men to the same point. It quickens, stimulates, and elevates the Greenlander: it raises him to a sort of new life: it seems almost to bestow on him new senses: it opens his eye, and bends his ear, and rouses his heart: and what it adds, it sanctifies. The same grace tames the high spirit of the Indian: it reduces him to the meekness, and docility, and simplicity of a child. The evidence arising to Christianity from these facts is, perhaps, seldom sufficient by itself to convince the gainsayer: but, to a man who already believes, it greatly strengthens the reasons of his belief. I have seen also in these books, that, the fish-boat and the oil and the tomahawk and the cap of feathers excepted, a Christian minister has to deal with just the same sort of creatures as the Greenlander and the Indian among civilized nations."

From the diversity and unity which we have seen to characterize conversion, it follows, that the concern of those who profess faith in Christ should be not how they have been brought to its possession, but whether they really have it or not—that each one may be able to say, at the least, with the blind man of old, "One thing I know, that, whereas I was blind, now I see." Nothing can be more unsafe than to rest in the mere fact of having been the subjects of sudden impressions, whether of an awful or joyful character; while on the other hand the absence of such impressions should produce no misgiving in his mind who has other and more satisfactory evidence that he is a new creature in Christ Jesus.

Another lesson may be drawn from our histories, and it is this—at whatever stage of spiritual progress you have arrived, act up to your light. Dream not of going back. The "City of Destruction" is behind, the light of heaven is before. If you can only cry, What shall I do? continue to ask the question with deep and solemn earnestness. If you have only light enough to see it your duty to read and pray, go and do it. If conscience tells you to abandon certain sins and companions, obey, and do it with all the decision of one who feels that life and death are in the balance.

But, at the same time, let no one be satisfied till he has placed his soul in the hands of the loving and all-sufficient Saviour. Reading and praying, if rested in, will prove not helps, but hindrances. Even the abandonment of sinful habits, if trusted in as a qualification for coming to Christ, or as constituting any claim to his favour, will prove, as it did in the case of John Bunyan, a vain attempt to establish one's own righteousness, instead of submitting to the divinely appointed way of pardon and life. The awakened inquirer should come to the Saviour as he is, "nor of fitness fondly dream." The biographer of Hewitson remarks well, that when he came to Christ and rejoiced in the freeness of the gift of life, it was not in virtue of, or as qualified by, the two years' anguish through which he had passed, but simply in virtue of the Divine authority which he had from the beginning, "Come unto me, and I will give you rest."

"Oh, how unlike the complex works of man,
Heaven's easy, artless, unencumbered plan!
No meretricious graces to beguile,
No clustering ornaments to clog the pile;
From ostentation, as from weakness, free,
It stands like the cerulean arch we see,
Majestic in its own simplicity.
Inscribed above the portal from afar,
Conspicuous as the brightness of a star,
Legible only by the light they give,
Stand the soul quickening words—BELIEVE AND LIVE."

PART THE THIRD.

THE DIVINE LIFE: PROVIDENTIAL OCCASIONS.

FACTS.

CONTENTS.—Events divided into Two Classes—The Casual, a Storehouse of Divine Weapons — Gifford — Bunyan — Alderman Kiffin—Lady Huntingdon and Capt. Scott—Robinson—Simeon — Wilberforce — Legh Richmond — Chalmers — Doddridge—R. Haldane—Students in Geneva—John Williams—Dr. Judson—Budgett—Hewitson—Dr. Hope—Narrative by Dr. Malan — The Influence of Affliction — Howels — Cecil—Waldo—John Newton—Remarks by Tholuck—The Finger of God.

"The manifold wisdom of God is conspicuously exhibited, no less than his inexpressibly condescending love, in the variety of leadings by which men are brought to the attainment of the one great object—Redemption." —NEANDER.

"This also cometh forth from the Lord of hosts, which is wonderful in counsel, and excellent in working."—ISAIAH.

"What is His Creation less
Than a capacious reservoir of means,
Formed for His use, and ready at His will?"—COWPER.

"Lord, with what care hast Thou begirt us round!
Parents first season us: then schoolmasters
Deliver us to laws; they send us bound
To rules of reason, holy messengers,
Pulpits and Sundays, sorrow dogging sin,
Affliction sorted, anguish of all sizes,
Fine nets and stratagems to catch us in;
Bibles laid open, millions of surprises,
Blessings beforehand, ties of gratefulness,
The sound of glory ringing in our ears;
Without, our shame; within, our consciences;
Angels and grace, eternal hopes and fears."—HERBERT.

THE DIVINE LIFE:

PROVIDENTIAL OCCASIONS.

THE author of the "Natural History of Enthusiasm" proposes a beautiful analysis of the order and harmony of Providence. He says, that "events may be divided into two classes—first, those which arise in the ordinary course of experience, and which being regulated by certain known laws, natural or moral, may, to a certain and often a great extent, be calculated beforehand, and thus bring into exercise the quality of prudence, or the useful faculty of long-sightedness. Indeed, a careful observation and right estimate of such causes and effects may be said to constitute the best kind of worldly wisdom. Another and more limited class of events may be described as incidental or fortuitous. These intersect the common course, the straightforward line of our experience, from a multitude of different points. They bear laterally upon us, and arise out of an endless and ever-varied train of causes, connected very probably with the life and conduct of others—originating, it may be, in some idle word, or some thoughtless action, of some unknown person, whose mortal existence has been closed for centuries. And yet these apparently stray circumstances often intersect our path just at such a time and in such a manner as to enable them to serve the most important purposes for our temporal and spiritual good."

In reference to these two distinguishable classes

of events, namely, those which may be foreknown by human sagacity, and those which may not, "it is manifest that the former exclusively is given to man as the sphere of his labours, and for the exercise of his skill; while the latter is reserved as the royal domain of sovereign bounty and infinite wisdom." To the former class, as providential occasions of spiritual life to the souls of men, belong the regular ministrations of Christ's gospel, the habitual reading of Holy Scripture, parental instruction, Sabbath school tuition, and every other form of systematic endeavour to bring men's minds under the influence of the truth as it is in Jesus. To the latter belong those apparent fortuities by which men are brought into contact with the truth, or disposed to open their ears and hearts to it. And it is to the illustration of these we now proceed. The hand of God may be very clearly seen in them. To use the words of Mr. Isaac Taylor, they "constitute a *superstratum* in the system of human affairs, wherein, peculiarly, the Divine Providence holds empire for the accomplishment of its special purposes. It is from this hidden and inexhaustible mine of chances—chances as we must call them—that the Governor of the world draws, with unfathomable skill, the materials of his dispensations towards each individual of mankind. The world of nature affords no instances of complicated and exact contrivance comparable to that which so arranges the vast chaos of contingencies as to produce, with unerring precision, a special order of events adapted to the character of every individual of the human family. Amid the whirl of myriads of fortuities, the means are selected and combined for constructing as many independent machineries of moral discipline as there are moral agents in the world; and each apparatus is at once complete in itself, and complete as part of a universal movement.

"If the special intentions of Providence towards individuals were effected by the aid of supernatural interpositions, the power and presence of the Supreme Disposer might indeed be more strikingly displayed than it is; but his skill much less. And herein especially is manifested the perfection of the Divine wisdom, that the most surprising conjunctions of events are brought about by the simplest means, and in a manner so perfectly in harmony with the ordinary course of human affairs, that the hand of the Mover is ever hidden beneath second causes, and is descried only by the eye of pious affection. This is, in fact, the great miracle of Providence, that no miracles are needed to accomplish its purposes. Countless series of events are travelling on from remote quarters towards the same point, and each series moves in the beaten track of natural occurrences; but their intersection, at the very moment in which they meet, shall serve, perhaps, to give a new direction to the affairs of an empire. The materials of the machinery of Providence are all of common quality; but their combination displays nothing less than infinite skill." "This also cometh forth from the Lord of hosts, which is wonderful in counsel, and excellent in working."

It would be difficult to name a man whose labours or writings have contributed to the character of this age, in whose history we shall not find remarkable chances—as men would call them—chances which, in some instances, involved the life of the man, and in others formed the crisis of his spiritual history. John

Bunyan and his "Pilgrim's Progress," for instance, have contributed more, perhaps, to the thinking and feeling of the last two hundred years than any other book and man that can be named. But on how many contingencies was Bunyan's life suspended, and how many contributed to his conversion!

The history of his instructor—the "Evangelist" of his immortal allegory, who directed him to the wicket-gate—comes first before us. GIFFORD had been a royalist in his youth. He was arrested for his concern in the rising in Kent, and, with eleven of his comrades, was doomed to die. The night before the day fixed for his execution, his sister came to visit him. She found the guard asleep, and assisted her brother to effect his escape. For three days the fugitive lay hid in a field, in the bottom of a deep ditch, but at last got away to a place of safety in the neighbourhood of Bedford. There, being a perfect stranger, he ventured on the practice of physic, and abandoned himself to reckless habits and outrageous vice. One evening he lost a large sum of money at the gaming table; and, in the fierceness of his chagrin, his mind was filled with the most desperate thoughts of the providence of God. In his vexation he snatched up a book. It was a volume of Bolton, "a solemn and forceful writer" then well known. A sentence of this book so fixed itself on Gifford's conscience that for many weeks he could get no rest in his spirit. At last he found peace through the blood of the cross, and his joy was extreme. For some time the few pious individuals in that neighbourhood would not believe that such a reprobate was really converted. But, nothing daunted by their distrust, like his prototype of Tarsus, he began to preach

Gifford of Bedford.

the word with boldness, and, endowed with a vigorous mind and a fervent spirit, great success attended his ministry. Imagination could not feign a more fitting history for the pastor of John Bunyan.

William Kiffin; born 1616; died 1701.

William Kiffin lived through one of the most eventful periods of English history, from 1616 to 1701, and was one of the most influential merchants and eminent Christians in the city of London. His position brought him into contact with the great statesmen, good and bad, of the reigns of the two Charleses and of James II., while his principles exposed him to frequent and cruel persecution.

When a great plague desolated London in 1625, William Kiffin was nine years of age. Almost all his relations were swept away by the deadly scourge, and his life was for a time despaired of. On his recovery he was placed under the charge of surviving relatives, who soon failed in business, and lost what of property belonged to him. At the age of thirteen he was apprenticed to "a mean calling," and, two years after, the melancholy which preyed on his mind induced him to run away from his master. For hours he wandered up and down the streets with almost as little of plan or intention as the leaf that is driven, now in one direction and now in another, by the fitful winds. But the winds, lawless though we call them, are obedient to natural laws which govern all their currents and powers, and every leaf that is tossed by them hither and thither, is moved according to the force that propels it. In like manner does Providence invisibly govern the most chanceful and accidental occurrences of life. The boy Kiffin was like a leaf or straw driven by the winds when he passed St. Antholin's church, and saw people going in to worship. He followed without knowing why. The preacher took for his text the fifth commandment, and dwelt specially on the duty of servants to their masters. The run-away apprentice was bewildered, imagined himself discovered, and thought the minister preached to him. On the dismissal of the congregation he returned to his home, and found his master unaware of his intention to forsake his service. Soon after he went to the same sanctuary and heard a sermon on the words: "There is no peace," saith my God, "to the wicked." The minister showed what true peace was, and that no man could obtain it but by faith in Jesus Christ. Young Kiffin was impressed, and felt that he was a stranger to that peace. His perplexity of mind was great. "I saw myself," he says, "every day more and more sinful and vile; pray I could not; believe in Jesus Christ I could not. I thought myself shut up in unbelief; and although I desired to mourn under the sense of my sins, yet I saw there was no suitable proportion of sorrow to that evil nature which I found strongly working in my soul." From this time he attended a faithful ministry, by which he was led gradually to the enjoyment of peace. In a sermon on 1 John i. 7, "The blood of Jesus Christ his Son cleanseth us from all sin," the minister showed the efficacy of the blood of Christ both to pardon and to cleanse from sin, and answered many objections which the unbelieving heart of man brings against that full satisfaction which Jesus Christ has made for sinners. "I found many of them were such as I had made in my own heart; such as the sense of unworthiness, and willingness [desire] to be better before I would come to Christ for life, with many other of the like kind. This sermon was of great use to my soul. I thought I found my heart greatly to close with the riches and freeness of grace which God held forth to poor sinners. I found my fears to vanish, and my heart filled with love to Jesus Christ. I saw sin viler than ever, and felt my heart more abhorring it." His growing faith and holiness soon proved that he was now a new creature in Christ Jesus. And the design of that providence which led the wandering steps of the boy into St. Antholin's church, was manifested in the future character and usefulness of the man.

Lady Huntingdon.

In the history of the COUNTESS OF HUNTINGDON there are many instances of providential occurrences of an unexpected character leading to the most lasting spiritual results.

Captain Scott.

A Captain Scott had been exposed to many dangers as a soldier, and had been frequently awakened by them to think of the claims of religion. It was his daily practice, though felt to be a toilsome duty, to read the psalms and lessons of the day, a practice well known to his brother officers; but as his conduct, in other respects, conformed to theirs, they gave him no opposition. On one occasion, when out on a shooting party in the neighbourhood of Oathall, in Sussex, he was driven by a storm, for cover, to the house of a farmer. There he found several labourers who had taken shelter in the same cottage. The conversation of the farmer and his labourers struck the soldier with surprise. Where had they obtained their knowledge and acquired the sentiments they expressed? "At the hall yonder," they told him, "where there was now a very famous man, a Mr. Romaine, preaching for lady Huntingdon;" and they importunately invited him to come and hear for himself. The following Sunday he went, and was struck with the solemnity of the congregation and the impressive manner in which the service was conducted. Mr. Romaine preached on our Lord's words in John xiv. 6, "I am the way." The truth then delivered was exactly suited to the case of captain Scott. It emancipated him from the bondage of fear, and inspired him with a love to God, under whose influence religion ceased to be a form, or a thing of fits and starts, and became the habitual temper of his mind and law of his life. He became a preacher of the gospel, and hundreds were afterwards converted under the ministry of one who was thus *casually* brought to a knowledge of saving truth.

Lady Huntingdon was a frequent visitor in the cottages of the poor, ministering with a liberal hand to their temporal wants, praying beside the beds of the sick, interesting herself in their every concern, and, above all, ever directing them to the all-sufficient Friend above. On one occasion, we are told, her ladyship spoke to a workman who was repairing a garden-wall, and pressed him to take some thought concerning eternity and the state of his soul. Some years afterwards she was speaking to another on the same subject, and said to him, "Thomas, I fear you never pray, nor look to Christ for salvation." Your ladyship is mistaken," answered the man; "I heard what passed between you and James at such a time, and the word you designed for him took effect on me." "How did you hear it?" inquired lady Huntingdon. "I heard it," answered the man, "on the other side of the garden, through a hole in the wall, and shall never forget the impression I received."

There are few names more honoured among the useful working clergy of the church of England than that of the late THOMAS ROBINSON, vicar of St. Mary's, Leicester. The eulogy pronounced upon him by a member of another communion, the eloquent Robert Hall, is well known. "Who ever heard him," said Mr. Hall, "without feeling a persuasion that it was a man of God that addressed him; or without being struck with the perspicuity of his statements, the solidity of his thoughts, and the rich unction of his spirit? It was the harp of David, which, struck by his powerful hands, sent forth more than mortal sounds, and produced an impression far more deep and permanent than the thunder of Demosthenes, or the splendid coruscations of Cicero. . . . Through the protracted period of his labours, many thousands, who have finished their course with joy, derived from his ministry, there is every reason to believe, the principle of a new life. His residence in Leicester forms an epoch in the religious history of this country. From that time must be dated, and to his agency under Providence must be ascribed, a decided improvement in the moral and religious state of this town and its vicinity; an increase of religious light; together with a general diffusion of a taste and relish for the pure word of God. It is only once in an age that an individual is permitted to confer such benefits on the place of his residence as this ancient and respectable borough derived from the labours of Mr. Robinson; and the change which Baxter accomplished at Kidder-

Thomas Robinson; born at Wakefield, 1749; died at Leicester, 1813.

minster, he effected at Leicester. It was the boast of Augustus, that he found the city of Rome composed of brick, and left it marble; Mr. Robinson might say, without arrogance, that he had been the instrument of effecting a far more beneficial and momentous change. He came to this place while it was sunk in vice and irreligion; he left it eminently distinguished by sobriety of manners, and the practice of warm, serious, and enlightened piety. He added not aqueducts and palaces, nor did he increase the splendour of its public edifices; but he embellished it with undecaying ornaments; he renovated the minds of the people, and turned a large portion of them 'from darkness to light, and from the power of Satan unto God.' He embellished it with living stones, and replenished it with numerous temples of the Holy Ghost."

The providential means by which this man of "masculine understanding" and "capacious heart" became a Christian, were, some of them at least, of that apparently casual order in which many fail to see more than chance. Thomas Robinson's early youth was not characterized by any strong impressions of religion. His attention was much engrossed with the fascinations of art, literature, and the drama. But just before his departure from home for the commencement of a college life, he met a poor man, a shoemaker of Wakefield, who asked him whether he was not going to be a clergyman. On receiving an answer in the affirmative, the poor man added, "Then, sir, I hope you will study your Bible, that you may be able to feed the flock of Christ with spiritual food." Robinson was much impressed with the kindness and honesty of his poor friend, and cheerfully accepted the loan of a few humble volumes of practical and experimental piety. About the same time he was visited by a severe illness which threatened his life. And the seriousness of spirit produced by these two circumstances was further confirmed by a dream, of which he was afterwards accustomed to relate, that it brought before his eyes a lively representation of Wakefield church in flames; that awful appearances in the sky ensued; till at last the conflagration of the world began, and he was hurried up into the air to meet his Judge. For this and similar dreams we claim no supernatural character—nothing could be more entirely natural, or more naturally suggested by his circumstances and his waking thoughts. But its beneficial influence is not, on this account, to be treated as other than providential.

Thomas Robinson was no longer a trifler, but deeply in earnest. Still he was far from being a new creature in Christ Jesus. For two years he continued in great perplexity of mind, not knowing whither to turn or what to do. And then he had recourse to scenes of gaiety and dissipation. But the misgivings of his conscience interrupted his enjoyment of sinful pleasure, and his soul became like the troubled sea which cannot rest. At length, in 1768, he took up his residence within the walls of Trinity College, Cambridge. He was elated with the novelty of the scene, and its associations of age, and wisdom, and piety, and devoted himself to his studies with zeal and interest. His religion, too, such as it was, rendered his habits and conversation very different from those of the greater part of his cotemporaries. But he was still without peace with God. It was about a year after his arrival at the university that the perusal of Hervey's "Theron and Aspasio" was the means of turning him from darkness to that light in which he saw clearly the ground of pardon and peace, and found at the same time the spring of true godliness. He now understood the great and fundamental doctrine that it is "not by works of righteousness" which we can do, but "according to his own mercy" God will save us. And being saved by grace, instead of continuing in sin, it was his early and constant endeavour to have his whole body, soul, and spirit sanctified to the will and service of God. The truths which proved his own deliverance from the bondage of a burdened conscience, and from the power of an evil heart, formed the staple of his after ministry, and were the instruments of that spiritual reformation which, in the terms we have already quoted, Robert Hall ascribed to his labours in Leicester.

Charles Simeon; born at Reading, Sep. 24, 1758; died at Cambridge, Nov. 13, 1836.

The name of CHARLES SIMEON is still more intimately connected with the revival of evangelical religion in England than that of Thomas Robinson. The influence of the latter, great and beneficial as it was, was chiefly local. Before the close of Mr. Simeon's ministry, it would have been difficult to find in England the district in which one would not meet with a clergyman, or other educated gentleman, who was teaching and adorning the precious truths which he had first heard at Trinity Church, Cambridge, or in the faith of which he had been there greatly strengthened and encouraged. And yet the turning point of Simeon's own spiritual history was of a most unlikely and unexpected character.

While a boy at Eton College, Charles Simeon, though governed by no better principles than his schoolfellows, was distinguished for energy and vigour. On one of the public fast days, during the American war, he was particularly struck with the idea of the whole nation uniting in fasting and prayer on account of the sins which had brought down divine judgments upon it; and he thought that if there was one who had more displeased God than others it was he. Few of his schoolfellows had any notion of a fast, except that they were to abstain from meat and amusement till the afternoon after the second service. But young Simeon felt that to humble himself before God was a duty of immediate necessity. Accordingly he spent the day in fasting and prayer. His companions exclaimed "Woe, woe unto you, hypocrites!" Before this blast of scorn his good resolutions were dissipated, and he became as thoughtless as ever. The only trace of religious impression that remained was that, in the true spirit of a Pharisee, he had a small box with several divisions in it, into which, on having been tempted to say or do what he afterwards considered unlawful or immoral, it was his custom to put money for the poor.

In 1779 young Simeon entered King's College, in the university of Cambridge. And on the third day after his arrival a circumstance took place which might have hardened him in formality, or produced infidelity, but which was overruled by divine grace to the saving of his soul. He was told that he was expected in the space of about three weeks to attend the Lord's supper. "What," he said, "*must* I attend?" On being informed that he *must*, the thought rushed into his mind that Satan himself was as fit to attend as he, and that if he must attend he must prepare. Without a moment's loss of time he bought the old "Whole

Duty of Man" (the only religious book, he says, he had ever heard of), and began to read it with great diligence, at the same time calling his ways to remembrance, and crying to God for mercy; and so earnest was he in these exercises, that within the three weeks he made himself quite ill with reading, fasting, and prayer.

On Easter Sunday Mr. Simeon must receive the Lord's supper again, and he continued with unabated earnestness to search out and mourn over what he describes as the numberless iniquities of his former life; and so greatly was his mind oppressed with the weight of them, that, like colonel Gardiner, he frequently looked upon the dogs with envy, wishing, if it were possible, that he could be blessed with their mortality, and they be cursed with his immortality in his stead. He set himself to undo his former sins, and in his endeavours to this end practised great self-denial. After three months of deep mental distress, the day of peace and hope dawned upon his soul. In the week before Easter, as he was reading bishop Wilson on the Lord's supper, he met with an expression to this effect: "That the Jews knew what they did when they transferred their sin to the head of their offering." This remark opened to him a new world of spiritual vision, and the thought rushed into his mind, "What! may I transfer all my guilt to another? Has God provided an offering for me that I may lay my sins on his head? Then, God willing, I will not bear them on my own soul one moment longer." The great sacrifice that was offered on the cross appeared to him now in an altogether new light. He understood in some measure how "He who knew no sin" had become "sin for us, that we might be made the righteousness of God in him." His hope of mercy grew brighter and brighter, till on the morning of Easter-day he awoke early, with those words in his heart and on his lips, "Jesus Christ is risen to-day! Hallelujah! Hallelujah!" "From that hour," he says, "peace flowed in rich abundance into my soul, and at the Lord's table I had the sweetest access to God through my blessed Saviour." The fancy of his Eton days, that he made amends for his sins by giving money to the poor, was now for ever at an end; but the freeness of the mercy in which he now rejoiced was only a motive to serve God and his fellow-men with the more zeal and self-denial.

Dr. Stewart, of Moulin.

The Rev. ALEXANDER STEWART was the minister of a Highland parish in the end of the last century. He was a young man of unblemished reputation and amiable manners. To the outward proprieties of his station there was nothing wanting. But the power of godliness was unfelt. In his parish there was a scene of the wildest grandeur, the Pass of Killiecrankie, a savage defile, just beyond which lies the battle-field on which the viscount Dundee endeavoured to retrieve the fortunes of James II. In the year 1796, Mr. Simeon, of Cambridge, and Mr. James Haldane,* visited the Highlands. They had never heard of Mr. Stewart, but when they were leaving Edinburgh, a "random thought" occurred to one of their friends to introduce them to the minister of Moulin, as they expected to visit the Pass of Killiecrankie. On their way they visited Dunkeld, and, after surveying its beauties, intended to proceed north-

* See Biographical Tract, "Rev. Charles Simeon," published by the London Religious Tract Society.

ward. This was on a Friday. The carriage was at the door at the appointed time, but Mr. Simeon was too much fatigued to proceed. By this unexpected circumstance their visit to the parish of Moulin took place on a Saturday. And this Saturday was a high day there; it was the day preceding the annual celebration of the Lord's supper; and the travellers were easily persuaded to prolong their visit. After feasting their eyes on the awful magnificence of the Pass, and listening to the tumultuous roar of the Garry, storming its angry way along the bottom of the deep gorge below, they returned to enjoy the hospitality of the manse, and to take part in the solemnity of the following day. When on Sabbath evening Mr. Simeon retired to his chamber, his host accompanied him, and on the conversation into which they then fell were suspended issues of the greatest moment. Mr. Stewart was not without some feeling of the unprofitableness of his ministry, and as his heart was drawn out to his English guest, he did not conceal his thoughts; while Mr. Simeon spoke to him from the fulness of his heart of the grace of God and the gospel of Jesus Christ. "I know nothing," wrote Mr. Stewart afterwards, "to which I can so fully compare myself, as to Ezekiel's dry bones, when they were covered with flesh and skin, but were without life or sensation. It was reserved for Mr. Simeon to be the man who should be appointed to prophesy to the wind and say, 'Come from the four winds, O breath, and breathe upon this dead body, that it may live.'" How marvellous in working is the providence of God! Two strangers from a distance must be sent to Moulin; their plans must be once and again changed that they may be there at a season of peculiar solemnity, to become the instruments of good to the soul of a man they had never heard of. And the man thus visited, by the grace of God, became thereafter the means of the conversion of many. From the hour when he experienced Christ to be the power of God unto salvation, the strain of his preaching was entirely changed. He determined to know nothing among men, save Jesus Christ, and him crucified. And immediately there appeared in his parish a great awakening—one of those seasons when the Spirit of God comes down with pentecostal power. Within a few months of Mr. Simeon's visit, many were turned to the Lord. And only the eye of Omniscience can trace in their course from one generation to another all the streams of blessing which still flow from the fountain thus opened.

Mr. Simeon and a poor woman.

We select another instance from the life of CHARLES SIMEON to illustrate those singular providential coincidences which prove the occasion of the conversion of souls to God. In 1783, just at the beginning of his ministry, Mr. Simeon was invited to be present at a brother's marriage in London, and to perform the ceremony. On his arrival in town he undertook to perform the "occasional duty" of a clergyman at Horselydown for a week. And on the very day of his brother's marriage, when a large and splendid party had assembled to celebrate the event, notice was sent to him that there would be a funeral at his friend's church. He was thus withdrawn from an uncongenial scene of gaiety, and that to do a work which he knew not. While waiting in the churchyard for the corpse which was about to be laid in its narrow house, he occupied his time in reading the epitaphs on the tombstones. Many of them were such as might adorn a Jew's or a heathen's grave. But at last he came to one which characterized a Christian:—

> "When from the dust of death I rise,
> To claim my mansion in the skies,
> E'en then shall this be all my plea—
> 'Jesus has lived and died for me.'"

Struck with the sentiment, he looked around to see if there were any one to whom God might render it the means of spiritual instruction, and at a little distance he saw a young woman "of a sorrowful countenance" reading an epitaph. She had ruined her health in labouring for the support of an aged mother and two children. Having just been to a sister who lived in that neighbourhood, instead of receiving help or sympathy, she had been sent away with reproaches; and now, after wandering among the tombs for five hours, and regarding herself as forsaken of God, her misery was insupportable, her resolution was taken, she would drown herself. Directed by a Providence which knew these things, Mr. Simeon accosted her:—"You are reading epitaphs, mistress—read that; when you can say the same from your heart, you will be happy indeed; but till then you will enjoy no real happiness in this world or in the next." She read the words without any apparent emotion, and coolly remarked that a churchyard was a very proper place for her, for that she was much distressed. On hearing her burden of domestic care, Mr. Simeon turned to some passages in his Bible, and endeavoured to turn her eyes to Him who gives rest to heavy-laden souls. The arrival of the corpse put an end to the conversation, but he took her address and visited her wretched home, two miles off, the following evening. There he found the aged mother very ill of asthma, two little babes lying in bed, and the young woman sitting like a statue of sorrow. The next evening, and the next, he visited them again; and it was only on the third visit that he heard the tale of intended suicide. "But now, sir," concluded the poor woman, "instead of despairing of bread to eat, I am enabled to see that God, who is the Father of the fatherless, and the Husband of the widow, is my friend; that Jesus Christ has washed me from all my sins in the fountain of his own blood, and that it is my privilege to be careful for nothing; and, blessed be God, I am enabled to cast all my care on him who careth for me." Twelve months after, Mr. Simeon had the satisfaction to find that while the aged mother had died in the peace of the gospel, the younger widow was leading a holy and consistent life. The invitation which brought him to London was kindly but ignorantly designed by his relations, who at that time did not sympathize with his religious feelings, to divert him from the over-intense pursuit of the objects which lay nearest to his heart. But his Master had another design than theirs, and gave him a work to do which will be gratefully remembered throughout eternity.

W. Wilberforce; born in Hull, Aug. 24, 1759; died in London, July 29, 1833.

WILLIAM WILBERFORCE had impressions of religion when, as a child, he lived under the roof of a pious aunt at Wimbledon. "But when he entered parliament as member for his native borough, Hull, he was utterly without God in the world. This, too, was his melancholy state when in 1783, in a season of intense political excitement, he was returned for the county of York. When parliament was prorogued the following summer he went down to York, and was 'the joy of the races.' He spent his twenty-fifth birthday at the top wave and highest flow of those frivolous amusements which had swallowed up so large a portion of his youth." Nothing could be further from his thoughts at this time, than to make any arrangement by which he should be won from the world, and taught to serve a better Master. But it was so ordered by One whose hand he saw not. When at York, he invited a friend to accompany him in a continental tour, and was surprised that he declined it. He then invited Isaac Milner in his stead. This was the *chance*, as it seemed, by which the whole of his life was turned into another channel. There was nothing apparently in the companionship which he had chosen to produce a new state of feeling. "Though Milner's religious opinions," Wilberforce wrote afterwards, "were even now in theory much the same as in later life, yet they had at this time little practical effect on his conduct. He was free from every taint of vice, but not more attentive than others to religion." Before they set out on their journey, Mr. Wilberforce discovered the opinions of his companion, but it was now too late to revoke an invitation which, had he known them sooner, he never would have given. On the shores of the Mediterranean, where they luxuriated for months, they had frequent discussions on religious subjects, but they were merely speculative. There was too little of the power of evangelical religion manifested at this time in the life of one who became afterwards one of its ornaments, to give much weight to his reasonings, and his gay and sprightly friend held on his ungodly course unmoved.

And now we find another of the innumerable lines

of providential arrangement made strikingly visible in the circumstances which contributed to Mr. Wilberforce's conversion. Dr. Doddridge, long before this time in his grave, had been the friend of Mr. Unwin, Cowper's well-known correspondent. Mr. Unwin had been the friend of the mother of one of Mr. Wilberforce's female relatives now of his party at Nice, and had presented to her a copy of Dr. Doddridge's "Rise and Progress of Religion in the Soul." That copy lay casually on a table in their winter retreat, just as Mr. Wilberforce was preparing to return to his parliamentary duties. Casting his eye over it hastily, he asked Milner's opinion of it. "It is one of the best books ever written," was the reply; "let us take it with us, and read it on our journey." He consented, they read it together carefully, and Wilberforce determined to examine the Scriptures for himself at some future season, and see if things were stated there in the same manner. On his arrival in England, all concern about religion was swallowed up in the excitement of politics, and in a constant round of company and amusement. The villa at Wimbledon, where his infant lips had been taught hosannas by his pious aunt, was now his own, and resounded with songs of another order. There many an evening assembly filled with its gay festivities the former abode of peaceful piety.

The following summer, however, Wilberforce and Milner returned to Italy, and their conversation became more serious than before. They began to read the Greek Testament together, and to examine its doctrines. By degrees Wilberforce became interested in the opinions of his companion, and at length became impressed with a sense of their practical importance.

"Often (he says) while in the full enjoyment of all that this world could bestow, my conscience told me that in the true sense of the word I was not a Christian. I laughed, I sang, I was apparently gay and happy; but the thought would steal across me—'What madness is all this; to continue easy in a state in which a sudden call out of the world would consign me to everlasting misery, and that when eternal happiness was within my grasp!'" At length such thoughts as these completely occupied his mind, and he began to pray earnestly. When he reflected on these subjects, "the deep guilt, and black ingratitude" of his past life forced itself upon him in the strongest colours, and he condemned himself for having wasted his precious time and opportunities and talents. "It was not so much," he said, "the fear of punishment by which I was affected, as a sense of my great sinfulness in having so long neglected the unspeakable mercies of my God and Saviour; and such was the effect which this thought produced, that for months I was in a state of the deepest depression from strong convictions of my guilt." His guilty conscience soon found peace, however, through faith in an all-sufficient Saviour. And when he made a frank avowal of the change which he had undergone to those who had hitherto been the companions of his thoughtlessness, some treated the announcement as the effect of a temporary depression, which social intercourse would soon relieve; one threw his letter angrily in the fire; others, knowing that his past life had not been vicious, imagined that he could but turn ascetic. But it was not so; Mr. Wilberforce did not "flee from men's pursuits" to cultivate a hot-house piety, but devoted his life to manful struggles with the great evils of his time; and with what success the history of his country will long record. The freedom of the negro in the British colonies is his noblest monument; and in his example, both the loftiest potentate and the humblest peasant may find instruction and blessing.

A few months after the publication of Wilberforce's "Practical View of Christianity," in 1797, a young Cambridge man entered on the curacies of Brading and Yaverland, in the Isle of Wight. He was orthodox and moral; the regularity and decorum with which he discharged his duties far exceeded those of many. A college friend, who was about to take orders, received Mr. Wilberforce's book from a near relative, and sent it to the curate of Brading for his opinion of it; the young clergyman no sooner began to read it than he found himself so deeply interested in its contents, that the volume was not laid down till the perusal of it was completed. "The soul of the reader was penetrated to its inmost recesses. A change was effected in his views of divine truth, as decided as it was influential. He was no longer satisfied with the creed of the speculatist; he felt a conviction of his own state as a guilty, condemned sinner, and under that conviction he sought mercy at the cross of the Saviour. There arose in his mind a solemn consciousness that however outwardly moral and apparently irreproachable his conduct might appear to men, yet within there was wanting that entire surrender of the heart, that ascendency of God in the soul, and that devotedness of life and conduct which distinguishes holiness from morality, and the external profession of religion from its inward and transforming power." It was in this unlooked-for manner that Mr. LEGH RICHMOND received his first sacred impressions, to use his own words, as to the vital character of personal religion, the corruption of the human heart, and the way of salvation by Jesus Christ. The stream of blessing which the "Dairyman's Daughter," and other "Annals of the Poor," convey to the cabins and hamlets of the peasantry of England, had its fountain head in the regenerate heart of the Christian senator, and was directed to the parsonage of Brading by one who was altogether unconscious of the providential importance of what he was doing.*

Legh Richmond; born Jan. 29, 1772: died May 8, 1827.

Fourteen years after Wilberforce's book was published, a Scottish clergyman sat in his quiet parsonage, brooding over his spiritual state, seeking comfort, and finding none.† He was a man of mighty eloquence, and high literary ambition. Hitherto he had preached a gospel which contained little more that was adapted to man's condition than what Seneca and other heathen moralists had taught. But death had visited his father's house, and the hand of God was on his own person. Eternity had now acquired a befitting importance in his esteem, and he set himself manfully to prepare for its awful realities. But he knew not how. There was a certain class of doctrines which were very precious to a venerable father, and had given much comfort to a dying brother and sister. These doctrines, however, had been often denounced from his pulpit as visionary and fanatical. The awakened clergyman set himself to work out a righteousness of

* See Biographical Tract, "William Wilberforce," published by the London Religious Tract Society.

† Ibid.

his own. He attempted in an agony of soul to "scale the heights of perfection, to quell the remonstrances of a challenging, and not yet appeased commandment;" but it was "like the laborious ascent of him, who, having so wasted his strength that he can do no more, finds that some precipice still remains to be overcome, some mountain brow that scorns his enterprise, and threatens to overwhelm him." He tried to mix the merit of Christ with the sincerity of his repentance, and the pains-taking of his obedience; yet his soul knew no solid peace. In his father's house he found Wilberforce's "Practical View," and, in his own humble manse, he pored over its pages with an interest which such books had never awakened before. As he read, "he felt himself on the eve of a great revolution in all his opinions about Christianity;" and, by the grace of God, this revolution was happily consummated. The gospel, which he had before despised, now gave peace and life to his own soul; and THOMAS CHALMERS became the spiritual son of William Wilberforce. There is no name with which the revival of evangelical religion in Scotland is more closely associated than that of Chalmers; and if Mr. Wilberforce's book had been the means of no other conversion than his, its publication would have been an event of historical importance.

Dr. Chalmers; born March 17th, 1780: died May 30, 1847.

The reader may pause to retrace the stream of holy influence, which thus widens and deepens as it flows on its blessed course. A gay young man, a man of mark and wealth, asks a friend to join him on a continental tour. The friend declines, and the request is made to another, who consents. The man whose society is thus casually sought holds certain opinions, the discovery of which, had it been made earlier, would have prevented the request being made to him. A lady friend and relative carries with her to their winter quarters on the Mediterranean, a copy of Doddridge's "Rise and Progress of Religion in the Soul," which Cowper's friend, Unwin (a cotemporary and friend of the author), had presented to her mother. The gay Wilberforce, in an idle hour, takes up the volume and asks his friend's opinion of it. He is told it is one of the best books ever written, and consents to read it. And the reading determines him to examine the Scriptures for himself, and see whether the teachings of Doddridge's book are true. Wilberforce ere long becomes a devout Christian, and addresses the world with all the earnestness of his fervid nature on the defective views of religion which generally prevailed around him. His book comes into the hands of Legh Richmond in a way as undesigned as was the association of Wilberforce and Milner; and in a manner equally undesigned it is taken up by Thomas Chalmers at the very moment when it is most likely to affect his heart and enlighten his mind—and both of them become converts to the truth as it is in Jesus.

This complication of lines of influence, intersecting each other, and, chanceful as they seem to be, producing results so great, becomes the more remarkable when it is remembered that the life of Philip Doddridge was preserved when he was an infant by what we call the merest chance. Philip Doddridge was the twentieth child of his parents, and at his birth there was only one other child surviving. When born he was so destitute of any appearance of vitality, that the attendants thought the child dead, and laid it aside accordingly. One of them, however, soon afterwards happening to cast a glance upon the infant, fancied that she perceived a feeble heaving of its chest, and took upon herself the apparently futile task of its resuscitation. Her care was providentially rewarded, for while she continued to cherish it, a faint moaning became audible, evincing that the babe was indeed alive; and thus, apparently by accident, was that voice called into action on whose eloquent accents thousands afterwards hung in hushed delight, while their hearts grew warm with the holy love of God. How much had the world lost if that babe had been carried from the chamber of his birth to his grave! The eternal God could raise up other instruments to accomplish his purposes, but this feeble infant was *the* instrument on which he had ordained so much to depend; and in the accident by which it was preserved from an untimely grave we see his hand as plainly working as in the most startling miracle of holy writ. How true it is that the chances of life "constitute a superstratum in the system of human affairs, wherein peculiarly the Divine Providence holds empire for the accomplishment of its special purposes."

Robert Haldane: born in London, Feb. 28, 1764; died in Edinburgh, Dec. 12, 1842.

ROBERT HALDANE retired from the navy at the early age of twenty, and spent the next ten years of his life in the improvement of his paternal estate of Airthrey, honoured by his friends and neighbours, but careless of his spiritual interests. The providential means by which he was awakened from the sleep of spiritual death was the excitement of the French revolution. That great political convulsion came upon Europe like an earthquake, casting down thrones, mitres, and altars, mingling in one heap of ruins the trophies of feudal grandeur and the monuments of sacerdotal tyranny. Like most young men of ardent, generous, and energetic minds, Robert Haldane was roused as from a lethargy by the events passing around him. He saw, or imagined he saw, loom ing through the mist, the prospect of a new and better order of things. He admitted that good and evil were wildly contending for the mastery, but he was sanguine as to the result, and dropped out of his calculation the corruption of human nature, and the hopelessness of any solid reformation apart from the influence of a divine agency.

No sooner was Robert Haldane's mind directed to "the concerns of his immortal soul," than he pursued the momentous subject with characteristic intensity. And we can trace the providence of God in his intercourse at this juncture with enlightened Christian ministers, and especially in what will be called his *casual* intercourse with a journeyman mason that was working on his estate. This good man was well read in his Bible and in the best old Scottish divines. While the mason and his employer were walking from one part of the estate to another, the conversation turned from the subject of masonry to the glory of the great Architect of the universe. The views of divine truth, and of faith in the finished work of Christ, which this humble but intelligent Christian unfolded as they went along, were so plain and scriptural, that Mr. Haldane saw the gospel to be indeed glad tidings, and ever afterwards looked back with thankfulness to that memorable walk, "in which he began to discern more clearly that, in the matter of justification, faith must cast away all reliance on the shifting sands of frames and feelings, and fasten only upon the Rock of ages."*

The name of Robert Haldane is identified with the revival of Scriptural Christianity on the continent of Europe, and the circumstances are perhaps still more strikingly providential than even those of his own conversion.

Robert Haldane in Geneva.

In the beginning of this century the city of GENEVA had fallen from her ancestral faith, and proved how vain are historic names and scriptural formularies, when the spirit has ceased to animate the lifeless frame. Her pastors and professors had abandoned the doctrines of the Godhead and atonement of our Lord Jesus Christ, and were Arians and Socinians. Her Sabbaths were profaned and trampled under feet. On God's holy day the theatres were opened, and even the pastors on certain solemn festivals dismissed their congregations earlier that they might themselves participate in the festivities of the Lord's day, which was closed with fireworks and the discharge of cannon. It was at this period of its history (in 1816) that Robert Haldane passed through the ancient gates of Geneva, not to gratify his tastes as a traveller, but to make known the blessed gospel. But how was he to discharge his mission?

On his arrival he called on a pastor who was understood to hold Bible truth in reference to the person and work of our Lord, and was kindly received. The pastor acquiesced in all the views of his visitor, but he seems to have been a man of an easy or immovable temper, with whom no progress could be made. Mr. Haldane quitted Geneva for Berne, where, for eight

*See Biographical Tract, "Robert and James Haldane," published by the London Religious Tract Society.

days, he was permitted to converse with a pastor who was no Arian or Socinian, and was willing to hear concerning the great truths of the gospel. He was about to quit Geneva a second time, hopeless of finding any one with whom he might converse on gospel truth, when a trivial circumstance, as men judge, was the means of opening a wide and effectual door. "M. Moulinie had politely offered to conduct Mrs. Haldane to see the model of the mountains, a little way out of town, and with this object he promised to call on us (says Mr. H.) the day following. In the morning, however, we received a note from him, saying that, having suffered from a severe headache during the night, he was himself unable to come, but had sent a young man, a student of divinity, who would be our conductor. On this providential circumstance depended my continuance at Geneva, which I had been on the point of leaving. With this student I immediately entered into conversation respecting the gospel, of which I found him profoundly ignorant, although in a state of mind which showed that he was willing to receive information. He returned with me to the inn and remained till late at night. Next morning he came with another student, equally in darkness with himself. I questioned them respecting their personal hope of salvation, and the foundation of that hope. Had they been trained in the schools of Socrates or Plato, and enjoyed no other means of instruction, they could scarcely have been more ignorant of the doctrines of the gospel. They had, in fact, learned much more of the opinions of the heathen philosophers than of the doctrines of the Saviour and his apostles. To the Bible and its contents their studies

M. James, Evangelical Pastor at Breda.

M. Charles Rieu.

had never been directed. After some conversation, they became convinced of their ignorance of the Scriptures and of the way of salvation, and exceedingly desirous of information. I, therefore, postponed my intended departure from Geneva."

Within a few weeks from this period we find Mr. Haldane surrounded by almost all the students of the Theological Seminary, who braved the frowns and threats of their professors, and received from him a course of conversational prelections on the Epistle to the Romans, till the period of their vacation in the summer of 1817. And not a few of these students were converted to Christ. Of these Rieu, Pyt, and Gonthier have long since finished a brief but brilliant course with joy; and there yet remain Frederick Monod, Merle D'Aubigné, Gaussen, Galland, Guers, James, and others, to testify how great the work was of which Mr. Haldane was providentially the instrument. "The work," says M. Monod, writing thirty-six years after, "which Mr. Haldane began in 1817, has been advancing ever since, and the extent of it will not be known until the day of the revelation of all things."

The well known author of the "History of the Reformation," to whose writings the world is so deeply indebted, has himself stated the providential circumstances which led to his conversion. "When I and M. Monod attended the university of Geneva, there was a professor of divinity who confined himself to lecturing on the immortality of the soul, the existence of God, and similar topics. As to the Trinity, he did not believe it. Instead of the Bible, he gave us quotations from Seneca and Plato. St. Seneca and St. Plato were the two saints

Merle D'Aubigné.

whose writings he held up to admiration." And thoroughly did the disciple whose words we are quoting enter into the opinions and spirit of his master. About the time of Mr. Haldane's arrival in Geneva there appeared a pamphlet entitled, "Considerations on the Divinity of Jesus Christ," by Henri Empeytaz. This pamphlet produced great excitement among the students in theology, to whom it was addressed. They assembled in the "grand hall," chose for their president one of their own number, and addressed to the "Venerable Company" a letter in which they solemnly protested against what they termed the "odious aggression." The foremost man on this occasion, the chosen president of the assembled students, was no other than Merle D'Aubigné. "But the Lord sent one of his servants to Geneva," he says, "and I well remember the visit of Robert Haldane. I heard of him first as an English or Scotch gentleman who spoke much about the Bible, which seemed a very strange thing to me and the other students, to whom it was a shut book. I afterwards met Mr. Haldane at a private house, along with some other friends, and heard him read from an English Bible a chapter from Romans, about the natural corruption of man—a doctrine of which I had never before heard. In fact, I was quite astonished to hear of men being corrupt by nature. I remember saying to Mr. Haldane, 'Now I see that doctrine in the Bible.' 'Yes,' he replied, 'but do you see it in your heart?' That was but a simple question, but it came home to my conscience. It was the sword of the Spirit; and from that time I saw that my heart was corrupted, and knew from the word of God that I can be saved by grace alone: so that if Geneva gave something to Scotland at the time of the Reformation—if she communicated light to John Knox—Geneva has received something from Scotland in return, in the blessed exertions of Robert Haldane."

John Williams; born at Tottenham, June 29, 1796; died at Erromanga, Nov. 20, 1839.

The missionary JOHN WILLIAMS, known as the Martyr of Erromanga, enjoyed from childhood the advantage of Christian instruction and example, his mother being a woman of consistent and earnest piety; and his constant observance of private devotion awakened the hope that maternal prayers were not in vain. In his fourteenth year he came into London and was apprenticed to an ironmonger in the City-road. Happily he was surrounded in his new home with the same spiritual influences which rendered his mother's house a school for Christ. His skill in workmanship, and his genial, obliging disposition soon rendered him a universal favourite. But although John Williams was an upright and estimable youth, "one thing" he lacked. The promise of his early years had not been realized. Those blossoms, which in childhood awakened the hope of his mother, did not set. With "godly jealousy" she marked the progress of his mind, and perceived with pain the decay of those serious impressions which she had once beheld with so much joy. Under these circumstances she could do little more than continue to commend her child to God, and, when on the Sabbath day he visited his family, improve the opportunity for restoring those thoughts and feelings, the traces of which were now becoming every year more illegible. But these efforts appeared to be in vain. Amidst all that was affectionate and respectful to herself, Mrs. Williams saw but too clearly that "his heart was not right with

God." One obvious indication of this was his growing disregard to the Sabbath and its sacred services. He was, according to his own after testimony, a lover of pleasure more than a lover of God, and often scoffed at the name of Christ and his religion.

In his eighteenth year John Williams appeared to be rapidly sinking down into a state of settled "hardness and impenitence of heart." His Christian friends looked on with sorrow and solicitude; and these feelings were augmented by the discovery that he had become the associate of several irreligious young men, and had recently more than ever disregarded the Sabbath and forsaken the sanctuary. His position now was most perilous; and even his mother's entreaties had become too feeble to restrain him. But prayer was made by her on his behalf continually, and God heard her cry. The circumstances were these.

In conformity with what had now become a common practice, John Williams had engaged to spend a Sabbath evening with several of his young associates at a tea-garden near his master's residence, or more correctly, at a tavern connected with one of these scenes of Sabbath desecration and sensual indulgence. But, happily, his giddy companions did not keep their time. Had they been as punctual as himself, that evening would have been spent in the tavern. But providentially, while he was sauntering near the place of meeting, greatly annoyed by their delay, and by the observation of those who knew his face and were hastening to the house of God, Mrs. Tonkin, his master's wife, came by, and on discerning his features by the light of a lamp, inquired the reason of his remaining there. This he frankly avowed, and at the same time expressed great vexation at his disappointment; when, with affectionate earnestness, this pious friend endeavoured to induce him to accompany her to the Tabernacle in Moorfields. He yielded to her importunity, but rather from a feeling of mortification than from any better principle; and few ever entered the house of God less prepared to profit by its services. The preacher's text was the weighty question, "What is a man profited, if he shall gain the whole world and lose his own soul? or what shall a man give in exchange for his soul?" This solemn inquiry was carried home by the preacher with point and energy, and the word came with power and with the demonstration of the Holy Spirit upon the mind of his youthful auditor. This was a night to be remembered—and it was remembered with vividness and interest. Speaking of it from the same pulpit, when he was about to leave his country a second time to preach the gospel in Polynesia, he said, "It is now twenty-four years ago since, as a stripling youth, a kind female friend invited me to come into this place of worship. I have the door in my view at this moment at which I entered, and I have all the circumstances of that important era of my history vividly impressed upon my mind, and I have in my eye at this instant the particular spot on which I took my seat. I have also a distinct impression of the powerful sermon that was that evening preached by the excellent Mr. East, now of Birmingham; and God was pleased, in his gracious providence, to influence my mind so powerfully, that I forsook all my worldly companions." Nor was this the only effect. "From that hour," he wrote subsequently, "my blind eyes were opened, and I beheld wondrous things out of

God's law. I diligently attended the means of grace. I saw that beauty and reality in religion which I had never seen before. My love to it and delight in it increased; and I may add in the language of the apostle, that I 'grew in grace, and in the knowledge of my Lord and Saviour Jesus Christ.'" Old things had passed away, all things had become new. And from that hour the young disciple manifested great decision of character. His convictions were converted at once into practical principles; and his early piety was marked by the same simplicity and firmness which distinguished and dignified his more matured experience.

When the work, "Missionary Enterprises in the South Sea Islands" was published in 1837, the book was very appropriately called by an English prelate, a new chapter of the Acts of the Apostles. And if in the call of this modern apostle there was no supernatural appearance of the ascended Lord, such as arrested the youthful Saul on his way to Damascus, it was the providence of that Lord that directed and used the commonest accidents of life to turn him from the vanities of the world, that he might go far hence among the Gentiles to preach the unsearchable riches of Christ. The work which was assigned him he ceased not to perform till he fell beneath the club of the savage on the shores of Erromanga.

If John Williams may be called the apostle of Polynesia, Dr. Judson has equal claim to be called the apostle of Burmah. And his decision for God may be ascribed to a circumstance equally fortuitous with that which turned the feet of John Williams into the Tabernacle at Moorfields.

Dr. Judson; born in Massachusetts, Aug. 9, 1788: died April 12, 1850.

Young Judson is described as possessed of an acute intellect, with great powers of acquisition and unflagging perseverance. His temper was amiable, but his natural love of pre-eminence was unduly encouraged and fostered by his father, who fondly but unwisely told him he expected him to become a great man. When about fourteen years of age, his studies were interrupted by a serious attack of illness, and for a year after he was unable to resume his wonted occupations. When the violence of the disease subsided, he spent many long days and nights in reflecting upon his future course. His plans were of the most extravagantly ambitious character. Now he was an orator, now a poet, now a statesman; but whatever his character or profession, he was sure in his castle-building to attain to the highest eminence. After a time one thought crept into his mind, and embittered all his musings. Suppose he should attain to the highest pinnacle of which human nature is capable, what then? Could he hold his honour for ever? What would it be to him, when a hundred years had gone by, that America had never known his equal? He did not wonder that Alexander wept when at the summit of his ambition: he felt very sure that he should have wept too. Then he would become alarmed at the extent of his own wicked soarings, and try to comfort himself with the idea that it was all the result of the fever in his brain.

One day his mind reverted to religious pursuits. Yes, an eminent divine was very well: though he should of course prefer something more brilliant. Gradually, and without his being aware of his own train of thought, his mind instituted a comparison between the great worldly divine, toiling for the same perishable objects as his other favourites, and the humble minister of the gospel, labouring only to please God and benefit his fellow-men. There was (so he thought) a sort of sublimity about that, after all. Surely the world was all wrong, or such a self-abjuring man would be its hero! Ah! but the good man had a reputation more enduring. Yes, yes, his fame was sounded before him as he entered the other world; and that was the only fame worthy of the possession, because the only one that triumphed over the grave. Suddenly, in the midst of his self-gratulation, the words flashed across his mind, "Not unto us, not unto us, but unto thy name give glory." He was confounded. Not that he had actually made himself the representative of this last kind of greatness—it was not sufficiently to his taste for that; but he had ventured on dangerous ground, and he was startled by a flood of feelings that had till now remained dormant. He had always said and thought, so far as he had thought any thing about it, that he wished to become truly religious; but now religion seemed so entirely opposed to all his ambitious plans, that he was afraid to look into his heart, lest he should discover what he did not like to confess, even to himself—that he did not want to become a Christian. He was fully awake to the vanity of worldly pursuits, and was on the whole prepared to yield the palm of excellence to religious ones; but his father had often said he would one day be a great man, and a great man he had resolved to be.

The transition from this state of mind to infidelity was very easy. French infidelity was at this period sweeping over the land like a flood. At Providence

College there was a young man, who was amiable, talented, witty, exceedingly agreeable in person and manners, but a confirmed deist. A very strong friendship sprang up between the two young men, founded on similar tastes and sympathies, and Judson soon became, at least professedly, as great an unbeliever as his friend. The subject of a profession was often discussed between them. At one time they proposed entering the law, because it afforded so wide a scope for political ambition; and at another they discussed their own dramatic powers, with a view to writing plays.

During a part of his collegiate course Judson was engaged in the instruction of a school at Plymouth, and on closing school set out on a tour through the northern states, and thence to New York. Before setting out on this tour, he had unfolded his infidel sentiments to his father, and had been treated (as we are informed by his sister, from whose reminiscences we derive these facts) with the severity natural to a masculine mind that has never doubted, and to a parent, who, after making many sacrifices for the son of his pride and of his love, sees him rush recklessly on his own destruction. His mother was none the less distressed, and she wept, and prayed, and expostulated. He knew his superiority to his father in argument; but he had nothing to oppose to his mother's tears and warnings, and they followed him now wherever he went. He knew he was on the verge of such a life as he despised. For the world he would not see a young brother in his perilous position; "but I," he thought, "am in no danger. I am only seeing the world—the dark side of it as well as the bright; and I have too much self-respect to do anything mean or vicious." In this spirit, while in New York, he attached himself to a theatrical company, not with the design of entering upon the stage, but partly for the purpose of familiarizing himself with its regulations, in case he should enter on his literary projects, and partly from curiosity and the love of adventure.

After seeing what he wished of New York he pursued his journey westward, and visited the home of an uncle, a Christian minister. The uncle was absent, and the conversation of the young man who occupied his place was characterized by a godly sincerity, a solemn but gentle earnestness, which addressed itself to the heart, and Judson went away deeply impressed. The next night he stopped at a country inn. The landlord mentioned, as he lighted him to his room, that he had been obliged to place him next door to a young man who was exceedingly ill, probably in a dying state; but he hoped that it would occasion him no uneasiness. Judson assured him that, beyond pity for the sick man, he should have no feeling whatever. But it was nevertheless a very restless night. Sounds came from the sick chamber—sometimes the movements of the watchers, sometimes the groans of the sufferer; but it was not these which disturbed him. He thought of what the landlord had said—the stranger was probably in a dying state; and was he prepared? Alone, and in the dead of night, he felt a blush of shame steal over him at the question, for it proved the shallowness of his philosophy. What would his late companions say to his weakness? The clear-minded, intellectual, witty E——, what would he say to such consummate boyishness? But still his thoughts *would* revert to the sick man. Was he a Christian, calm and strong in the hope of a glorious immortality? or was he shuddering upon the brink of a dark, unknown future? Perhaps he was a "free-thinker," educated by Christian parents, and prayed over by a Christian mother. The landlord had described him as a *young* man; and in imagination he was forced to place himself upon the dying bed, though he strove with all his might against it. At last morning came, and its light dispelled all his "superstitious illusions." As soon as he had risen, he went in search of the landlord, and inquired for his fellow-lodger. "He is dead," was the reply. "Dead!" "Yes; he is gone, poor fellow! The doctor said he would probably not survive the night." "Do you know who he was?" "Oh yes; it was a young man from Providence College, a very fine fellow; his name was E——." Judson was completely stunned. After hours had passed, he knew not how, he attempted to pursue his journey. But one single thought occupied his mind, and the words, dead! lost! lost! were continually ringing in his ears. He knew the religion of the Bible to be true, he felt its truth, and he was in despair. In this state of mind he resolved to abandon his scheme of travelling, and at once turned his horse's head towards Plymouth.

This was the very crisis of young Judson's history. The two unbelieving friends pursue their travels hither and thither, and, by the merest accident, as it seems to the eye of man, cross each other's path, or rather meet, but meet unconsciously; and, unknown to each other, occupy adjoining chambers—the one to die, the other to be awakened by that death out of his unbelieving reverie, and to seek a better preparation for both living and dying than a sceptical philosophy could give him. "This also cometh forth from the Lord of hosts, which is wonderful in counsel, and excellent in working."

Within a few months after this occurrence, Mr.

Judson, now twenty years of age, entered Andover College, not as a professor of religion and candidate for the ministry, but as a person deeply in earnest on the subject, and desirous of arriving at the truth. He had become thoroughly dissatisfied with the views of life which he formerly cherished. Aware of his personal sinfulness, and conscious that he needed some great moral transformation, he yet doubted the authenticity of revealed religion. His mind did not readily yield to the force of evidence. This is by no means an uncommon case, as is remarked by Judson's biographer; nor is it all difficult of explanation. A deeply seated disinclination to the humbling doctrines of the cross frequently assumes the form of inability to apply the common principles of evidence to the case of revealed religion. Men of unusual strength of will, and a somewhat too confident reliance on the decisions of their individual intellect, are peculiarly liable to fall into this error.

Mr. Judson's moral nature was, however, thoroughly aroused, and he was deeply in earnest on the subject of religion. Light gradually dawned upon his mind, and he was enabled, six weeks after his removal to Andover, to surrender his whole soul to Christ as his atoning Saviour. The change in Mr. Judson's religious character was not attended by those external indications of moral excitement which are frequently observed. The reformation wrought in him was, however, deep and radical. With unusual simplicity of purpose, he yielded himself up once and for ever to the will of God, and without a shadow of misgiving, relied upon Christ as his all-sufficient Saviour. From the moment of his conversion, he seemed never, through life, to have been harassed by a doubt of his acceptance with God. The new creation was so manifest to his consciousness, that, in the most decided form, he had the witness in himself. His plans of life were, of course, entirely reversed. He banished for ever those dreams of literary and political ambition in which he had formerly indulged, and simply asked himself, How shall I so order my future being as best to please God? That he was moved by no transient impulse, nor fit of enthusiasm, but was made partaker of a new *life*—the divine life—is sufficiently attested by the devotion of six-and-thirty years of unwearied toil to the salvation of idolatrous Burmah.

Samuel Budgett; born July, 1794; died May, 1851.

"Samuel Budgett," says his biographer, "was early taught to worship, and obey, and seek the God from whose hand his young being had come. What Lamartine so beautifully says of his own mother, might be said equally of Budgett's:—'We could not remember the day when she *first* spoke to us about God.'" One of the friends of his after life thus states one of those events which pass silently within the bosom of Christian families, but which re-appear in the life of their members, in blessed and memorable fruit:—"He was about nine years of age, when one day, in passing his mother's door, he heard her engaged in earnest prayer for her family, and for himself by name. He thought, 'My mother is more earnest that I should be saved than I am for my own salvation.' In that hour he became decided to serve God, and the impression then made was never effaced." In this providential manner began the Christian life of one of the most useful and honoured of the sons of commerce, who, rising from poverty, acquired wealth, and devoted it with a liberal hand to the service of religion and humanity.

W. H. Hewitson; born Sept. 16, 1812; died Aug. 7, 1850.

When WILLIAM HEPBURN HEWITSON* entered the university of Edinburgh, in the autumn of 1833, his soul was filled with the intensest ambition to acquire fame. And "verily he had his reward." He was "facile princeps" in most of his classes, and carried off a variety of prizes amid the plaudits of his fellow-students. In the spring of 1837, just as he was completing his literary course, a university prize was proposed for the best essay on the Nature, Causes, and Effects of National Character; and Hewitson's ambition was stirred. He wrote at Leamington on the prescribed theme, and on the 27th of December the Senatus Academicus adjudged the prize to him. Meanwhile, Providence interposed to teach him the vanity of his aims, and to prepare him to reap disappointment from his honours—the blessing which at that time he most needed. In the month of November he happened one day to turn up to the mineral spring at Leamington. A young man entered the building, whose appearance at once attracted his observation; the coarse linen frock was in strange contrast with the gay apparel of the groups around. The humble youth was emaciated, and walked forward with a feeble step. After drinking of the water, he slowly withdrew. After a little, Mr. Hewitson descended the hill, in the middle of which the spring was situated, and found him sitting at one of the bends of the winding path which slopes gently down the

* See Biographical Tract, "William H. Hewitson," published by the London Religious Tract Society.

declivity. "I spoke to him," he says. "His diffident tone of voice, and his modesty of manner, at once enlisted my sympathies. During several weeks afterwards I frequently visited his father's lowly cottage. My intercourse with the young man soon gave me ground to conclude that if my theoretic knowledge of gospel truths was greater than his, he, unlike myself, had experienced their sanctifying power. Truly his was the better portion. When he spoke of the Saviour's love to sinners, and his obedience unto death for their redemption, he at times gave vent to his gratitude by tears of joy. He seemed like one who had obtained everlasting consolation and good hope through grace, to have not a shadow of doubt or anxiety on his soul as to the prospect of eternal glory. One evening, about sunset, he fell asleep."

The impressions which were produced by Mr. Hewitson's visits to this happy deathbed could not be effaced. The question flashed on him, "Could I thus calmly pass into the immediate presence of the just and holy Jehovah? Am I, like him, sheltered from the wrath to come?" It was amidst these deep anxieties that, in January, 1838, he was summoned to Edinburgh to receive the honours which were awarded to his essay on National Character. The essay was read in the presence of all the professors and students. It is said to have been a noble production, embodying in one masterly work the accumulated resources of his entire past studies. And the applause bestowed upon it was more than sufficient to feed and inflame the literary ambition of a less aspiring mind than that of Mr. Hewitson. But now all is changed. Like Henry Martyn, he found that he had grasped a shadow, or rather, his biographer says, he had grasped not a shadow, but a stinging serpent. "Ambition," we find Hewitson himself writing, while the crown of laurel is still fresh upon his brow—"ambition is a devil, and public praise is a syren, which soothes while it destroys." And but for the interposition of a gracious Providence, he says, it had accomplished his final destruction. The crowned academician became miserable in the enjoyment of his honours; and two years passed over him before he found peace. From the time that his heart was maddened, as he expressed it, by the unsatisfactoriness of fame, the "strong divinity of soul" within him—to use the language of his earlier life—was waked up to contend against the sins of his own heart, to "crucify the flesh with its affections and lusts;" and he knew full well that it was only in Christ Jesus he must find acceptance; but still he was in bondage. And the secret of his difficulty is revealed in his own words: "For long, the painful feeling still preyed upon my mind, that I must do some good works myself, or God would not accept me in Christ Jesus." His wrestlings with sin and a corrupt heart were not unreal or uncalled for. But the subtle spirit of self-righteousness which pervaded them blinded him to the truth in which, through divine teaching, he afterwards rejoiced—that the gospel offer is "free and full, and wholly of grace."

Dr. James Hope; born at Stockport, 1801; died 1841.

Dr. Hope was the son of a wealthy merchant, and enjoyed the greatest educational advantages in every department but one. His parents, at least when their children were young, belonged to that numerous class who deem morality to be religion, and who think that by setting a good example to their families and the poor, by a regular attendance at church, and by a consistent course of honesty and integrity, they are performing all the requirements of religion. During his medical studies in Edinburgh, young Hope's character was quite unsullied by any of the dissipations of youth, but this he ascribed to the natural refinement of his feelings, and not to religious principle. He continued the observance of Sunday in the same manner as he had been taught to do at home, never studying on that day; and during his earlier medical practice, while he was yet a stranger to the power of the gospel, he did the same, and he ever after thought that a blessing attended even this partial and imperfect observance of the Sabbath.

This eminent physician was at first stimulated to exertion only by motives of worldly ambition, and by the desire to add lustre to the name he bore. His father had pushed these principles to their utmost limit, and, by keeping in the shade the more sordid inducements of wealth, and that aggrandizement which is strictly selfish and personal, had inspired his son with notions which many would have considered enthusiastic. This ambition led him to use the greatest diligence, to practise remarkable self-denial and control over his natural tastes and feelings, and to rest unsatisfied so long as there was one individual who surpassed him. It was so far removed from all vainglorious desires to enjoy the appearance of greatness without its reality, and so united to a real elevation of character, that, in ordinary language, it would have been called a laudable ambition. But God was not in all the young doctor's thoughts. Eternity had no place in his reckonings and pursuits. And the turn ing point of his spiritual history is found in a circum stance which common speech would call casual or accidental.

In the winter of 1826–7, while in Paris, a friend, Dr. Nairne, happened to call on him one Sunday, and inquire whether he was going to church. Dr. Hope answered in the negative, assigned some trivial reason for not going to the ambassador's to divine service, and added that there was no other place to which he could go. "Oh," said Dr. Nairne, "I will show you where to go;" and he accordingly took him to the chapel of Mr. Lewis Way. This was the first time Dr. Hope had heard evangelical preaching, and what his first impressions were we are not informed. But he now perceived that if religion was anything, it must be everything. The same activity of mind which spurred him on in the pursuit of scientific truth prompted him to bring his whole mental faculties to the investigation of that immutable truth, the importance of which so infinitely surpasses that of all others. During the remainder of his residence abroad he eagerly embraced every opportunity of conversing on the subject, and of eliciting the opinions of those whose conduct bore evidence of their being under the influence of religion. After his arrival in London he found more time to investigate the subject calmly and dispassionately. He was always slow, we are told, in forming a conclusion on a new subject; not because be experienced difficulty in comprehending it, but because of his high opinion of its importance; and his comprehensive mind could see further, and discover more intricacies to unravel, than a more superficial intellect would have done. The result was that his conduct answered to the Scriptural definition of the kingdom of heaven, in the comparison of it to leaven which, put into one corner, worked imperceptibly till the whole was leavened. Within a few years it was evident that ambition was no longer the mainspring of his actions. He desired henceforward to devote all his talents, his professional eminence, and the influence accruing from it, to the service of religion. And how thoroughly his life was imbued and governed by its principles will be seen from the testimony of Dr. Thomas H. Burder, author of "Letters from a Senior to a Junior Physician." In reference to the early period of their acquaintance, he says, "Some years ago, before I was aware of Dr. Hope's religious principles, I had sometimes said to Mrs. Burder, after observing him narrowly, 'Well, if Dr. Hope is not a pious man, he is the most perfect man without religion I ever met with.' But the more I knew of him, the more anxious was I to discover whether *any* principles short of those which teach repentance towards God, faith in our Lord Jesus Christ, and an unreserved consecration of heart and life to his service, could have yielded such transparency of conduct, such humanity, disinterestedness, humility, guileless simplicity, and undeviating integrity, as I observed in him. At length I learned that he lived 'as seeing Him who is invisible.'" The faith which sanctified Dr. Hope's life, cheered his death. Within a few hours of his departure he said, "I will not make speeches; but I have two things to say." The first was an affectionate farewell to his wife. He then added, "The second is soon said. Christ is all in all to me. I have no hope except in him. He is, indeed, all in all."

Narrative by Dr. Cæsar Malan.

Dr. Cæsar Malan received the following narrative from the subject of it. A young man, the son of French Protestant parents, was turned aside from the paths of religion and virtue, during his attendance at the university of Paris. In the pursuit of sinful pleasure, instead of enjoying satisfaction, he was a terror to himself. "When I reached the age of twenty-six (he said) I was in the sight of God as a madman, or like the horse which spurns the bridle, rushes furiously into the battle, and falls, being wounded suddenly from every quarter. . . . I had taken my degree, and entered on the duties of my profession (as a barrister), when, in one of my fits of ungovernable passion, I had a quarrel, which ended in a challenge to a duel with one whom I thoroughly hated, as I regarded him as a rival. Our combat (why not call it our mutual purpose of assassination?) was to take place in secret. I spent a whole day and night in preparing for it, and still I could not look forward to it without horror. Not that I dreaded either being wounded or killed, for I was unfeeling, and my heart was hardened. But, sir, my Bible frightened me. I had laid it aside in a closet, and to this closet I went to seek the sword with which I intended to meet my opponent. I opened the closet; it was nearly midnight. I climbed a chair, and reached to the highest shelf, feeling for my sword, when I laid my hand on my Bible. A sudden chill ran through my veins, and, without any time for deliberation, I took the book, opened it, and still standing on the chair, I read the tenth Psalm, which was the first passage on which my eyes rested. Thus, sir, the voice of the Lord once more resounded through the dark recesses of my soul.

I read with breathless eagerness, and still I went on reading, though my uneasiness increased, till I came to this verse: 'Wherefore doth the wicked contemn God? He hath said in his heart, Thou wilt not require it.'

"I felt confounded, and throwing myself prostrate on the floor of my room, I sobbed aloud and groaned, praying for pardon from God for the sake of Jesus. I dared not rise; I was afraid even to look up. I felt that the eye of God was upon me, and my sorrow is not to be described. The tortured criminal does not suffer what I then felt; and about an hour passed away, at the end of which time I felt somewhat more calm, and sat down, still holding my Bible in my hand. God had thus rescued me. The prayers of my poor mother were heard, and my sinful soul was restored to the narrow way of life, which, indeed, I had never totally forgotten, though I had in so great a degree trodden under foot the truths I had learned, seeking to crush them as I should a serpent.

"What followed? My duel was a painful subject, and I resolved to give it up. But this was not all; I was filled with sympathy for him whom I had regarded as my adversary, and I longed to make this known to him, and also to those who were to have been the witnesses of our crime. The day began to dawn, and the hour for our meeting arrived. My companions came to seek me; but I had gone on first, and hastened to the wood, which had been the place chosen for the duel. I reached it first, and felt that the Lord was graciously present with me. My adversary, accompanied by his second and mine, arrived there, and perceiving me, he cried out, 'Here I am; make ready!' I answered seriously, but with much feeling, 'I am ready, in the presence of God, to ask pardon of you, if I have offended you, and to forgive you any wrong you may have done to me.' 'Coward! scoundrel!' he exclaimed; 'this is your meanness.' 'You need not insult me,' I added, 'I speak in the presence of God, who sees us both. He has humbled me and touched my heart, and I repent, and acknowledge my folly before him, and entreat you also to fear him, and no longer to reject his mercy.' . . .

"Thus, sir," said the narrator to Mr. Malan, "God prevailed. The contest was dropped, and I returned to the town, urging my companions no longer to live in rebellion against God. I know not if they yielded to my entreaties, for I left the town shortly afterwards, and had no further intercourse with them. But I cannot describe the joy of my pious mother, when she saw me to be such as she desired, and felt that the infinite love and mercy of the Lord had been manifested towards me."

Influence of affliction.

The instances are innumerable in which the stray events of Divine Providence become the occasions and crises of the greatest moral changes. We now proceed to trace the agency of a mean which God uses, perhaps more than any other of a providential order, to bring thoughtless men to himself. It is that of affliction.

> "The God our light proud hearts deny,
> Our grief-worn hearts adore."

But yet it is not that affliction has any power either to awaken a contrite sense of sin, or to inspire a man with the new sentiments which characterize the Christian convert. So far from it, that it often proves the means of steeling the heart against the claims of God; and many come out of the furnace not melted, far less refined, but only hardened into an obduracy which nothing will move. Of this we have a memorable instance in the case of Pharaoh. God determined to deliver his people, and he commanded their oppressor to let them go. The effect of that command, however, was only to irritate and provoke him. But "God not only sent the command to Pharaoh, but sent one punishment after another to him for resisting that command. It does not surprise us to be told that some of these punishments shook the heart of the king for a moment, but that presently he relapsed into his previous determination, and that after each new act of remorse, and each new effort to throw it off, he became harder and more obstinate. We know enough of ourselves and our fellow-men to feel that such a statement has a great air of probability. . . . The awful contradiction between the will of man and the will of his Creator is aggravated by what seemed to be means for its cure. . . . Great and severe troubles come upon us. We say that God has sent them. We actually think so. Friends who look on observe that God is trying us, doubtless for our benefit. They complain afterwards that we are not better than we were before, not gentler, more resigned, more humble. Our sufferings have only embittered us. They wonder at it. God has shown us his great power. We have said it was his. Should it not have changed the whole course and habit of our lives?" Instead of this, it often hardens that which it seemed to soften.

But affliction is not always in vain. Accompanied by a divine agency it becomes the means of turning men to God. And more appropriate means cannot be imagined. The case of Manasseh presents itself as a contrast to that of Pharaoh. "Manasseh would find himself surrounded in Babylon by the gods of whom he had set up images in Jerusalem; he would see that in its perfection which he had tried to imitate on a poor and insignificant scale. And he would be under the rod with which he had wished to scourge his subjects. This was the kind of lesson which all the prophets had prepared their kings for. They had dallied with idolatry; there was something in it specially attractive, it seemed so much more passionate, devout, sympathetic, than that worship which the law of their fathers had prescribed. Their taste would be gratified. They should experience this worship in the length, and depth, and breadth of it. They had dallied with tyranny; what old decrees and statutes had power to bind them, the rulers of the land? What obligations had they to their serfs and bondsmen? No remedy can be effectual for such thoughts but that which is said to have been tried upon the Sicilian masters in the days of Timoleon—the becoming serfs and bondsmen themselves. In this case we are told it was effectual. Manasseh humbled himself, turned to the Lord God of Israel, and was brought back to Jerusalem another man."

We shall trace the influence of affliction on the minds of some of the most eminent Christians, such as Howels, Cecil, Peter Waldo, and John Newton. It will be seen that its forms were various, sometimes personal disease, sometimes domestic bereavement, sometimes startling natural occurrences awakening fear and thoughtfulness, sometimes mental sorrow from dissatisfaction and disgust with the world; and it will be found, moreover, that the casual is often combined with the afflictive in turning sinners to God.

The Reverend WILLIAM HOWELS was known and honoured in London for many years, as a faithful servant of Jesus Christ. When a child, he was taught to pray by a pious mother, and used, according to his own statement, to run into holes and corners, and hide himself, and weep over his sins. His impressions of the evil of sin, of the holiness of God, and of his omniscience, omnipresence, and omnipotence, are said to have been deep and powerful. Throughout his early years, he was known as a youth of scrupulous morality and unflinching integrity, while his temper was cheerful and sociable. His talents and acquirements gained him great esteem in the cultivated ranks of society; while the amiable qualities of his heart, his warmth of affection, and readiness to fulfil every kind office, joined to unreserved frankness of manners, rendered him beloved by all classes in his neighbourhood. "As to religion," says his biographer, "he was strictly moral and conscientious; but his acquaintance with divine doctrines was at this period very imperfect, and of a legal kind."

William Howels; born 1778, in Glamorganshire; died in London, 1832.

In 1800, William Howels entered the university of Oxford, full of ambition and expectation. As sub-librarian of the Bodleian library, the stores of academical learning were thrown open to him; but an invisible hand soon obstructed his way. His career of application and progress was arrested by the failure of his health. But the ardent and persevering youth was not easily diverted from his purpose, and for some time strove hard, in spite of incipient indisposition, to continue the pursuit of his favourite studies. A pious clergyman found the pale and sickly student one day in the Bodleian library, intent on perusing a Greek poet, and affectionately remonstrating with him, inquired why he did not rather read his Greek Testament. The inquiry, however, did not lead to any religious thoughtfulness; and his letters of this date show that God had no place in his affections and aims. "My ambition, and it is a laudable ambition, is of that painful, restless kind, that it would urge me to be a critic in classical learning. My passions are of a fiery nature; whatsoever I take in hand, I cannot help pursuing to excess."—"Illness alone I could bear with patience; but what I chiefly regret is, that I am not able to prosecute my studies."—"I feel this moment all the agonies of the most exquisite sensibility. It is, however, one comfort to reflect that I have run my career of folly; I have resisted every temptation I have been exposed to at Oxford. This is the race week, but I have not been at the races. We have very elegant balls here, as I have been informed, frequented by several persons of high rank. My being a gownsman entitles me to go to any of them; but I have wasted so much time already, that I shun them as I would Satan. I have two years yet before I can be made a Bachelor of Arts. I do not intend leaving Oxford this summer. Oh, had I health! Illness weakens the mind as well as the body; but I must be content. It is useless to struggle. Rubs and difficulties, after all, are the best tutors for a young man; they teach him more wisdom than all the sages of antiquity."

It is impossible to read these words without respect and sympathy. They embody much of the spirit of a popular ode, entitled " A Psalm of Life." "Life was real, life was earnest" in the estimate of William Howels. He could eschew the fashionable dance and the exciting race-course to concentrate time and energy on the acquisition of knowledge, and the attainment of fame. Even affliction he could philosophically declare to be the young man's best tutor. And he could say :—

" Let us, then, be up and doing,
 With a heart for any fate;
Still achieving, still pursuing,
 Learn to labour and to wait."

But his words as clearly indicate the absence of Christian principle as a source either of strength or of solace. They exhibit nothing of the humiliation of the penitent sinner, bowing under the chastisement of his heavenly Father—no looking to Jesus for pardon, peace, and spiritual health—no application to the Divine Comforter for support or holiness. And in a letter in which he notices the departure of his beloved mother, there is no trace of a mind that has found a refuge for its cares and troubles in the bosom of a Saviour. The character of the philosopher appears to have been hitherto, in his view, the model of perfection, the sum of religion.

But now a new scene of intense interest opened in the history of the invalid student, and a spiritual change was experienced, which influenced with all-commanding power the whole of his subsequent life. The circumstances are thus related by a friend :— " Whilst dear Mr. Howels was in a painful state as to bodily health and mental feeling at Oxford, and as yet an utter stranger to the effectual support and heavenly solace of vital religion, a fellow-collegian,

Mr. Lewis, proposed to go with him, one Sabbath evening, to a Baptist chapel in the city, to hear a popular preacher (the Rev. James Hinton), and to see a respectable congregation, as a means of relieving the tedious hours of solitude. This proposal, made in the spirit of youthful levity, was acceded to by the sickly student, with no higher views than the hope of a temporary relaxation of thought by the change of scene and objects. Both accordingly went to the chapel. Howels was much taken up with the elegant language and general ministerial talents of the preacher, and returned home well satisfied. He was induced, for the gratification of his taste for eloquence, to repeat his visit to the same chapel. But it pleased the Lord, who overrules the steps of man to his own ends, to take occasion thereby to bring his purposes to pass, by applying the great truths of the gospel with irresistible power to his heart. The eyes of his mind were now enlightened to see his lost state, as a sinner, with great clearness; and in due proportion were the suitableness, glory, and value of the Saviour revealed to him by the Spirit. Nothing less than the divine righteousness of Immanuel could give peace of conscience and effectual rest to the troubled mind. Could moral integrity and decent conduct avail at such a crisis? This exemplary and amiable youth had as much to repose his hopes on as most men; yet when the commandment came in the light and power of the Spirit, sin revived, and he died to all self-righteous confidence, and henceforth became a most determined opposer of human pretensions to merit, and a most energetic, uncompromising advocate of justification by faith in the sole merits of a crucified Redeemer. He was thus effectually converted from worshipping the vain idol of literary fame, to the saving knowledge and service of the only true God and Saviour Jesus Christ. Our devoted student had been led into the university in the pleasing hope of attaining honours, but he had met with a painful disappointment, which made his situation in college comfortless and dreary as a desert. The Lord was pleased to reveal himself to him in the midst of his 'trouble' in a way of mercy and grace through the gospel, and to give him 'a good hope' and an earnest of a better 'and more enduring substance,' than the shadowy object of his former anxious pursuit. The Lord 'is able to do exceeding abundantly above all that we ask or think.'"

When the value of divine things beamed clearly on the mind of William Howels, his energetic spirit (to use the words of his biographer) was characteristically actuated by them. He gave them deep and intense consideration. The conviction of sin within him was deep-wrought and searching, unfolding the innermost recesses of his heart, inducing a spirit congenial with the apostle's when he exclaimed, "Oh wretched man that I am!" His views, on the other hand, of the excellency and divine glory of the person of Christ, together with the complete efficacy of his merits for the salvation of the believing sinner, were clear, full, and strong, indicative of the teaching of that Spirit whose office it is to glorify Christ. When we review the circumstances of Howels' conversion, and connect them with his subsequent ministry, so fruitful of other conversions, we can only exclaim, "This also cometh forth from the Lord of hosts, which is wonderful in counsel, and excellent in working."

R. Cecil; born Nov. 8, 1754; died Aug. 15, 1810.

RICHARD CECIL became one of the most honoured and useful of Christ's ministers; but let us see how the providence of God must first reduce him to misery before he will appreciate or receive the gospel.

There was a decision, a daring, an untamableness, we are told, in the structure of Cecil's mind, even when a boy, to which the minds of his associates yielded an implicit subjection. Yet this bold spirit was allied to a noble and generous disposition. He had a native and thorough contempt of what was mean and little. Early religious impressions, which were produced by "Janeway's Token for Children," soon wore away, and gave place to the follies and vices of youth. By degrees he listened to infidel principles, till he avowed himself an unbeliever. And in his unbelief he was one of the boldest of the bold. The natural daring of his mind allowed him to do nothing by halves. He soon became a leader and apostle of infidelity, and laboured to banish the scruples of more cautious minds. In this he was too successful; and, in after life, he met with more than one of his converts to infidelity, who laughed at all his affectionate and earnest endeavours to pull down the fabric which had been cemented by his own hands.

With all his infidel daring, however, he found it difficult thoroughly to believe the lie which he loved, as this record of his pen shows:—"When I was sunk in the depths of infidelity, I was afraid to read any author who treated Christianity in a dispassionate, wise, and searching manner. He made me uneasy. Conscience would gather strength. I found it more difficult to stifle her remonstrances. He would recall early instructions and impressions, while my happiness could only consist with their obliteration." Again he tells us:—"My father had a religious servant. I frequently cursed and reviled him. He would only smile on me. That went to my heart. I felt that he looked on me as a deluded creature. I felt that he thought he had something which I knew not how to value, and that he was therefore greatly my superior. I felt there was a real dignity in his conduct. It made me appear little even in my own eyes. If he had condescended to argue with me, I could have cut some figure; at least by comparison, wretched as it would have been. He drew me once to hear Mr. Whitefield; I was seventeen or eighteen years of age; it had no sort of religious effect on me; nor had the preaching of any man in my unconverted state."

How shall this proud spirit be subdued and changed? His infidelity plunged him into every species of licentiousness, but could not satisfy his soul. He felt the littleness of every object which engages the ambition and desires of carnal men, and acquired a thorough disgust of the world before he gained any hold of higher objects and better pleasures. "When I was about twenty years old (he says) I became utterly sick of the vanity, and disgusted with the folly of the world." This was the turning point of his life. Into this misery, as deep, though not of the same outward character, as that of the prodigal son in our Lord's parable, he was allowed by Providence to sink, that he might feel the insufficiency of all expedients of human device to satisfy or sustain a human soul. In the midst of his misery, he tells us that his mind revolted from Christianity. The very notion of Jesus Christ and of redemption repelled him. He thought there might possibly be a Supreme Being, and if there were, he might hear him when he prayed. There was something grand and elevating in the idea of worshipping the Supreme Being; but the whole plan and scheme of redemption appeared degrading, and it seemed impossible to believe in it as a religion suitable to man. But the Providence which let him work himself into misery by his infidelity, surrounded him with circumstances which were blessed as the means of overcoming his aversion to the faith of Jesus Christ. He was connected with sincere Christians, whom he knew to be both holy and happy. "It was one of the first things," he writes, "which struck my mind in a profligate state, that in spite of all the folly and hypocrisy and fanaticism which may be seen among religious professors, there was a mind after Christ, a holiness, a heavenliness, among real Christians." "My first convictions on the subject of religion were confirmed from observing that really religious persons had some solid happiness among them, which I had felt that the vanities of the world could not give. I shall never forget standing by the bed of my sick mother. 'Are not you afraid to die?' I asked her. 'No.' 'No? Why does the uncertainty of another state give you no concern?' 'Because God has said to me, Fear not: when thou passest through the waters, I will be with thee; and through the rivers, they shall not overflow thee.'" The remembrance of this scene ofttimes drew from him the ardent prayer that he might die the death of the righteous. His mind opened very gradually to receive the truths of the gospel. The religion which began in disgust with the world, rose by degrees superior to his disaffection to the peculiar doctrines of the gospel. The seed sown in tears by his inestimable mother, though long buried, burst into life, and shot forth with vigour, and he became a preacher of that truth which once he laboured to destroy.

Peter Waldo; A. D. 1160-1185.

Peter Waldo was a rich merchant of Lyons, and enjoyed his opulence without thoughts of a hereafter, till he was startled out of his pleasant dreams by an alarming providence. One evening, as he sat after supper with his friends, one of the party fell lifeless on the floor. This incident reminded him of his own mortality, and made so powerful an impression on his mind, that he resolved to abandon all other concerns, and occupy himself wholly with the concerns of religion. Happily his attention was drawn to the Holy Scriptures, and he resolved to know, from the original fountain itself, the way of life and salvation. He read the Vulgate for himself, and, in addition, employed learned men to translate the Gospels and other portions of the Bible into the Romance language. He thus acquired a correct idea of Christ's gospel, and found peace with God. Peter Waldo now distributed his wealth among the poor, and proposed to form a spiritual society of apostolicals, a society for the spread of evangelical truth among the neglected people in city and country. He employed for this purpose multiplied copies of his Romance version of the Scriptures, which, by degrees, was extended to the whole Bible. He and his companions laboured with great zeal, and without any thought, at first, of separating themselves from the Roman communion, but simply aiming at a spiritual society, like many others, in the service of the church; with this difference, that while other founders of such societies were animated with a zeal for the church, and its laws possessed for them all the force of truth drawn directly from the word of God, Peter Waldo, on the other hand, was influenced more by the truth derived immediately from the Scriptures. But an influential union of laymen, associated for the purpose of preaching to the people—a union which made the Sacred Scriptures themselves the source of religious doctrine, could not long escape opposition and persecution. The archbishop of Lyons forbade Peter Waldo and his companions to expound the Scriptures and to preach. But they did not think they ought, in obedience to this magisterial decree, to desist from a calling which they were conscious was from God. They declared that they were bound to obey God rather than man, and persevered in the work which they had begun. The anathema of the pope, however, soon drove Waldo from Lyons. His flock were scattered, and "went everywhere preaching the word." Many of them found an asylum in the valleys of Piedmont, where they took with them their new translation of the Bible, and were united with others of the same faith. Waldo himself, after many wanderings, carrying with him everywhere the glad tidings of salvation, settled at length in Bohemia, where the fruit of his labours was seen, "after many days," in the rapid extension throughout that country of the principles of the Reformation, and where, in the fourteenth century, as many as eighty thousand persons are said to have been put to death for the word of God, and for the testimony which they held. That sudden death in the house and presence of the rich merchant of Lyons was indeed a fruitful providence, the occasion of spiritual benefits and moral changes, which, in the course of centuries, became too widely spread to be traced or numbered.

In the history of JOHN NEWTON, we find the providence of God preserving, in a remarkable manner, a life that was to become one of great value to the world, and in a manner equally remarkable, turning that life from courses of desperate wickedness into the way of holiness and peace.

John Newton; born in London, July 24, 1725; died Dec. 21, 1807.

The pious mother who had taught him to bend his infant knees before the throne of the heavenly grace was taken from him before he was seven years old. At the age of fifteen he had religious convictions, which were soon dissipated, and he learned to curse and blaspheme. Upon his being thrown from a horse, near a dangerous hedgerow, his conscience suggested to him the dreadful consequences of appearing as he was before God, and he abandoned his profane practices for a time—but only for a time; and the consequence of such struggles between sin and conscience was that, on every relapse, he sank into still greater depths of wickedness. While yet a youth, he had an engagement to go on board a man-of-war one Sunday with a companion. The appointed hour arrived—Newton was not there—and the boat went without him. But that boat never reached the ship. She was overset, and Newton's companion, and several others, were drowned. He had been but a few minutes too late to be of that lost party.

Referring to his religious impressions and temporary reformations, he wrote afterwards: "All this while my heart was insincere. I often saw the necessity of religion as a means of escaping hell; but I loved sin, and was unwilling to forsake it. I was so strangely blind and stupid, that sometimes, when I have been determined upon things which I knew were sinful, I could not go on quietly till I had first discharged my ordinary task of prayer, in which I have grudged every moment of the time: when this was finished, my conscience was, in some measure, pacified, and I could rush into folly with little remorse."

In one of his reforming moods, Newton became a Pharisee. "I did everything (he says) that might be expected from a person entirely ignorant of God's righteousness, and desirous to establish his own. I spent the greatest part of every day in reading the Scriptures, and in meditation and prayer. I fasted often; I even abstained from all animal food for three months. I would hardly answer a question for fear of speaking an idle word: I seemed to bemoan my former miscarriages very earnestly, and sometimes with tears: in short, I became an ascetic, and endeavoured, as far as my situation would permit, to renounce society, that I might avoid temptation." This reformation continued for more than two years. But, he adds, "it was a poor religion; it left me in many respects under the power of sin; and, so far as it prevailed, only tended to make me gloomy, stupid, unsociable, and useless."

From an ascetic, John Newton became an infidel. In 1743 he was "impressed" into the royal navy. His mind had already been poisoned by sceptical reading, and now his principal companion on board the man-of-war was an expert and plausible infidel, whose zeal was equal to his address. By the objections and arguments of this man, Newton's heart was soon gained, and he plunged into infidelity with all his spirit. "Like an unwary sailor who quits his post just before a rising storm," religion was renounced at the very time when its restraints and comforts were most needed.

The wickednesses in which John Newton now indulged were as varied as his circumstances permitted. And his misery was complete. There seemed no alternative but to throw himself into the sea, and thus put a period, as his infidelity taught him, to all his sorrows at once. One reason that prevented the commission of suicide was the vindictive hope of taking the life of his captain. Conscious that he had deserved all that he suffered from his captain's hands (for he had deserted and been punished), his pride suggested that he was grossly injured. And his purposes wavered between murder and suicide, not thinking it practicable to effect both. His love to the young lady who afterwards became his wife was the only restraint that was now left, and though he neither feared God nor regarded man, he could not bear that *she* should think meanly of him when he was dead.

After a series of sins and sufferings, we find him on the coast of Africa in the employment of a slave-dealer, reduced to wants which made him a literal representative of the prodigal son. Sometimes it was with difficulty he could procure a draught of cold water when burning with a fever. His bed was a mat, spread upon a board or chest, with a log for his pillow. Upon his appetite returning after the fever left him, he would gladly have eaten, but "no man gave unto him." In his distress he would go by night into the plantation and pull up roots and eat them raw upon the spot, for fear of discovery. The very slaves shunned him, yet sometimes pitied him and relieved his wants out of their own slender pittance. He was a very outcast, ready to perish. But, unlike the prodigal in our Lord's parable, his distress did not at this time awaken him out of the stupor of sin to say, "I will arise and go to my Father."

Unexpectedly rescued from this life of degradation, it was only to encounter fresh disaster and peril at sea. But "God moves in a mysterious way, his wonders to perform." He was regarded as a Jonah on board the ship which carried him from off the coast of Africa. Though not ordinarily addicted to drunkenness, he challenged four or five of his comrades one evening to try who could hold out longest in drinking rum. Dancing on the deck like a madman, his hat fell overboard, and seeing the ship's boat by moonlight, he endeavoured to throw himself into it to recover his hat. His sight, however, had deceived him—the boat was twenty-feet from the ship's side. He was half overboard, and would in one moment have plunged into the water had not some one caught hold of him and pulled him back. The tide ran very strong at the time; his companions were too much intoxicated to save him, and the rest of the ship's company were asleep; and as for himself, he could not swim even had he been sober. An unseen Providence watched over a life that was yet to be made a blessing.

Among the few books that were on board the ship was "Thomas à Kempis." Newton took it up carelessly one day as he had often done before; but now the thought occurred to him, "What if these things should be true?" He could not bear the force of the inference, and shut the book, concluding that, true or false, he must abide the consequences of his own choice, and put an end to these reflections by joining in the foolish conversation of those around him. But now the conviction which he was so unwilling to receive was forced upon him amid the terrors of a storm. He went to bed that night in his usual spiritual indifference, but was awakened from a sound sleep by a violent sea, which broke on the vessel and filled the cabin where he lay with water. The cry arose immediately that the ship was sinking. He essayed to go on deck, but was met upon the ladder by the captain, who desired him to bring a knife. On his return for the knife, another person went up in his place, and was instantly washed overboard. For four weeks the vessel, an almost perfect wreck, was at the mercy of the winds and waves, and the men were constantly at the pumps. Provisions grew short; they had no bread, hardly any clothes, and the weather was cold. Then the bold heart of the sailor quailed at the thought of meeting that God whom he had rejected and blasphemed. But at first he could not pray, and he remained for a time in a sullen frame, a mixture of despair and impatience. While holding the helm at the solemn midnight hour, his former religious professions, his many warnings and deliverances, his licentiousness, his profane ridicule of Holy Scripture—all rose up before him, and his sins seemed too great to be forgiven. He waited with fear and impatience to receive his inevitable doom. But it was otherwise appointed by Him who is over all. With an ordinary cargo the vessel must have sunk, but the wood and beeswax with which she was partly laden kept her afloat. And with the hope of safety there gleamed into his soul some hope towards God. He began to pray. "I could not utter the prayer of faith (he says); I could not draw near to a reconciled God, and call him Father; my prayer was like the cry of the ravens, which yet the Lord does not disdain to hear. I now began to think of that Jesus whom I had so often derided; I recollected the particulars of his life and of his death—a death for sins not his own, but, as I remembered, for the sake of those who, in their distress, should put their trust in him." "O God, save me, or I perish," was the cry of the returning prodigal. "The God of the Bible forgive me, for his Son's sake." "My mother's God, the God of mercy, have mercy on me." "The comfortless principles of infidelity were rivetted" on Newton's soul. But before reaching port he felt he had satisfactory evidence of the truth of the gospel, and of its exact suitableness to his necessities He saw that God might declare not his mercy only, but his justice also, in the pardon of sin, on account of the obedience and sufferings of Jesus Christ. "Till then he was like the man possessed with the *legion*. No arguments, no persuasion, no views of interest, no remembrance of the past, no regard to the future, could restrain him within the bounds of common prudence; but now he was restored to his senses." He had yet much to learn, but he left that broken ship a new man. And after a few years he became a devoted minister of Jesus Christ, and one of the most useful men of his age. The storm was in this instance the minister of Providence to arrest a godless youth, and to give to Christ's church one of the holiest men that have ever ministered at her altar.

The conversion, of which affliction is so often the means or occasion, is not to be regarded as a being frightened into religion. If it issued only in a constrained abandonment of certain follies, and a constrained observance of certain rites, we should give it no higher character. And the asceticism or virtue, whose only motive is fear, we should regard as of no higher spiritual value than the worldliness or vice which it succeeded. But when we find a man emerge from sorrow and suffering with new spiritual tastes, and thereafter living a life, not of forced conformity to hated precepts from the fear of dreaded judgments, but a life of loving devotion to Christ and the good of men, we can regard his affliction as nothing less than a visitation of God to bring that soul to himself.

It is true that of old God appeared to Elijah not in the storm and tempest, but in the still small voice. Yet who does not know that God maketh the winds his messengers likewise, and useth the flames of fire as his ministers? "Yea, who is not aware," to use the words of Dr. Tholuck, "how much more infrequent have been the times when God appeared to him in the mild gentle sunshine, than those in which he came as the storms roared, and the clouds of the tempest gathered? . . . . Is it not true that, when the sun shines upon us, and we feel its gentle warmth in our life, we become indifferent to its mild beams, and do not so much as ask whence comes the pleasant light? Because it is grateful to our feelings, we think that it is a matter of course. Not until the tempest comes, which we dread, do we look around us and inquire, Whence comes this? Before the eye of the Christian there rises to the clouds from every event in life a thread, on which the eye moves along up to the source where all gifts begin and end. But the eye of the natural man sees not the thread, so long as the sun shines. When it is night, and the lightning gleams through the darkness, then only does he discern the thread; then for the first time do his tardy affections rise upward to God. Oh, what an image of the heart of man, in this respect, is the history of Israel! What Moses says in his parting song, how it is confirmed in the history of us all! The Lord found them in the desert, in the barren wilderness; and as an eagle fluttereth over her young, and beareth them away, so the Lord spread out his wings and took them, and bore them on his wings, and nourished them with the fruits of the field, and let them suck honey from the rock, and oil from the hard stone. But when they were satiated and had become fat they were insolent. They grew strong, and neglected the God who made them. As David confesses of himself, 'Before I was afflicted I went astray; but now have I kept thy word;' so do the greater part of Christians confess, each of himself, 'As long as thou, eternal God, heldest back thy lightning and thunder, I went astray; but when they prostrated me upon the ground, I then attended, for the first time, to thy word, and learned by experience that the Lord cometh to men in storm and tempest.' And this is not only the fact at the first return to God at conversion—ah! is it not our general experience, that the star of faith never shines brighter than when it is night all around us? and that the field of our life never brings forth better fruit than when the storm and tempest come over it? What but this is the reason that you, who are the most experienced Christians, when you look back upon your days gone by, think of the days of storm and commotion with no less gratitude than those of peace? For all chastisement, when it is upon us, seemeth to be not a matter of joy but of sorrow; yet afterwards it will yield the peaceable fruit of righteousness to those who are exercised thereby."

Plutarch relates how Timoleon was miraculously delivered from the conspiracy of two murderers, by their meeting "in the very nick of time" a certain person who, to revenge the death of his father, killed one of them, just as they were ready to give Timoleon the fatal blow, though he knew nothing of the business, and Timoleon escaped the danger. "And what," says good old Flavel, "did this wonderful work of Providence, think you, yield the relator? Why, though he was one of the most learned and ingenious among the heathen sages, yet all he made of it was this, 'The spectator wondered greatly at the artifice and contrivance which fortune uses!' This is all he could see in it. Had a spiritual and wise Christian had the dissecting and anatomizing of such a work of Providence, what glory would it have yielded to God! What comfort and encouragement to the soul! The bee makes a sweeter meal upon one single flower than the ox doth upon the whole meadow, where thousands of them grow."

Let not the reader rise from the review of those facts and histories by which we have endeavoured to illustrate the providential occasions of conversion, without exclaiming, "This is the finger of God." It has been remarked by one of the most learned of men, as characteristic of the poetry of the Hebrews, that "as a reflex of monotheism it always embraces the universe in its unity." "The Hebrew poet does not depict nature as a self-dependent object, glorious in its individual beauty, but always as in relation and subjection to a higher spiritual power. Nature is to him a work of creation and order, the living expression of the omnipresence of the Divinity in the visible world." So are all the occurrences of Providence as well as the phenomena of nature. And this is no mere poetry. The "monotheism" of the Hebrews was not idea or sentiment; it was truth; there *is* one God, ever living, over all. And the inspired literature of the nation was indeed a "reflex" of this truth. The Hebrew bards saw God's hand everywhere, creating, renewing, working, governing; and in the operations of this hand they saw the principle that bound into one harmonious whole the wide and varied universe of matter and of mind. We only follow in their wake. The trifles of life become great, the chances of life orderly and regular, the ills of life turn into blessings, the very dreams of life become grave realities, when, by the unseen power which controls and guides them, they become the occasions of spiritual good to immortal souls. And it is reason, no less than religion, that says, "This is the Lord's doing, and it is marvellous in our eyes."

PART THE FOURTH.

THE DIVINE LIFE: TRUE MEANS.

FACTS.

CONTENTS.—Pilgrim and the Cross—Allegory by Dr. James Hamilton—Moravian Missions—Testimony of John Williams—Cannibal Priest—Rammohun Roy—Banerji—Experience of Dr. Duff—John Wesley—C. Wesley—Whitefield—Kingswood Colliers—David Hume—Hervey—Walker—Toplady—Berridge—Baxter—A. Fuller—Dr. MacAll—Quotations from Isaac Taylor, Chalmers, and Professor Butler.

CONCLUSION.—The Standing Miracle—Argument for Divinity of Gospel—What Conversion does not do—What it is not—Am I a Partaker of the Divine Life?—Dying Young Lady—"The Sand and the Rock."

"The Christian scheme, the cause and the source of spiritual life to the individual human spirit."—THE RESTORATION OF BELIEF.

"As blossom and fruit grow only from a sound root, so too it is only from faith in Christ, and in the redemption wrought by him, that the true moral life proceeds."—OLSHAUSEN.

"Where is the wise? where is the scribe? where is the disputer of this world? hath not God made foolish the wisdom of this world? For after that in the wisdom of God the world by wisdom knew not God, it pleased God by the foolishness of preaching to save them that believe. For the Jews require a sign, and the Greeks seek after wisdom; but we preach Christ crucified, unto the Jews a stumblingblock, and unto the Greeks foolishness; but unto them which are called, both Jews and Greeks, Christ the power of God, and the wisdom of God. Because the foolishness of God is wiser than men; and the weakness of God is stronger than men."—THE APOSTLE PAUL (1 Cor. i. 20–25.)

"Transformation of apostate man
From fool to wise, from earthly to divine,
Is work for Him, that made him. He alone,
And he by means in philosophic eyes
Trivial and worthy of disdain, achieves
The wonder; humanizing what is brute
In the lost kind; extracting from the lips
Of asps their venom; overpowering strength
By weakness, and hostility by love."—COWPER.

THE DIVINE LIFE:

TRUE MEANS.

We distinguish the occasions and even the instruments of conversion from the true means; and what we intend by the latter will be best illustrated by two allegories, one of them from the ever new story of the "Pilgrim's Progress," and the other from a modern author.

In Bunyan's great allegory the pilgrim is introduced to us clothed with rags, standing in a certain place, with his face from his own house, a book in his hand, and a burden on his back. He reads the book, and weeps and trembles. Unable to contain, he cries out, "What shall I do?" He is undone, he tells his wife, by reason of the burden that lieth hard upon him. Moreover, their city is to be burned with fire from heaven, and he sees no way of escape. His relations imagine that some "frenzy distemper" hath got into his head, and hope that sleep may settle his brains. But he spends the night in sighs and tears, and in the morning tells his friends that he is worse and worse. While walking solitarily in the fields, reading and praying, he is met by Evangelist, who, on hearing the recital of his fears and anxieties, directs his attention to a shining light over a wicket gate beyond a very wide field, and says to him, "Keep that light in your eye, and go up directly thereto, so shalt thou see the gate; at which, when thou knockest, it shall be told thee what thou shalt do."

The pilgrim now runs across the plain, resists every entreaty to return, and cries, "Life, life, eternal life." Soon, however, he and one whom he had induced to flee with him from the City of Destruction fall into the Slough of Despond. Here they wallow for a time and the pilgrim, whose name is Christian, begins to sink in the mire, "because of the burden on his back." He struggles, however, to the side of the slough that is furthest from his own house, and next to the wicket gate. And by the assistance of one whose name is Help, he gets out, and walks once more on solid ground. Danger of another order now awaits him, in the counsel of Mr. Worldly Wiseman. "In yonder village," (the name is called Morality,) says this plausible, but unsafe guide, "there dwells a gentleman, whose name is Legality, a very judicious man, and a man of very good name, that has skill to help men off with such burdens as thine is from their shoulders; yea, to my knowledge, he hath done a great deal of good this way: ay, and, besides, he hath skill to cure those that are somewhat crazed in their wits with their burdens. To him, as I said, thou mayest go, and be helped presently. His house is not quite a mile from this place; and if he should not be at home himself, he hath a pretty young man to his son, whose name is Civility, that can do it as well as the old gentleman himself. There, I say, thou mayest be eased of thy burden."

So, says our author, Christian turned out of his way to go to Mr. Legality's house for help; but, behold, when he was got now hard by a high hill which stood by the way-side, it seemed so high, and also that side of it that was next the way did hang so much over, that Christian was afraid to venture further, lest the hill should fall on his head: Wherefore there he stood still, and wot not what to do. Also, now his burden seemed heavier to him than while he was on his way. There came also flashes of fire out of the hill that made Christian afraid that he should be burned; here, therefore, he did sweat and quake for fear.

His confusion is increased by meeting his old instructor, Evangelist, who asks him, "Did not I direct thee the way to the little wicket gate?" "Stand still," said Evangelist, "that I may show thee the words of God." So he stood trembling, while Evangelist read, "The just shall live by faith; but if any man draw back, my soul shall have no pleasure in him." Then Christian fell down at his feet as dead, crying, "Woe is me, for I am undone!"

Admonished and instructed by Evangelist, Christian resumes his onward course to the wicket gate, and, on reaching it, announces himself as a poor burdened sinner, come from the City of Destruction, and going to Mount Zion, that he may be delivered from the wrath to come. He is admitted and instructed on many points of which he is yet ignorant. And then he girds up his loins to address himself to his journey. But still the burden is not removed, it weighs him down, and makes him sad. The crisis of his deliverance is, however, at hand.

"Now I saw in my dream (says our author) that the highway up which Christian was to go, was fenced on either side with a wall, and that wall was called *Salvation*. Up this way, therefore, did burdened Christian run, but not without great difficulty, because of the load on his back.

"He ran thus till he came at a place somewhat ascending; and upon that place stood a cross, and a little below in the bottom, a sepulchre. So I saw in my dream that just as Christian came up with the cross his burden loosed from off his shoulders, and fell off his back, and so it continued to do till it came to the mouth of the sepulchre, where it fell in, and I saw it no more.

"Then was Christian glad and lightsome, and said, with a merry heart, 'He hath given me rest by his sorrow, and life by his death.' Then he stood still awhile to look and wonder, for it was very surprising to him that the sight of the cross should thus ease him of his burden. He looked, therefore, and looked again, even until that the springs that were in his head sent the water down his cheeks. Now as he stood looking and weeping, behold, three shining ones came to him, and saluted him with, 'Peace be to thee.' So the first said to him, 'Thy sins be forgiven thee.' The second stripped him of his rags, and clothed him with a change of raiment. The third also set a mark on his forehead, and gave him a roll with a seal upon it, which he bid him look on as he ran, and that he should give it at the Celestial Gate; so they went their way. Then Christian gave three leaps for joy, and went on singing:—

'Thus far did I come loaden with my sin;
Nor could aught ease the grief that I was in
Till I came hither. What a place is this!
Must here be the beginning of my bliss?
Must here the burden fall from off my back?
Must here the strings that bound it to me crack?
Bless'd cross! Bless'd sepulchre! Bless'd rather be
The man that there was put to shame for me.'"

The truth which is thus taught in Bunyan's allegory is the doctrine of this part of our book. It is the cross of our Lord Jesus Christ, the atonement which he offered for sin, that brings peace to the conscience, removes the burden of guilt, and at the same time inspires the soul with those principles of godly obedience which constitute the divine life in the soul of man. There is a most intimate connection between the removal of the burden of guilt and the removal of the bondage of sin, and the cross is the means of both. Other truths have their place and power in the awakening and instructing of the soul, but the truth that the God-man, the Lord Jesus, hath died for man's sin, is the turning point of the soul's conversion. As the fact that Christ hath died for men is the basis on which the holy God is propitious to men, and pardons and saves them, so our knowledge and belief of the fact brings peace to our conscience, and inspires our heart with filial love to God, and filial confidence in him as our Father and Friend. Another allegory will illustrate our doctrine.

Some people once lived in a happy isle, but for their misdeeds they had been banished. Their place of exile was a cheerless coast; but it lay within distant sight of their former home. Soon after their expulsion a message had come from their injured sovereign, offering to all who pleased an amnesty. Few minded it. They had grown sour and sullen, and they tried to persuade themselves that the earth-holes in which they burrowed were more comfortable than the mansions of his land, and that the mallows among their bushes were more nutritious than all the fruits of his gardens. One man, however, was of a different mind. He was a musing, thoughtful person. Often might you have seen him pacing the beach when the rays of evening shone on the happy isle, and . . from his dreary prison he wistfully eyed the forests on its coast, and the mountains of purple streaked with silver which sat enthroned in its interior; and as he fancied that he could sometimes hear faint murmurs of its joy, he wished that he was there. One morning when he awoke, it struck him that the opposite shore was unusually nigh, and so low was the tide that he fancied he might easily ford it, or swim across. And so he hastened forth. First over the dry shingle, then over the solid sand till he reached the damper sand, and then he was astonished at his own delusion; for it was still a mighty gulf, and even whilst he gazed the tide was rising. But another time he tried another plan. To the right of his dwelling the line of coast stretched away in a succession of cliffs and headlands, till the view was bounded by a lofty promontory, which seemed to touch the furthest side. To this promontory he resolved to take a pilgrimage, in the hope that it would transport him to the long-sought realm. The road was often a steep clamber, and for many an hour the headland seemed only to flee away. But after surmounting many a slope and swell, at last he reached it. With eager steps he ran along the ridge, half hoping that it was the isthmus which would bear him to the happy isle. Ah, no! He has reached its extremest verge, and here is that inexorable ocean still weltering at its base. Baffled in this last hope, and faint with his ineffectual toil, he flung himself on the stones and wept. But, by and by, he noticed off the shore a little boat, with whose appearance he was quite familiar. It used to ride at anchor opposite his own abode, and had done so for ever so long; but like his neighbours, he got so used to it that it never drew his notice. Now, however, seeing it there, he looked at it, and as he looked it neared him. It came close up to the rocks where he was seated. It was a beautiful boat, with snowy sail and golden prow, and a red cross was its waving pennon. There was one on board, and only one. His raiment was white and glistening, and his features betokened whence he came. "Son of man," he said, "why weepest thou?" "Because I cannot reach the blessed isle." "Canst thou trust thyself with me?" the stranger asked. The poor wayfarer looked at the little skiff leaping lightly on the waves, and he wondered, till he looked again at the pilot's kind and assuring countenance, and then he said, "I can." And no sooner had he stepped on board, than swift as a sunbeam it bore him to the land of light; and, with many a welcome from the pilot's friends, he found himself among its happy citizens, clothed in their bright raiment, and free to all their privileges, as now a subject of their king.

"The happy isle," says the author of the allegory,* "is peace with God—that position which man occupied whilst innocent. The dreary land is that state of alienation and misery into which fallen man is banished. The little skiff denotes the only means by which the sinner may pass from nature's alienation over into the peace of God. It is a means, not of the sinner's devising, but of God's providing. It is the ATONEMENT, and He who so kindly invites sinners to avail themselves of it, is the Lord Jesus himself."

The doctrine which these allegories teach is that which the apostle Paul taught of old. "The Jews require a sign, and the Greeks seek after wisdom: but we preach Christ crucified, unto the Jews a stumbling-

* Dr. James Hamilton. See "The Royal Preacher," Lecture xx.

block, and unto the Greeks foolishness; but unto them which are called, both Jews and Greeks, Christ the power of God, and the wisdom of God."* The apostolic ministry was one of "reconciliation," and its great theme was "that God was in Christ, reconciling the world unto himself, not imputing their trespasses unto them." It was this "word of reconciliation" that the apostles addressed to the hearts and consciences of men to bring them back to God. "We are ambassadors for Christ, as though God did beseech you by us: we pray you in Christ's stead, be ye reconciled to God. For he hath made him to be sin for us, who knew no sin; that we might be made the righteousness of God in him."† The death of Christ in man's stead was the only basis of reconciliation between the offended God and the offending creature, and the announcement of it was the only means by which the heart of the offender could be subdued and won back to loyalty, and the belief of it the only means by which his conscience could be freed from the burden of guilt. These positions receive illustration and proof from the facts and histories which have already passed before the reader's attention. He has only to recall the names of Paul, Luther, Latimer, Gardiner, Bunyan, Simeon, Chalmers, Wilberforce, and the other worthies, whose conversion we have recorded, to be impressed with the fact that by whatever means their attention was drawn to religion, or their interest in it awakened, it was by faith in Christ they found peace and became partakers of a true holiness. The facts and instances which follow are intended further to illustrate and confirm this important principle.

* 1 Cor. i. 22—24. † 2 Cor. v. 19—21.

When the Moravian missionaries went to Greenland, in 1733, they thought that the most rational way of instructing the heathen was to speak first of the existence and perfections of God, and to enforce obedience to the divine law; and they hoped, by these means, gradually to prepare their minds for the reception of the sublimer and more mysterious truths of the gospel. But this plan proved wholly ineffectual. For five years they laboured in this style, and could scarcely obtain a patient hearing from the savages. But circumstances, unexpected and uncontrived by themselves, led to an entire change of procedure.

The Moravians in Greenland.

In the beginning of June, 1738, Brother Beck, one of the missionaries, was copying a translation of a portion of the Gospels. He read a few sentences to the heathen, and after some conversation with them, he gave them an account of the creation of the world, the fall of man, and his recovery by Christ. In speaking of the redemption of man, he enlarged with more than usual energy on the sufferings and death of our Saviour, and exhorted his hearers seriously to consider the vast expense at which Jesus had ransomed the souls of his people. He then read to them out of the New Testament the history of our Saviour's agony in the garden. Upon this, the Lord opened the heart of one of the company, whose name was Kayarnak, who, stepping to the table in an earnest manner exclaimed, "How was that? tell me that once more; for I, too, desire to be saved." These words, which were such as had never before been uttered by a Greenlander, penetrated the soul of Brother Beck, who, with great emotion, gave them a fuller account of the life and death of our Saviour, and the scheme of salvation through him. Some of the pagans laid their hands on their mouth (which is their usual custom when struck with amazement.) On Kayarnak an impression was made that was not transient, but had taken deep root in his heart. By means of his conversation, his family, or those who lived in the same tent with him, were brought under conviction; and before the end of the month three large families came with all their property and pitched their tents near the dwelling of the missionaries, in order, as they said, to hear the joyful news of man's redemption. Kayarnak became eminently serviceable to the mission as a teacher of his countrymen, and adorned his Christian profession till his death."

The missionaries now understood the divine mode of reaching and changing the heart of savage or of civilized. They determined, in the literal sense of the words, to preach at once Christ and him crucified. And "no sooner," says Mr. James Montgomery, "did they declare unto the Greenlanders 'the word of reconciliation' in its native simplicity, than they beheld its converting and saving power. This reached the hearts of their audience, and produced the most astonishing effects. An impression was made which opened a way to their consciences, and illuminated their understandings. They remained no longer the stupid and brutish creatures they had once been; they felt they were sinners, and trembled at their danger; they rejoiced in the Saviour, and were rendered capable of sublimer pleasures than those arising from plenty of seals, and the low gratification of sensual appetites. A sure foundation being thus laid in the knowledge of a crucified Redeemer, the missionaries soon found that this supplied their young converts with a powerful motive to the abhorrence of sin, and the performance of every moral duty towards God and their neighbour; taught them to live soberly, righteously, and godly in this present world; animated them with the glorious hope of life and immortality; and gave them the light of the knowledge of the glory of God as the Creator, Preserver, and Moral Governor of the world, in a manner far more correct and influential than they could have hoped to attain had they persevered in their first mode of instruction. The missionaries themselves derived benefit from this new method of preaching. The doctrines of the cross of Christ warmed and enlivened their own souls in so powerful a manner, that they could address the heathen with uncommon liberty and fervour, and were often astonished at each other's power of utterance. In short, the happiest results have attended this practice, not only at first, and in Greenland, but in every other country where the Moravian brethren have laboured for the conversion of the heathen."

The principle on which the successful labours of the Moravian missionaries have been conducted, has often been misunderstood. "Of all who have attempted to teach Christianity to barbarous or savage nations," wrote a celebrated essayist in the beginning of this century, "the Moravian brethren may be fairly placed at the head. They begin with civilizing their pupils, educating and instructing them in the useful arts. It is by this kind of practical instruction alone that those in a certain degree of ignorance and barbarism are to be gained over to the truth." In reply to this statement, Dr. Chalmers showed that it was founded on ignorance of the means which the Moravians had adopted ever since their first convert was won by the simple story of the cross. "The truth is," he remarked, "that the Moravians have of late become the objects of a sentimental admiration. Their numerous establishments, and the many interesting pictures of peace, and order, and industry which they have reared among the wilds of heathenism, have at length compelled the testimony of travellers. It is delightful to be told of the neat attire and cultivated gardens of savages; and we can easily conceive how a sprig of honeysuckle at the cottage door of a Hottentot may extort some admiring and poetical prettiness from a charmed spectator who would shrink offended from the peculiarities of the gospel. Now they are right as to the fact. It is all very true about the garden and honeysuckle; but they are most egregiously wrong as to the principle. And when they talk of these Moravians as the most rational of missionaries, because they furnish their converts with the arts and comforts of life before they ever think of pressing upon them the mysteries of their faith, they make a most glaring departure from the truth, and that, too, in the face of information and testimony afforded by the very men whom they profess to admire. It is not true that Moravians are distinguished from the other missionaries by training their disciples to justice, and morality, and labour, in the first instance, and by refraining to exhort to faith and self-abasement. It is not true, nor does it consist with the practice of the Moravians, that in regard to savages, some advance towards civilization is necessary, preparatory to any attempt to christianize them."

The question thus raised is now settled, not on theoretic grounds, but on the conclusive evidence of experiment and fact. "I am convinced," said the late John Williams, after many years of labour among savage tribes, "that the first step towards the promotion of a nation's temporal and social elevation is to plant amongst them the tree of life, when civilization and commerce will entwine their tendrils around its trunk, and derive support from its strength. Until the people are brought under the influence of religion, they have no desire for the arts and usages of civilized life; *but that invariably creates it.* The missionaries were at Tahiti many years, during which they built and furnished a house in European style. The natives saw this, but not an individual imitated their example. As soon, however, as they were brought under the influence of Christianity, the chiefs, and even the common people, began to build neat plastered cottages, and to manufacture bedsteads, seats, and other articles of furniture. The females had long observed the dress of the missionaries' wives, but while heathen, they greatly preferred their own, and there was not a single attempt at imitation. No sooner, however, were they brought under the influence of religion, than all of them, even to the lowest, aspired to the possession of a gown, a bonnet, and a shawl, that they might appear like Christian women. While the natives are under the influence of their superstitions, they evince an inanity and torpor from which no stimulus has proved powerful enough to arouse them but the new ideas and the new principles implanted by Christianity."

The Polynesians

When Christianity was introduced into the island of Rarotonga, two-and-thirty years ago, there was a native priest, a savage cannibal, who was so enraged at the success of the

Cannibal Priest.

gospel, that, with seventy men of like character, he vowed a vow to die rather than submit to the new faith. This man assisted in burning down the first chapels and school-houses on the island, and for fifteen years was a determined, violent, and constant enemy to the truth. By some means he was induced to attend the preaching of the gospel, became convinced of his sins, and understood something of Christian truth, but only enough to make him unhappy. When, five years afterwards, he was admitted into the fellowship of the Christian church, he spoke to this effect:—"Brethren, am *I* here? I who have been so wild a savage? Ah! *brethren* is a new name to us—we knew not what that meant in our heathenism." Pointing to the old men, he said, "You know me." To one of them he said, "You and I killed so and so in yonder mountain, and, with others, revelled in a cannibal feast on his body." He then mentioned three persons by name whom he and they had murdered and eaten. "But you young men," he said, "know me, too; I burned down the chapel and schools; but you do not know all. These hands have murdered eleven persons in yonder mountains, and I have partaken of more than twice that number of feasts of human bodies. Am *I* here? I who have done these deeds? Some of you have been expecting me to come and make profession of my faith in Jesus long before now. But whenever I have thought of doing so, the sin and guilt of my cannibalism have prevented me. This has been the barrier, until the other day I heard the missionary preach from that text in Isaiah, 'I have blotted out, as a thick cloud, thy transgressions, and, as a cloud, thy sins.' That was the gospel to me. Amongst the sins making up that cloud, the sin of cannibalism was noticed, and all its enormity described; but it was shown that even that could be blotted out by the blood of Jesus. My burden was that moment removed. My heart found peace. I had conversation with the missionary, and now, as the result of the love and death of Jesus, it is true that I, even I, am here." And this man, from whom the demon of sin and savageism was expelled by the cross of Christ, is now one of the most intelligent and consistent elders in the Rarotongan church.*

In the course of five-and-thirty years, five-and-thirty islands in these southern seas have wholly cast away their idols as the fruit of the labours of one society. And other societies have been equally successful, so that there are now in these regions 240,000 persons who profess the faith of.the Bible, and of these 46,000 are in actual membership as communicants at the table of our Lord. Will it be said that these were savages, and that the universal adaptation of the gospel is not to be inferred from their conversion? The answer is obvious—that the power which effected the greater change is competent to effect the less. It is not among the snows of Greenland and the sunny isles of the Pacific alone that the efficacy and adaptation of the gospel of the love of God through Jesus Christ have been tested in modern times by missionary societies. There is not a land under heaven, nor a class of men in any land, that does not supply its living witnesses.

"Ah!" said the celebrated Brahmin, Rammohun Roy, when the conversion of the Greenlander by the

* The above fact has been kindly supplied by the Rev. W. Gill; and this experienced missionary speaks of it as "one of ten thousand which illustrate the power of the gospel in the South Seas."

story of the cross was mentioned in illustration of the principle that nothing but the simple preaching of the gospel can convert the world—"Ah," said he, all the pride of the Brahmin rising in his breast, "that was very good—but you must not suppose the same method which succeeded with the rude, the ignorant, the barbarous Esquimaux, would do for the polished, the learned, the enlightened Brahmins of India." "But all hearts are essentially alike, Greenlanders and Esquimaux," to use the words of Dr. Raffles, when mentioning this circumstance; "and this gospel of the kingdom which suits the one will suit the other. It will—it must; for, if it does not, there is nothing else." Facts confirm this expectation. There are now in India many Brahmins who are "obedient to the faith," simple-hearted believers in the truth which warmed and won the heart of the Greenlander, and which softened and humanized the heart of the Rarotongan. Pariah and Brahmin are found rejoicing together in the same gospel, and in the same Saviour.

"I believe," says the Rev. Benjamin Rice, "that the universal experience of missionaries in India is, that when the doctrine of the cross is first propounded to any Hindoo, and especially to a Brahmin, it is regarded by him, as it was by the ancient Greeks, as utter 'foolishness.' But when any educated Hindoo, whether Brahmin or otherwise, can be brought to give sufficient attention to the subject to understand the gospel system, the evidence on which it is based, and the complete and satisfactory provision which it makes for those spiritual wants of humanity which Hindooism itself professes to meet, but does not—I have almost uniformly found that *then* the doctrine of the cross commands the respect of such a man. The numerous conversions that have actually taken place amongst the Brahmins—conversions which have led to the renunciation of home, kindred, and property, and submitting to a life of contempt amongst their own people for the sake of Christ—sufficiently disprove the truth of Rammohun Roy's assertion."

A converted Hindoo, an educated man, informed a missionary some years ago, that in reading the Bible he had been very much struck with the fact, that while all the Hindoo incarnations had been assumed for the most trivial objects, and the incarnate deities had led lives of the most degrading character, Jesus Christ, the Son of God, from pure love to a sinful world, became incarnate that he might save them from ruin.

The Rev. Krishna Mohan Banerji.

The Rev. KRISHNA MOHAN BANERJI, formerly a Brahmin, and now an ordained minister at Calcutta, in connection with the church of England, states that while the doctrines of Christianity were under discussion by Dr. Duff and the young infidel Hindoos of Calcutta, his mind particularly revolted against the doctrine of the atonement, "till God," he says, "by the influence of his Holy Spirit, was graciously pleased to open my soul to discern its sinfulness and guilt, and the suitableness of the great salvation which centered in the atoning death of a Divine Redeemer. And the same doctrine of the atonement which, when not properly understood, was my last great argument against the divine origin of the Bible, is now, when rightly apprehended, a principal reason for my belief and vindication of the Bible as the production of infinite wisdom and love."

The experience of Dr. Duff, in his discussion with the class to which this young man belonged, is deeply interesting and instructive. They were youths who had been educated in the Government college at Calcutta, an institution from which all reference to religion was, on system, excluded. The result of such training was what might have been anticipated. Class after class issued forth from this college, who, by the course of enlightened study pursued, were made alive to the gross absurdities of their own systems. These, therefore, says Dr. Duff, they boldly denounced as masses of imposture and debasing error, and the Brahmins as deceivers of the people, though many of themselves belonged to that exalted and sacred class. But they were in a state of mind utterly blank as regards moral and religious truth—moral and religious obligation. They were infidels or sceptics of the most perfect kind, believing in nothing, believing not even in the existence of a Deity, and glorying in their unbelief. All subjects seemed to be more or less tolerated but religion. Against religion in every form they raged and raved. They scrupled not to scoff at Christianity; they scrupled not to avow their disbelief in the very being of a God; thus realizing the condition of the men described by an ancient author, who "fled from superstition, leaped over religion, and sunk into atheism." They despised the character of a missionary, whom they thought fit for nothing but to stand in lanes and corners of the streets, and there address the Pariahs and lowest castes of the people. Dr. Duff succeeded at last in bringing them to a public disputation, met them on their own ground, and argued with them the question of the being of God, "with a determinate view," he says, "to this noblest end—the getting a hearing on the higher and more glorious subject of Christ crucified." At the end of the disputation the young men for the most part declared, "We now believe there is a Great First Cause, the intelligent Author of all things."

Still these young Hindoos were not prepared to listen to the gospel message. Was it from God? they demanded. And the evidences of revealed religion must be discussed in detail. Night after night these young men brought forward the old and now exploded arguments of Hume on the subject of miracles; and night after night had the Christian missionary, on the banks of the Ganges, and for the satisfaction of Hindoos, to combat the plausible reasonings and deductions of that great but misguided man.

"The evidences in favour of Christianity as a revelation from God having been admitted by several as irresistible, and by others no longer opposed, we last of all (says Dr. Duff) came to the grand terminating object of all our labours, namely, the announcement of the message itself, the full and free declaration of the essential doctrines of the gospel. It was then, and then only, as might have been expected, that vital impressions began to be made. Hitherto we were engaged in the removal of obstacles that opposed our entrance into the temple of truth. Having now reached the threshold, we crossed it in order to discover and admire the beauties of the inner workmanship. Hitherto the intellect chiefly was called into exercise. We had now something suited to the feelings and conscience. The word of God is the alone direct and efficacious instrument in awakening and regenerating a guilty and polluted world; and the Holy Spirit of God the alone almighty Agent in crowning this instrumentality with triumphs that shall issue in the glories of eternity. Accordingly it was when unfolding, in simple and absolute dependence on divine grace, the Scripture doctrine of the sinfulness, depravity, and helplessness of human nature, that the heart of the first convert became seriously affected under a sense of the guilt and vileness of sin; and, when unfolding the inexpressible love of the Divine Redeemer to our apostate world, that another heart was touched, yea, melted, under the display of such infinite tenderness. Thus it was that the gospel triumphed; and the doctrine of the cross, brought home to the heart and conscience, and sealed by the Divine Spirit, maintained its high pre-eminence as the only antecedent to the conversion of a soul towards God."

The Brahmins thus won to God exhibited a power of faith worthy of the best age of the church of Christ. One instance will be sufficient illustration. "It was about nine in the evening (said Dr. Duff, addressing the General Assembly of the church of Scotland), and if any one here has been in that far distant land, he will know what the external scene was, when I say it was on the banks of the Ganges, and under the full

A young Brahmin.

effulgence of an Indian moon, whose brightness almost rivals the noonday glory of the sun in these northern climes. Two or three had resolved, as friends, to go along with this individual, and witness a spectacle never before seen by us, and perhaps not soon again to be seen by Europeans. It was heart-rending throughout. Having reached the outer door of the house, the elder brother of this young man advanced towards him, and looking at him wistfully in the face, began first to implore him by the most endearing terms as a brother, that he would not bring this shame and disgrace upon himself and his family—which was a most respectable one. Again and again did he earnestly appeal to him by the sympathies and the tenderness and the affection of a brother. The young man listened, and, with intense emotion, simply in substance replied, 'That he had now found out what error was, that he had now found out what truth was, and that he was resolved to cling to the truth.' Finding that this argument had failed, he began to assert the authority of the elder brother, an authority sanctioned by the usages of the people. He endeavoured to show what power he had over him, if he cruelly brought this disgrace upon his family. The young man still firmly replied, 'I have found out what error is; I have found out what truth is; and I have resolved to cling to the truth.' The brother next held out bribes and allurements. There was nothing which he was not prepared to grant. There was no indulgence whatever which he would not allow him in the very bosom of the family—indulgences absolutely prohibited and regarded as abhorrent in the Hindoo system—if he would only stop short of the last and awful step of baptism, the public sealing of his foul and fatal apostasy. The young man still resolutely adhered to his simple but emphatic declaration.

"It was now, when every argument had finally failed, that his aged mother, who had all the while been present within hearing, though he knew it not, raised a howl of agony, a yell of horror, which it is impossible for imagination to conceive. It pierced into the heart, and made the very flesh creep and shiver. The young man could hold out no longer. He was powerfully affected, and shed tears. With uplifted arms, and eyes raised to heaven he forcibly exclaimed, '*No: I cannot stay.*' And this was the last time he ever expected to hold converse with his brethren or his mother.

"I could not help feeling then (continued Dr. Duff), and have often thought since, how wonderful is the power of truth—how sovereign the grace of God! If it be said that the Hindoo character is griping and avaricious, divine grace is stronger still, and is able to conquer it. If it is yielding and fickle —aye, fickle as the shifting quicksands—divine grace can give it consistency and strength. If it is feeble and cowardly, divine grace can make the feeble powerful, and convert the coward into a moral hero. What signal testimony do such triumphs bear to the power of the everlasting gospel!"

It is not maintained that the gospel of pardon through the atoning sacrifice of Christ is the only means of awakening religious earnestness. The most selfish fear, and the most mistaken apprehensions of the character of God, and of the way of obtaining life, may induce an agony of effort to please God and to win heaven. But the gospel is essential to the enjoyment of enlightened peace with God, and to the production in the soul of man of the principles of a free and loving obedience. And this is seen nowhere more remarkably than in the life and labours of Wesley, Whitefield, and their compeers.

John Wesley; born at Epworth, June 17, 1703; died March 2, 1791.

The father of JOHN WESLEY was an estimable and zealous clergyman of the church of England; and his mother was a woman of superior mental power, and of earnest religious character. The advantage of such a parentage was great. The young Wesleys had in their father an example of all that could render a clergyman respectable and influential; and in their mother there was a sanctified wisdom, a masculine understanding, and an acquired knowledge, which they regarded with just deference after they became men and scholars.* But over the minds of the rector of Epworth and his worthy wife there hung for many years, and, indeed, till towards the close of their life, considerable obscurity in regard to evangelical religion. And the influence of this obscurity is painfully traced in the spiritual history of their children.

John Wesley went to Oxford in his eighteenth year, full of gaiety and sprightliness. One who knew him during the earlier part of his college life speaks of him as a young fellow of the finest classical taste, and of the most liberal and manly sentiments. As a boy, he had been much impressed with religion, and had been admitted by his father to partake of the sacrament at the age of eight years. And when he proposed to himself to take deacon's orders, he was roused from the religious carelessness into which he had fallen at college, and applied himself diligently to the reading of books on theology. His mother observed the altered tone of his correspondence, and expressed her hope "that it might proceed from the operations of God's Spirit, that, by taking off her son's relish for earthly enjoyments, he might prepare and dispose his mind for a more serious and close application to things of a more sublime and spiritual nature." "If it be so," she said to him, "happy are you if you cherish those dispositions, and now in

* We follow Richard Watson's Life of John Wesley.

good earnest resolve to make religion the business of your life; for, after all, that is the one thing which, strictly speaking, is necessary: all things besides are comparatively little to the purpose of life. I heartily wish you would now enter upon a strict examination of yourself, that you may know whether you have a reasonable hope of salvation by Jesus Christ. If you have, the satisfaction of knowing it will abundantly reward your pains; if you have not, you will find a more reasonable occasion for tears than can be met with in a tragedy. The matter deserves great consideration by all, but especially by those designed for the ministry, who ought, above all things, to make their own calling and election sure, lest, after they have preached to others, they themselves should be cast away."

These maternal counsels were devout and earnest, and though not in all respects enlightened or fitted to instruct the heavy laden how he might be freed from the burden of sin, they produced a deep impression on young Wesley's mind. Of the same character were the books to which he now devoted himself—the "Christian's Pattern," by Thomas à Kempis; and Taylor's "Rules of Holy Living and Dying"—books which, whatever their excellencies or defects, are rather manuals for those who are Christians, than directories to those who are seeking to become such.

John Wesley was ordained deacon in September, 1725, and the year following he was elected Fellow of Lincoln College. His previous seriousness had been the subject of much banter and ridicule, and appears to have been urged against him, in the election, by his opponents; but his reputation for learning and diligence, and the excellence of his character, triumphed.

Two years later he became his father's curate; in 1728 he obtained priest's orders; and in 1729 he was required to take up his abode in Oxford as a tutor of his college. He now found, already in existence, a small society, of which he soon became the leader—its founder having been his brother Charles.

Charles Wesley; born 1708; died 1788.

Charles was five years younger than John, and though his outward conduct was unblamable, he repelled all those exhortations to a more strictly religious course which John seriously urged upon him after he was elected to Christ Church. But when John returned to Oxford, in 1729, he found his brother, he says, "in great earnestness to save his soul." His own account of himself is that he lost his first year at college in diversions; that the next he set himself to study; that diligence led him into serious thinking; that he went to the weekly sacrament, persuading two or or three students to accompany him; and that he observed the *method* of study prescribed by the statutes of the university. "This," he says, "gained me the harmless name of *Methodist.*" To the society of thoughtful young men which thus gathered around Charles Wesley, his brother John joined himself on his return to Oxford, and by his influence and energy gave additional vigour to their exertions to promote their own spiritual improvement and the good of others.

The strictly religious profession which Mr. Wesley and his companions now made excited both ridicule and opposition. But were these young men at this time partakers of the divine life? Were they new creatures in Christ Jesus? If entire sincerity be sufficient evidence of a new creation, there exists no room for doubt. And yet John Wesley thought himself, even at the time, to be but "almost" and not "altogether" a Christian—"a conclusion (says his biographer) of a very perplexing kind to many who have set themselves up for better judges in his case than he himself. From a similar cause we have seen St. Paul all but reproved by some divines for representing himself as the 'chief of sinners' at the time when he was 'blameless' as to 'the righteousness of the law;' and but for the courtesy due to an inspired man, he would probably, in direct contradiction to his own words, have been pronounced the chief of saints, although his heart remained a total stranger to humility and charity."

"If our views of personal religion must be taken from the New Testament (Mr. Watson continues), although as to men the Wesleys at Oxford were blameless and exemplary, yet in respect to God those internal changes had not taken place in them which it is the office of real Christianity to effect. . . . The very writers, Bishop Taylor and Mr. Law, who so powerfully wrought upon their consciences, were among the most erring guides to that peace of God which passeth all understanding for which they sighed; and those celebrated divines, excelled by none for genius and eloquence, who could draw the picture of a practical piety so copious and exact in its external manifestations, were unable to teach that mystic connection of the branches with the vine, from which the only fruits that are of healthy growth and genuine flavour can proceed. Both are too defective in their views of faith, and its object, the atonement of Christ, to be able to direct a penitent and troubled spirit into the way of salvation, and to show how all the principles and acts of truly Christian piety are sustained by a life of 'faith in the Son of God.'"

Bishop Taylor's chapter on purity of intention first convinced Mr. Wesley of the necessity of being holy in heart, as well as regular in his outward conduct; and he "began to alter the whole form of his conversation, and to set in earnest upon a new life." "He communicated every week," we are told in his Journal. "He watched against all sin, whether in word or deed, and began to aim at, and pray for, inward holiness;" but still with a painful consciousness, like Luther in his cell, that he found not that which he so earnestly sought. His error was drawn from his theological guides. He either confounded sanctification with justification, that is, a change of heart with a change of state before God; or he regarded sanctification as a preparation for, and a condition of, justification. He had not yet learned the apostle's doctrine, the gratuitous justification of "the ungodly," when penitent, simply through faith in Jesus Christ; nor that upon this there *follows* "a death" unto inward and outward sin, so that he who is so justified can "no longer continue therein." It was through the agitations, inquiries, hopes, and fears of several years, that the mind of John Wesley passed to the enjoyment of that steadfast peace which never afterwards forsook him, but gave serenity to his countenance, and cheerfulness to his heart, till the last hour of a prolonged life.

The young and learned "Methodists" of Oxford, while yet unacquainted with the secret of peace with God, and of filial affection and confidence towards him, devoted themselves earnestly to well-doing. They visited the prisoners in Oxford jail, and spent two or three hours a week in visiting and relieving the poor and the sick. Amidst the storm of opposition which practices so novel awakened, they were encouraged by the sanction and counsel of the father of the Wesleys. The rector of Epworth blessed God who had given him two sons together at Oxford who had received grace and courage to turn the war against the world and the devil. He bade them defy reproach, and animated them in God's name to go on in the path to which their Saviour had directed them.

The eye of man could see in these young men nothing but a mature and vital Christianity. That they had a "spirit of power" is very manifest, for they could endure toil and reproach, but it was still "a spirit of bondage unto fear;" and the reason is, that they were seeking justification "by the works of the law." "I was convinced more than ever," says John Wesley, "of the exceeding height, and breadth, and depth of the law of God. The light flowed in so mightily upon my soul, that everything appeared in a new view. I cried to God for help, and resolved not to prolong the time of obeying him as I had never done before. And by my continued endeavour to keep his whole law, inward and outward, to the best of my power, I was persuaded that I should be accepted of him, and that I was even then in a state of salvation." At the period to which these words refer, John Wesley was not altogether hopeless of finding acceptance with God by his own endeavours to keep the whole law. And he persevered diligently in the rigid practice of every discovered duty, in the hope of seizing the great prize by this means. But he soon became greatly surprised that he was so far from obtaining that settled enjoyment of conscious peace with God, that love to him, delight in him, and filial access to him, which the New Testament describes as the privilege of a true believer. The deep tone of feeling, and the earnestness of his inquiries, in his correspondence with his mother during 1732, present the state of his mind in a very affecting light. He then needed some one more fully instructed in the true doctrine of salvation than even this excellent and intelligent "guide of his youth," to teach him to lay down the burden of his wounded and anxious spirit, in self despair as to his own efforts, at the foot of the cross of Christ.

In 1735, the trustees of the new colony of Georgia directed their attention to Mr. John Wesley, and some of his friends at Oxford, as peculiarly qualified, by zeal and piety, and their habits of self-denial, to administer to the spiritual wants of the colonists, and also to attempt the conversion of the Indians. This mission was accepted by John Wesley because it was accompanied with the certainty of great hardships and sufferings, which he deemed necessary to his perfection. As yet he put mortification, retirement, and contempt of the world, too much in the place of that divine atonement, the virtue of which, when received by simple faith, at once removes the sense of guilt, cheers the spirit by a peaceful sense of acceptance through the merits of Christ, and renews the whole heart after the image of God.

On his voyage across the Atlantic, John Wesley was thrown into the society of pious Moravians, who were proceeding to settle in the new world, and saw in them the happy fruits of a genuine faith. Every day gave them occasion of showing meekness which no injury could move. But the absence of the spirit of fear struck the young Englishman still more than the absence of the spirit of anger and revenge. That they should not be afraid to die when the great deep seemed ready to swallow them up was to him a great mystery. And thus he had the first glimpse of a religious experience which keeps the mind at peace in all circumstances, and vanquishes that feeling which a formal and defective religion may lull to temporary sleep, but cannot eradicate—"the fear of death." In conversation with a Moravian pastor at Savannah, he was asked, "Do you know Jesus Christ?" He paused and said, "I know he is the Saviour of the world." "True," replied the Moravian; "but do you know he has saved you?" Wesley answered, "I hope he has died to save me." The other only added, "Do you know yourself?" "I do," was the reply. But the comment of later years was, "I fear they were vain words."

During his stay in Georgia, John Wesley spent his whole time in works of piety and mercy, and distributed his income so profusely in charity that for many months together he had not one shilling in the house. In the prosecution of his work he exposed himself to every change of season, frequently slept on the ground under the dews of night in summer, and in winter with his hair and clothes frozen to the earth. But his preaching was defective in that one great point which gives to preaching its real power over the heart, "Christ crucified."

On his homeward voyage, the language of his still restless heart was: "I went to America to convert the Indians; but oh! who shall convert me? Who is he that will deliver me from this evil heart of unbelief? I have a fair summer religion; I can talk well; nay, I believe myself safe, while no danger is present; but let death look me in the face, and my spirit is troubled; nor can I say, 'To die is gain.'" The returning missionary now longed for a faith that should deliver him entirely from guilty dread, but his notions of such a faith were very confused. He manifestly regarded it generally as a principle of belief in the gospel, which, by quickening his efforts after greater holiness, would raise him, through a renewed state of heart, into acceptance and peace with God.

John Wesley resorted finally to the mystic writers, "whose noble descriptions of union with God, and internal religion, made everything else appear mean, flat, and insipid. But in truth they made good works appear so too, yea, and faith itself, and what not? These gave me (he says) an entire new view of religion, nothing like any I had before. But, alas! it was nothing like that religion which Christ and his apostles lived and taught. I had a plenary dispensation from all the commands of God: the form ran thus: 'Love is all; all the commands besides are only means of love; you must choose those which you feel are means to you, and use them as long as they are so.' Thus were all the bands burst at once. And though I could never fully come into this, nor contentedly omit what God enjoined, yet, I know not how, I fluctuated between obedience and disobedience. I had no heart, no vigour, no zeal in obeying, continually doubting whether I was right or wrong, and never out of perplexities and entanglements."

Wesley, however, was delivered from the errors of the mystics, only to be brought back to the point from which he set out—with this difference, that he had now acquired correct views of his own spiritual character and of his spiritual wants. But his struggling soul cannot now be far from the kingdom of God. Not less earnest and conscientious in obeying God's will than before, he is no longer dreaming of finding acceptance through his own endeavours. He sees clearly that he must be justified on the ground of what Christ has done for him.

A few days after his arrival in London, John Wesley met with Peter Böhler, a minister of the Moravian church. It was on February 7, 1738, which he marks as "a day much to be remembered." In their conversation on saving faith, Böhler exclaimed more than once, "My brother, that philosophy of yours must be purged away." At Oxford, whither he had gone to visit Charles, who was sick, he again met with his Moravian friend, "by whom (he says), in the hand of the great God, I was clearly convinced of unbelief, of the want of that faith whereby alone we are saved with the full Christian salvation."

"He was now convinced (says one of his biographers) that his faith had been too much separated from an evangelical view of the promises of a free justification, or pardon of sin, through the atonement and mediation of Christ alone, which was the reason why he had been held in continual bondage and fear." In a few days he met with Peter Böhler again, "who now," he says, "amazed me more and more, by the accounts he gave of the fruits of living faith, and the holiness and happiness which he affirmed to attend it. The next morning I began the Greek Testament, again resolving to abide by 'the law and the testimony,' being confident that God would hereby show me whether this doctrine was of God."

On the 24th of May, 1738, Wesley emerged out of

his darkness into marvellous light, and experienced for the first time the full liberty of the sons of God. "In the evening," he says, "I went, very unwillingly, to a society in Aldersgate-street, where one was reading Luther's 'Preface to the Epistle to the Romans.' About a quarter before nine, while he was describing the change which God works in the heart through faith in Christ, I felt my heart strangely warmed. I felt I did trust in Christ, Christ alone, for salvation; and an assurance was given me that he had taken away my sins—even mine—and saved me from the 'law of sin and death.'"

"After this, he had some struggles with doubt," says Mr. Watson, "but he proceeded from strength to strength, till he could say, 'Now I was always conqueror.' His experience, nurtured by habitual prayer, and deepened by unwearied exertion in the cause of his Saviour, settled into that steadfast faith and solid peace which the grace of God perfected in him to the close of his long and active life."

His brother Charles (we still follow Mr. Watson's narrative) was also made partaker of the same grace. They had passed together through the briars and thorns, through the perplexities and shadows, of the legal wilderness, and the hour of their deliverance was not far separated. Böhler visited Charles in his sickness at Oxford; but the "Pharisee within" was somewhat offended when the honest German shook his head at learning that his hope of salvation rested upon "his best endeavours." After his recovery, the reading of "Halyburton's Life" produced in him a sense of his want of that faith which brings "peace and joy in the Holy Ghost." Böhler visited him again in London; and he began seriously to consider the doctrine which he urged upon him. His convictions of his state of danger, as a man unjustified before God, and of his need of the faith whereof cometh salvation, increased; and he spent his whole time in discoursing on those subjects, in prayer, and reading the Scriptures. Luther on the Galatians then fell into his hands; and on reading the preface he observes,—"I marvelled that we were so soon removed from him that called us into the grace of Christ unto another gospel. Who would believe that our church had been founded on this important article of justification by faith alone? I am astonished I should ever think this a new doctrine; especially while our articles and homilies stand unrepealed, and the key of knowledge is not yet taken away. From this time I endeavoured to ground as many of our friends as came to see me in this fundamental truth —salvation by faith alone; not an idle, dead faith, but a faith which works by love, and is incessantly productive of all good works and all holiness."

"On Whit-Sunday, May 21st, Charles Wesley awoke in hope and expectation of soon attaining the object of his wishes, the knowledge of God reconciled in Christ Jesus. In reading various portions of Scripture on that day, he was enabled to view Christ as set forth to be a propitiation for his sins through faith in his blood; and he received that peace and rest in God which he so earnestly sought. The next day he greatly rejoiced in reading the 107th Psalm, so nobly descriptive, he observes, of what God had done for his soul. He had a very humbling view of his own weakness; but was enabled to contemplate Christ in his power to save to the uttermost all those who ome unto God through him."

The comments of Mr. Richard Watson on this narrative are so appropriate to our purpose, that we shall quote some portion of them :—

"It is easy to assail with ridicule such disclosures of the exercises of minds impressed with the great concern of salvation, and seeking for deliverance from a load of anxiety 'in a way which they had not known,' and flippantly to resolve all these shadowings of doubt, these dawnings of hope, and the joyous influence of the full day of salvation, as some have done, into fancy, nervous affection, or natural constitution. To every truly serious mind these will, however, appear subjects of a momentous character; and no one will proceed either safely or soberly to judge of them, who does not previously inquire into the doctrine of the New Testament on the subject of human salvation, and apply the principles which he may find there, authenticated by infallible inspiration, to the examination of such cases. If it be there declared that the state of man by nature, and so long as he remains unforgiven by his offended God, is a state of awful peril, then the all-absorbing seriousness of that concern for deliverance from spiritual danger, which was exhibited by the Wesleys, is a feeling becoming our condition, and is the only rational frame of mind which we can cultivate. If we are required to be of a humble and broken spirit, and if the very root of true repentance lies in godly sorrow for sin, then their humiliations and self-reproaches were in correspondence with a state of heart which is enjoined upon all by an authority which we cannot dispute. If the appointed method of man's salvation, laid down in the gospel, be gratuitous pardon through faith in the merits of Christ's sacrifice; and if a method of seeking justification by works of moral obedience to the divine law be plainly placed by St. Paul in opposition to this, and declared to be vain and fruitless—then if in this way the Wesleys sought their justification before God, we see how true their own statements of necessity have been, that, with all their efforts, they could obtain no solid peace of mind, no deliverance from the enslaving fear of death and final punishment, because they sought that by imperfect works which God has appointed to be obtained by faith alone. . . . For the joyous change of Mr. Wesley's feelings, upon his persuasion of his personal interest in Christ through faith, those persons who, like Dr. Southey, have bestowed upon it several philosophic solutions, might have found a better reason had they either consulted St. Paul, who says, 'We joy in God, by whom we have received the reconciliation,' or their own church, which has emphatically declared that the doctrine of justification by faith is not only very wholesome, but also 'very full of comfort.' "

George Whitefield; born at Gloucester, Dec. 16, 1714; died Sept. 30, 1770, in New England.

The father of GEORGE WHITEFIELD was proprietor of the Bell Inn at Gloucester, and died when his youngest son, George, was two years old. The widowed mother was very careful of her Benjamin's education, and "always kept him in his tender years from intermeddling in the least with the tavern business." Writing of his childhood in after years, he said, "I can remember such early stirrings of corruption in my heart as abundantly convince me that I was conceived and born in sin. . . . . . . I was so brutish as to hate instruction, and used purposely to shun all opportunities of receiving it." Among "the iniquities of his youth," he charges himself with lying, filthy talking, foolish jesting, and profane swearing—charges which some who disliked the doctrines of his after ministry compared with the confessions of the "wild and fanatical Theresa," but with much injustice and ignorance, for they were recorded in a spirit of deep penitence. "It would be endless to recount the sins and offences of my younger days," he wrote. "They are more in number than the hairs of my head. My heart would fail me at the remembrance of them, were I not assured that my Redeemer liveth to make intercession for me. However the young man in the gospel might boast that he had kept the commandments from his 'youth up,' with shame and confusion of face I confess that I have broken them all from *my* youth."

In the midst of his follies he had some early convictions of sin, but they were transient and fruitless. During his first two years at the grammar school (from his twelfth to his fourteenth year) he bought, and read with much attention, "Ken's Manual for Winchester Scholars," a book commended to him by the use made of it by his mother in her afflictions. During a residence of two months in Bristol he experienced some awakenings of conscience. Once in St. John's church he was so affected by the sermon, that he resolved to prepare himself for the sacrament; and during his stay in Bristol reading Thomas à Kempis was his chief delight. "I was always impatient (he says) till the bell rang to call me to tread the courts of the Lord's house. But in the midst of these illuminations, something surely whispered, '*This will not last.*' And, indeed, so it happened. For—oh! that I could write it in tears of blood—when I left Bristol and returned to Gloucester, I changed my devotion with my place. Alas! all my fervour went off. I had no inclination to go to church, or draw nigh to God. In short, my heart was far from him."

"Having now, as I thought, nothing to do, it was a proper season for Satan to tempt me. Much of my time I spent in reading plays, and in sauntering from place to place. I was careful to adorn my body, but took little pains to deck and beautify my soul. Evil communications with my old schoolfellows soon corrupted my good manners. . . . . . Having thus lived with my mother for some considerable time, a young student, who was once my schoolfellow, and then a servitor of Pembroke college, Oxford, came to pay my mother a visit. Amongst other conversation, he told her how he had discharged all college expenses that quarter and saved a penny. Upon that my mother immediately cried out, 'This will do for my son!' Then turning to me, she said, 'Will you go to Oxford, George?' I replied, 'With all my heart.'"

The university had often been thought of, but the thought was dismissed as impracticable. The way seemed now to open. The friends who had procured for George Whitefield's schoolfellow a servitor's place, were his friends likewise; and the young aspirant resumed his classical studies. But while his scholarship advanced, his morals degenerated. "I got acquainted with such a set of debauched, abandoned, atheistical youths, that if God, by his free, unmerited, and special grace, had not delivered me out of their hands, I should have sat in the scorner's chair and made a mock at sin. By keeping company with them, my thoughts of religion grew more and more like theirs. I went to public service only to make sport and walk about. I took pleasure in their lewd conversation. I began to reason as they did, and to ask, why God had given me passions, and not permitted me to gratify them. In short, I soon made great proficiency in the school of the devil. I affected to look rakish, and was in a fair way of being as infamous as the worst of them."

Such was George Whitefield, when nearly seventeen years of age, and preparing for the university. But God stopped him when running on in a full career of vice; and he became morally reformed and outwardly religious. For a twelvemonth, he tells us, he went on in a round of duties, receiving the sacrament monthly, fasting frequently, attending constantly on public worship, and praying, often more than twice a day, in private.

When Whitefield entered Oxford, the small society of which the Wesleys were the centre and soul had been in existence for five years. Its members, as the reader is already aware, were earnest and zealous, but "ignorant of God's righteousness." One year after he entered the university, he formed their acquaintance. At this time, to use the words of a graphic writer, "his mind became so burdened with the great realities, that he had little heart for study. God and eternity, holiness and sin, were thoughts which haunted every moment, and compelled him to live for the salvation of his soul: but, except his tutor Wesley, and a few gownsmen, he met with none who shared his earnestness. And though earnest, they were all in error. Among the influential minds of the university there was no one to lead them into the knowledge of the gospel, and they had no religious guides, except the genius of the place, and books of their own choosing. The genius of the place was an ascetic quietism. Its libraries full of clasped schoolmen and tall fathers, its cloisters so solemn that a hearty laugh or hurried step seemed sinful, and its halls lit with mediæval sunshine, perpetually invited their inmates to meditation and silent reflection; whilst the early tinkle of the chapel bell, and the frosty routine of winter matins, the rubric and the founder's rules, proclaimed the religious benefits of bodily exercise. The Romish postern had not then been re-opened; but, with no devotional models save the marble Bernards and De Wykhams, and no spiritual illumination except what came in by the north windows of the past, it is not surprising that ardent but reverential young men should in such a place have unwittingly groped into a Romish pietism. With an awakened conscience and a resolute will, young Whitefield went through the sanatory specifics of à Kempis, Castanza, and William Law; and in his anxiety to exceed all that is required in the rubric, he would fast during Lent on black bread and sugarless tea, and stand in the cold till his nose was red, and his fingers blue, whilst, in the hope of temptation and wild beasts, he would wander through Christ-church meadows over dark." It was whilst pursuing this course of self-righteous fanaticism that he was seized with an alarming illness.

The seven weeks' sickness through which Whitefield now passed, he calls in his journal a "glorious visitation." The Wesleys were constant and brotherly in their attentions, but they were miserable comforters. Charles referred him to chapters in à Kempis: John to the maxims of quietism. But in vain. "All my former gross, notorious, and even my heart sins also, were now set home upon me," he writes. "Unable to sustain such views of the evil of sin, and having failed in all his former efforts to remove a sense of guilt by a series of observances, he was now 'shut up to the faith.'" "Whilst praying and yearning over his Greek Testament, the 'open secret' flashed upon his view." He discovered the true grounds of a sinner's hope and justification. The testimony of God concerning his Son brought peace and life. "I found and felt in myself, that I was delivered from the burden that had so heavily oppressed me. The spirit of mourning was taken from me, and I knew what it was truly to rejoice in God my Saviour. For some time I could not avoid singing psalms wherever I was; but my joy became gradually more settled. Thus were the days of my mourning ended: after a long life of desertion and temptation, the star which I had seen at a distance before began to appear again; the day-star arose in my heart."

Whitefield's youthful austerities and superstitions only increased the spirit of bondage, and diverted him from God's appointed remedy. It was faith in Christ that delivered him from the bondage of sin and fear. "The discovery of a completed and gratuitous salvation filled with ecstasy a spirit prepared to appreciate it, and, from their great deep breaking, his affections thenceforward flowed, impetuous and uninterrupted, in the one channel of love to the Saviour. . . . He traversed England, Scotland, and Ireland, for four-and-thirty years, and crossed the Atlantic thirteen times, proclaiming the love of God and his great gift to man. A bright and exulting view of the atonement's sufficiency was his theology; delight in God and rejoicing in Christ Jesus were his piety; and a compassionate solicitude for the souls of men was his ruling passion."

The great truth which stands forth so prominently in Whitefield's personal experience, is equally prominent in the history of his ministerial successes;—the love of God, as exhibited in the atoning death of his Son, is the mighty instrument by which souls are converted and made partakers of the divine life.

The manner of Whitefield as a preacher, it is true, was singularly effective. He had a voice of rich compass, which could equally thrill over Moorfields in musical thunder, or whisper its terrible secret in every private ear; and to this tuneful voice he added a most expressive and eloquent action. "Improved by conscientious practice, and instinct with his earnest nature, this elocution was the acted sermon, and by its pantomimic portrait enabled the eye to anticipate each rapid utterance, and helped the memory to treasure up the palpable ideas. . . . His thoughts were possessions, and his feelings were transformations; and if he spoke because he felt, his hearers understood because they saw. They were not only enthusiastic amateurs, like Garrick, who ran to weep and tremble at his bursts of passion, but even the colder critics of the Walpole school were surprised into momentary sympathy and reluctant wonder. Lord Chesterfield was listening in Lady Huntingdon's pew when Whitefield was comparing the benighted sinner to a blind beggar on a dangerous road. The beggar's little dog gets away from him when skirting the edge of a precipice, and he is left to explore the path with his iron-shod staff. On the very verge of the cliff this blind guide (the staff) slips through his fingers, and skims away down the abyss. All unconscious, its owner stoops down to regain it, and stumbling forward—'Good God! he is gone!' shouted Chesterfield, who had been watching with breathless alarm the blind man's movements, and who jumped from his seat to save the catastrophe. But the glory of Whitefield's preaching was its heart-kindled and heart-melting gospel. But for this all his bold strokes and brilliant surprises might have been no better than the rhetorical triumphs of Kirwan and other pulpit dramatists. He was an orator, but he only sought to be an evangelist."

The atheistic philosopher, David Hume, shall bear witness to the principle on which we insist. He heard Whitefield preach on one occasion, and gave this account of the sermon. Towards the end, "after a solemn pause, Mr. Whitefield thus addressed the audience: 'The attendant angel is just about to leave the threshold and ascend to heaven. And shall he ascend and not bear with him the news of one sinner, among all this multitude, reclaimed from the error of his ways?' The preacher then stamped with his foot, lifted up his hands and eyes to heaven, and with gushing tears cried aloud, 'Stop, Gabriel, stop ere you enter the sacred portal, and yet carry with you the news of one sinner converted to God.'" We can imagine the awe produced by such an appeal. But all that mode, and tone, and startling attitude could effect, would fall short of the conversion of the heart to God. Then let us hear the further statement of this unbelieving witness: "Mr. Whitefield then, in most simple but energetic language, described what he called a Saviour's dying love to sinful man, so that almost the whole assembly melted into tears." The secret is now out. "A Saviour's dying love to sinful man." This is the mighty charm of the gospel. This is the banner which Whitefield unfurled, and "by this" he conquered.

"This is the word of truth and love,
Sent to the nations from above.
. . . .
This remedy did wisdom find
To heal diseases of the mind;
This sovereign balm, whose virtues can
Restore the ruined creature man."

Let one instance out of multitudes be taken as illustrative of the power of that gospel which Whitefield preached to reclaim and elevate the very lowest. Some ladies, who had gone to hear him at lady Huntingdon's request, reported their opinion in these terms :—"Oh! my lady, of all the preachers we ever heard, he is the most strange and unaccountable. Among other preposterous things (would your ladyship believe it?) he declared that Jesus Christ was so willing to receive sinners, that he did not object to receive even the devil's *castaways*. Now, my lady, did you ever hear such a thing since you were born?" To which her ladyship made the following reply:— "There is something, I acknowledge, a little singular in the invitation, and I do not recollect to have ever heard it before; but as Mr. Whitefield is below in the parlour, we'll have him up and let him answer for himself.' Mr. Whitefield immediately acknowledged having used the obnoxious expression, and added, "Whether I did what was right or otherwise, your ladyship shall judge from the following circumstance :— Did your ladyship notice, about half an hour ago, a very modest single rap at the door? It was given by a poor, miserable-looking, aged female, who requested to speak with me. I desired her to be shown into the parlour, where she accosted me in the following manner :—'I believe, sir, you preached last evening at such a chapel?'—'Yes, I did.'—'Ah! sir, I was accidentally passing the door of that chapel, and hearing the voice of some one preaching, I did what I have never been in the habit of doing, I went in; and one of the first things I heard you say, was that Jesus Christ was so willing to receive sinners, that he did not object to receiving the devil's castaways. Now, sir, I have been on the town for many years, and am so worn out in his service, that I think I may with truth be called one of the devil's castaways: do you think, sir, that Jesus Christ would receive me?'" Mr. Whitefield assured her there was no doubt of it, if she were but willing to go to him. From the sequel it appeared that this poor creature was truly converted to God. And on her deathbed she left the most satisfactory testimony that through the blood of Jesus Christ she had found peace with God, and had been restored to his likeness. If we admire the process by which the putrefying morass is turned into a fruitful field, and the malaria of death replaced by the breezes of life and health, shall we not much more admire the renewing of a soul so debasedly corrupt, and the blessed truth by which it was effected?

The Kingswood Colliers.

The colliers of Kingswood, in the neighbourhood of Bristol, were notorious for their wicked and brutal manners, and were a terror to their neighbourhood. It was in the midst of these English savages that Mr. Whitefield erected his first field pulpit. On the afternoon of Saturday, Feb. 17, 1739, two hundred of them gathered around him on Rose Green, attracted probably by the novelty of the scene. Every time he went to Kingswood, the number of his hearers increased. Thousands of all ranks flocked from Bristol and the neighbourhood, and the congregation was sometimes computed at twenty thousand. Many of the outcast colliers, who had never been in a place of worship in their lives, received the word with eagerness and gladness. "Having," as Mr. Whitefield writes, "no righteousness of their own to renounce, they were glad to hear of a Jesus who was a friend to publicans, and came not to call the righteous but sinners to repentance. The first discovery of their being affected was to see the white gutters made by their tears, which plentifully fell down their black cheeks, as they came out of their coal pits. Hundreds and hundreds of them were soon brought under deep convictions, which, as the event proved, happily ended in a sound and thorough conversion. The change was visible to all, though numbers chose to impute it to anything rather than the finger of God." "Many an evil life was fashioned anew, and many a wretched home lighted up with the charities and the joys of pure religion."

What, in this case, was the true means of conversion? What was it that reached the hearts of the colliers of Kingswood, and made them men by making them christians? There was much in the manner of the preacher to interest and move them, it is true; and perhaps something in the circumstances to awe them. "The open firmament above me," he writes himself, "the prospect of the adjacent fields, with the sight of thousands and thousands, some in coaches, some on horseback, and some on the trees, and at times all affected and drenched in tears together, to which sometimes was added the solemnity of the approaching evening, was almost too much for, and quite overcame me." All very natural—but neither in the eloquence of the preacher, nor in the circumstantial accompaniments of his preaching, do we find the secret of the power which reached his hearers' hearts and turned them to God. We must look for it in *the truth preached.*

And what was that truth? The orator "spoke of an infinite sin," says one writer; "he spoke of an infinite love: he spoke of that which was true then, whatever might be true hereafter. He said, Thou art in a wrong state: hell is about thee. God would bring thee into a right state; he would save thee out of that state." This statement is ambiguous and defective. "What the orator really talked of," says another writer, "was the wrath of God revealed from heaven against all ungodliness and unrighteousness of men; and the mercy of God also revealed from heaven in the gospel of his grace. He told collier, formalist, self-righteous boaster—all alike—that they were guilty and needed pardon, that they were corrupt and needed renovation—that Jesus Christ came into the world to save sinners, to give himself a ransom for them. He exhorted them to flee from the wrath to come, and lay hold on eternal life. . . . . The early triumphs of the Methodist preaching were based upon appeals to the conscience. The 'orator' spoke to men as criminals; guilty, condemned, depraved. Their own hearts confessed the charge to be true. The Holy Spirit convinced them. They were told that God in love had given his Son to die in their stead, and was giving his Spirit to make them new creatures in his Son. They believed that there was a righteous pardon for their deep guilt, and a complete renewal

29

for their impure and unholy nature, in Christ, presented to them in the gospel. And this faith was their victory."

James Hervey; born Feb. 26th, 1713; died Dec. 25th, 1758.

JAMES HERVEY, when twenty years of age, formed the acquaintance of Whitefield, Wesley, and their associates at Oxford, and imbibed their spirit of serious attention to the concerns of religion. He received the communion every Sabbath, visited the prisoners in the jail, and read the Scriptures to the sick and the poor. At this time, however, and during the earlier years of his ministry, he was practically a stranger to those views of christian doctrine which, as preached by his friend Mr. Whitefield, proved so mighty an instrument of converting many to God; he entertained the deepest aversion to them. He regarded salvation as a blessing which should be bestowed on sincere, pious, and worthy persons. And when he felt himself deficient in duty, he would comfort himself with saying, "Soul, thy God only requires sincere obedience, and perhaps to-morrow may be more abundant in acts of holiness." When overcome by sin, he would call to mind his righteous deeds, and so hope to commute with divine justice, and quit scores for his offences by his duties. In order to be reconciled to God, or to ease his conscience, he would promise stricter watchfulness, more alms, and renewed fastings. He did not overlook the death of Christ as procuring the remission of sins; but eternal life, he imagined, must be obtained by his own doings.

In the parish of Weston Favel, where he was his father's curate, there resided a ploughman, who usually attended the ministry of Dr. Doddridge in the neighbouring town of Northampton. Mr. Hervey frequently accompanied this ploughman in his rural employment for the sake of his health. Understanding the ploughman to be a religious person, he said to him one day, "What do you think is the hardest thing in religion?" To which he replied, "I am a poor illiterate man, and you, sir, are a minister; I beg leave to return the question." Then said Mr. Hervey, "I think the hardest thing is to deny sinful self," grounding his opinion on that solemn admonition of our Lord, "If any man will come after me, let him deny himself." "I argued," said Mr. Hervey, afterwards, "upon the import and extent of the duty, showing that merely to forbear the infamous action is little; we must deny admittance, deny entertainment, at least, to the evil imagination, and quench even the enkindling spark of irregular desire. In this way I shot my random bolt." The ploughman replied, "There is another kind of self-denial to which the injunction goes; it is of great consequence, and the hardest thing in religion, and that is to deny *righteous* self." He went on to say with what pleasure he and his family had for a long time enjoyed the ordinances of religion under the ministry of Dr. Doddridge, and added, "But to this moment I find it the hardest thing to deny righteous self; I mean the renouncing of our own strength, and of our own righteousness; not leaning on that for holiness, nor relying on this for justification." In repeating the story to a friend, Mr. Hervey observed, "I then hated the righteousness of Christ; I looked at the man with astonishment and disdain, and thought him an old fool, and wondered at what I then fancied the motley mixture of piety and oddity in his notions. I have since clearly seen who was the fool—not the wise old Christian, but the proud James Hervey; I now discern sense, solidity, and truth in his observations."

The change which this confession indicates took place in the twenty-seventh year of his age. The light which dispelled his errors was not instantaneous, he says, but gradual; "it did not flash upon his soul, but arose like the dawning of the day." The discovery of the extent of the requirements of the law of God proved fatal to the hopes he was building on his own doings, and happily there came along with it a discovery of the all-sufficiency of the atonement and righteousness of Jesus Christ. His own words are:— "The two great commandments, 'Thou shalt love the Lord thy God with all thine heart,' and 'Thou shalt love thy neighbour as thyself,' made the first awakening impression on my heart. Amazing! thought I; are these commands of God as obligatory as the prohibition of adultery, or the observation of the Sabbath? Then has my whole life been a continued act of disobedience; not a day, nor an hour, in which I have performed my duty. This conviction," he says, "struck me as the handwriting upon the wall struck the presumptuous monarch. It pursued me as Saul pursued the Christians, not only to my own house, but to distant cities, nor ever gave up the great controversy till, under the influence of the Spirit, it brought me weary and heavy laden to Jesus Christ."

Mr. Hervey now wondered how he could have read the Bible so often, and overlooked its revelation of righteousness. "When he saw it he rejoiced with exceeding joy. It solved every problem, and filled every void. It lit up the Bible, and it kindled Christianity. It gave emancipation to his spirit, and motion to his ministry; and whilst it filled his own soul with happiness, it made him eager to transmit the benefit." But his frame was feeble. He could not imitate his college tutor, John Wesley, and his college friend, George Whitefield, in their mode of labour, and he was constrained to use his pen. And with this instrument, dipped in love and beauty, he contributed much to the revival of genuine religion. And if his writings are too gorgeous to be purely classical, they were singularly adapted to their age. Their mellow influence may still be traced. Their spirit is that of "securest faith, and sunniest hope, and most seraphic love." And "it were a blessed ambition to emulate their author's large and lightsome piety—his heart 'open to the whole noon of nature,' and through all its brightness drinking the smile of a present God."

"In the middle of last century, evangelical religion derived its main impulse from Whitefield, Wesley, and Hervey. But though there was none to rival Whitefield's flaming eloquence, or Wesley's versatile ubiquity, or the popularity of Hervey's gorgeous pen, there were many among their contemporaries who, as one by one they learned the truth in their own department or district, did their utmost to diffuse it." The spiritual history of two or three of these worthies, Walker, Toplady, and Berridge, we abridge from graphic sketches by Dr. James Hamilton.

In the summer of 1746, SAMUEL WALKER became curate of the gay little capital of western Cornwall. He was clever and accomplished—had learned from books

Samuel Walker born 1714; died 1761.

the leading doctrines of Christianity, and, whilst mainly anxious to be a popular preacher, had a distinct desire to do good—but did none. The master of the grammar school was a man of splendid scholarship, but much hated for his piety. One day Mr. Walker received from him a note, with a sum of money, requesting him to pay it to the Custom House. For his health Mr. Conon had been advised to drink some French wine, but on that smuggling coast could procure none on which duty had been paid. Wondering whether this tenderness of conscience pervaded all his character, Mr. Walker sought Mr. Conon's acquaintance, and was soon as completely enchained by the sweetness of his disposition as he was awed and astonished by the purity and elevation of his conduct. It was from the good treasure of this good man's heart that Mr. Walker received the gospel. Having learned it, he proclaimed it. Truro was in an uproar. To hear of their general depravity, and to have urged on them repentance and the need of a new nature by one who had so lately mingled in all their gaieties, and been the soul of genteel amusement, was first startling and then offensive. But soon faithful preaching began to tell. And in a few years upwards of eight hundred parishioners had called on him to ask what they must do for their soul's salvation; and his time was mainly occupied in instructing large classes of his hearers who wished to live godly, righteously, and soberly in this evil world. One November a body of troops arrived in his parish for winter quarters. He immediately commenced an afternoon sermon for their special benefit. He found them grossly ignorant. But when they came under the sound of his tender but energetic voice the effect was instantaneous. With few exceptions, tears burst from every eye, and confessions of sin from almost every mouth. In less than nine weeks no fewer than two hundred and fifty had sought his private instructions; and though at first the officers were alarmed at such an outbreak of "methodism" among their men, so evident was the improvement which took place, so rare had punishments become, and so promptly were commands obeyed, that the officers waited on Mr. Walker in a body, to thank him for the reformation he had effected in their ranks. On the morning of their march many of these brave fellows were heard praising God for having brought them under the sound of the gospel, and, as they caught the last glimpses of the town, exclaimed, "God bless Truro."

In the adjacent county of Devon, and in one of its sequestered passes, with a few cottages sprinkled over it, mused and sang AUGUSTUS TOPLADY. When a lad of sixteen, and on a visit to Ireland, he had strolled into a barn, where an illiterate layman was preaching, but preaching reconciliation to God through the death of his Son. The homely sermon took effect, and from that moment the gospel wielded all the powers of his brilliant and active mind. Toplady became very learned, and at thirty-eight he died, more widely read in fathers and reformers than most academic dignitaries can boast when their heads are hoary. His chief publications are controversial, and in some respects bear painfully the impress of his over-ardent spirit. In the pulpit's milder urgency, nothing flowed but balm. In his tones there was a

Augustus Toplady; born 1740; died 1778.

commanding solemnity, and in his words there was such simplicity, that to hear was to understand. And both at Broad Hembury and afterwards in Orange-street, London, the happiest results attended his ministry. Many sinners were converted. And the doctrines which God blessed to the accomplishment of these results may be learned from the hymns which Toplady has bequeathed to the church:—"When languor and disease invade;" "A debtor to mercy alone;" "Rock of ages cleft for me;" and "Deathless principle, arise;"—hymns in which it would seem as if the finished work were embalmed, and the lively hope exulting in every stanza; whilst each person of the glorious Godhead radiates mercy, grace, and holiness through each successive line. During his last illness, Augustus Toplady seemed to lie in the very vestibule of glory. To a friend's inquiry he answered, with sparkling eye, "Oh, my dear sir, I cannot tell the comforts I feel in my soul, they are past expression. The consolations of God are so abundant that he leaves me nothing to pray for. My prayers are all converted into praise. I enjoy a heaven already in my soul." And within an hour of dying he called his friends, and asked if they could give him up; and when they said they could, tears of joy ran down his cheeks as he added, "Oh, what a blessing that you are made willing to give me over into the hands of my dear Redeemer, and part with me; for no mortal can live after the glories which God has manifested to my soul."

At Everton, in Bedfordshire, not far from the spot where John Bunyan had been a preacher and a prisoner, lived and laboured a man not unlike him, John Berridge. For long a distinguished member of Clare Hall, Cambridge, and for many years studying fifteen hours a day, he had enriched his masculine understanding with all sorts of learning; and when at last he became a parish minister, he applied to his labours all the resources of a mind eminently practical, and all the vigour of a very honest one. But his success was small—so small that he began to suspect his mode was wrong. After prayer for light it was one day borne in upon his mind, "Cease from thine own works, only believe;" and consulting his concordance he was surprised to see how many columns were required for the words *faith* and *believe.* Through this quaint inlet he found his way into the knowledge of the gospel, and the consequent love of the Saviour; and, though hampered with academic standing, and past the prime of life, he did not hesitate a moment to reverse his former preaching, and the efficacy of the cross was soon seen in his altered parish. His mind was singular. Full of wit and humour, he thought in proverbs and spoke in parables. In the pith of piety, love to the Saviour, he always abounded. "My poor feeble heart droops when I think, write, or talk of anything but Jesus. Oh that I could get near him, live believingly on him! I would walk, and talk, and sit, and eat, and rest, with him." And it was this absorbing affection which in preaching enhanced all his powers. The bluntest boor, as he listened to the homely colloquy of John Berridge, was delighted at his own capacity. But was not that rather a home-thrust? "Yes, but it is fact; and sure enough the man is frank and honest," and so the blow is borne

John Berridge; born 1716; died 1793.

with the best smile that can be twisted out of agony. "Nay, nay, he is getting personal, and without some purpose the bolts would not fly so true." And just when the hearer's suspicion is rising, and he begins to think of retreating, barbed and burning, the arrow is through him. His soul is transfixed, and his conscience is all on fire. And these shafts of living Scripture fly so fast that in a few minutes the congregation is all a field of slain. Such was the powerful and piercing sharpness of this great preacher's sentences—so suited to England's rustic auditories, and so divinely directed in their flight, that eloquence has seldom won such triumphs as the gospel won with the bow of old eccentric Berridge. Strong men, in the surprise of sudden self-discovery, or in the joy of marvellous deliverance, would sink to the earth powerless or convulsed; and in one year of "campaigning," it is said, that four thousand have been awakened to the worth of their souls and a sense of sin.

It was the same truths uttered by a spirit of similar fervour that produced so great a revolution in Kidderminster a century before. The young heart of RICHARD BAXTER was first religiously impressed by the holy character and serious conversations of his father. While a youth his impressions were deepened at Ludlow Castle by two circumstances which might have had an opposite effect, his temptation to become a gambler, and the religious apostasy of his most intimate friend. The first game he ever played in his life, he played with the best gamester in the castle. It was soon perceived that he must inevitably lose the game, un-

Richard Baxter; born 1615; died 1691.

less he obtained one particular cast of the dice each time in succession. The dice gave that particular cast each time, and he won the game. His astonishing success induced him to believe that the devil had managed the dice for the purpose of making a gamester of him. He therefore returned the money he had won, and determined never to play another game. The apostasy of his young friend was more dangerous to him than the temptation to gambling. His friend was a very devotional young man. They were much attached to each other, and were constantly studying together. He was the first that Baxter had ever heard pray extempore, and it was from him that Baxter himself acquired the habit. This youth became a reviler of all religion, and even scoffed at Baxter's devotions.

Soon after, young Baxter discovered in his father's house an old tattered book which a poor cottager had lent him. Fresh from the scenes and recollections of Ludlow Castle, he read this book very closely, and the reading produced in his mind strong convictions of the evil of sin. That tattered old book was Bunny's "Book of Christian Exercises appertaining to Resolution." Its real author was Parsons, a famous English Jesuit; but it was corrected and improved by Edmund Bunny, who was rector of Bolton Percy, and who, after a life of apostolic labours, died in 1617.

"Bunny's 'Resolution' deals much and vigorously with conscience, and rouses every man to the obligation of 'resolving ourselves to become Christians indeed.' It is probable that this work gave to Baxter's mind that awakening tone, and that eloquent energy which tell so mightily in his 'Call to the Unconverted.' The Jesuit, in composing this work, never thought that it would produce the author of the 'Certainty of Christianity without Popery.' Bunny's 'Resolution' was useful to Baxter, however, only so far as it awakened his mind, and directed him to caution, prayer, and firmness: it neither led him to Christ, nor brought him to the guidance and aid of the Holy Spirit, and therefore it gave him no joy and peace in believing. This was reserved for another, and a very different work: this honour was for Dr. Sibb's 'Bruised Reed.' This admirable little work brought him and his resolutions to the Saviour, and melted his heart into devotion. If Bunny's 'Resolution' strung Baxter's harp, it was Sibb's 'Bruised Reed' that tuned it to the love of Christ." We have in this instance another illustration of the truth, that by whatever means the soul is aroused to religious concern and earnestness, the turning of the heart to God in true conversion is effected only by the knowledge of forgiving mercy through our Lord Jesus Christ.

The character of the inhabitants of Kidderminster, at the period of Baxter's settlement amongst them, was extremely degraded and unpromising. The whole populace of the town had become a disorderly mass, and were violently hostile to real religion under every form and name, whether conformist or nonconformist. The methods of pastoral labour which Baxter adopted he has explained in his "Reformed Pastor." And his success may be told in a very few words. "When I came thither first," he says, "there was about one family in a street that worshipped God, and called on his name; and when I came away there were some streets where there was not more than one family in the side of a street that did not do so." This was the case even with the inns and public houses of the town. Speaking of the Lord's day, he says, "You might hear a hundred families singing psalms and repeating sermons, as you passed through the streets." The number of his regular communicants averaged, before he left, sixteen hundred; "of whom," he says, "there were not twelve that I had not good hopes of as to their sincerity." "And though I have been absent from them now six years, and they have been assaulted with pulpit calumnies and slanders, with threatenings and imprisonments, with enticing words and seducing reasonings, they yet stand fast and keep to their integrity. Many of them are gone to God, and some are removed, and some are now in prison (for conscience sake), and most are still at home; but none that I hear of are fallen off, or forsake their uprightness." With deep humility and with thanksgiving to God he contemplated what God had wrought by him. "Oh! what am I, a worthless worm, not only wanting academical honours, but much of that furniture that is needful to so high a work, that God should thus abundantly encourage me?"

There was much in Baxter's manner to move his hearers. "Into his pulpit he brought all the energies and sympathies of his entire nature. Being deeply earnest himself, he wished his hearers to be deeply earnest." His own immortal lines best explain the simplicity of his style and purpose:—

"I preached, as never sure to preach again,
And as a dying man to dying men."

But this earnestness would have been in vain but that it was used to enforce the great converting truth, that "God so loved the world, that he gave his only begotten

Son, that whosoever believeth in him should not perish, but have everlasting life."

One other instance, and that of more modern date, we give in illustration of our theme. It is that of "a man," to use the words of Robert Hall, "whose sagacity enabled him to penetrate to the depth of every subject he explored; whose conceptions were so powerful and luminous that what was recondite and original appeared familiar; and who has left monuments of his piety and genius which will survive to distant posterity."

Andrew Fuller; born in Cambridgeshire, Feb. 6, 1764; died May 7, 1815.

ANDREW FULLER was born of Christian parents, and, though freely indulging in youthful sins and follies, was the subject of early religious impressions. One day, he tells us, as he was walking alone he began to think seriously what would become of his soul. He felt himself the slave of sin. He saw that if God would forgive him all the past, and offer him the kingdom of heaven on condition of giving up his wicked pursuits, he should not accept it, so conscious was he of the power of sin within him. And he walked sorrowfully along, repeating these words:—"Iniquity will be my ruin." While in this unhappy mood, the words of the apostle suddenly occurred to his mind:—"Sin shall not have dominion over you: for ye are not under the law, but under grace." He had been taught to regard the suggestion of a text of Scripture to the mind, especially if it came with power, as a promise coming immediately from God. He therefore understood this Scripture as a revelation from God to himself, and was instantaneously filled with transport. Tears of joy flowed profusely, till his face was swelled with weeping. But according to his own confession, before night all was gone and forgotten, and he returned to his former vices "with as eager a gust as ever." Twelve months after, as he walked by himself, he thought of his former hopes and affections, and how he had forgotten them and returned to all his wicked ways. Instead of sin having no more dominion over him, he pereeived that its dominion was increased. He was greatly dejected, but these words came into his mind:—"I have blotted out, as a thick cloud, thy transgressions, and, as a cloud, thy sins." As before, he received this as a message from God, and shed a multitude of tears, not of sorrow, but of joy and gratitude. He now judged that he had been in a backsliding state, and that God had graciously restored him; "though in truth," he said years after, "I have every reason to think that the great deep of my heart's depravity had not yet been broken up, and that all my religion was mere transient impression, without any abiding principle. Amidst it all, I had lived without prayer; and was never, that I recollect, induced to deny myself of one sin when temptations were presented. I now however thought, Surely I shall be better for the time to come. But, alas! in a few days this also was forgotten, and I returned to my evil courses with as much eagerness as ever."

At the age of sixteen he formed connections with other wicked youths, which accelerated his progress in evil. "Being of an athletic frame and daring spirit, I was often engaged (he says) in such exercises and exploits as might have issued in death, if the good hand of God had not preserved me." But conviction of sin returned to him, and for a time he was "like a drunkard who carouses in the evening, but mopes about the next day like one half dead." His mental anxieties increased till "the gnawings of a guilty conscience seemed to be a kind of hell within him." "Nay," he says, "I really thought at the time that this was the fire and brimstone of the bottomless pit, and that in me it was already kindled." Perplexity and despair took hold upon him. What to do he knew not. "To think of amendment, and much more to make vows concerning it as heretofore, were but a mockery of God and my own soul; and to hope for forgiveness in the course that I was in, was the height of presumption. . . . . . I was not then aware that any poor sinner had a warrant to believe in Christ for the salvation of his soul; but supposed there must be some kind of qualification to entitle him to do it; yet I was aware that I had no qualifications. On a review of my resolution at that time, it seems to resemble that of Esther, who went into the king's presence 'contrary to the law,' and at the hazard of her life. Like her I seemed reduced to extremities; impelled by dire necessity to run all hazards, even though I should perish in the attempt. Yet it was not altogether from a dread of wrath that I fled to this refuge; for I well remember that I perceived something attracting in the Saviour. I must—I will—yes, I will trust my soul, my sinful lost soul, in his hands. If I perish, I perish! . . . . . And as the eye of my mind was more and more fixed on Christ, my guilt and fears were gradually and insensibly removed. I now found rest for my troubled soul, and I reckon that I should have found it sooner, if I had not entertained the notion of my having no warrant to come to Christ without some previous qualification.

. . . . . When I thought of my past life, I abhorred myself, and repented in dust and ashes; and when of the gospel way of salvation, I drank it in, as cold water is imbibed by a thirsty soul. My heart felt one with Christ, and dead to every other object around me. I thought I had found the joys of the gospel heretofore; but now I seemed to *know* that I had found them, and was conscious that I had passed from death unto life. Yet even now my mind was not so engaged in reflecting upon my own feelings, as upon the objects which occasioned them."

"From this time," Mr. Fuller continues, "my former wicked courses were forsaken. I had no manner of desire after them. They lost their influence upon me. To those evils, a glance at which before would have instantly set my passions in a flame, I now felt no inclination. My soul, said I, with joy and triumph, is as a weaned child. I now know experimentally what it is to be dead to the world by the cross of Christ, and to feel an habitual determination to devote my future life to God. . . . . By the help of God I continue in his service to this day, and daily live in hope of eternal life, through Jesus Christ my Lord and only Saviour."

The peculiar and exclusive importance of the truth which we thus find to be the means of conversion, is seen in the experience of the deathbed, as well as in the first hour of the spiritual life. "Gentlemen," said Dr. R. S. MacAll to the medical men who stood around his dying bed,—"Gentlemen, I am no fanatic; rather I have been too much of a speculatist: and I wish to say this, which I hope you will all forgive me for uttering in your presence—I am a great sinner,

I have been a great sinner; but my trust is in Jesus Christ, and what he has done and suffered for sinners. Upon this, as the foundation of my hope, I can confidently rely, now that I am sinking into eternity." When asked by a brother minister if the gospel which he had preached to others now occupied his thoughts and was dear to his heart, he answered with a smile, "Yes, ITS VERY CORE; I cannot now trouble myself with its envelopments."

Christianity has been happily designated "a vast medical establishment for diseased minds." And the functions of those who teach its truth—"what are they but the solemn and public tender of divinely authorized remedies to the assembled patients in each ward of that mighty hospital, the sin-afflicted world? The physicians may vary in skill or activity, the sufferers in the virulence of the evil; but the relation between them remains substantially unchanged. Nor does it affect the truth of the representation that, in a vast majority of instances, the sick are unsuspicious of their sickness, any more than the confidence of the insane would be accepted as evidence of sanity. The ignorance is a part of the disease, and the first step to health is to know how far we are from it."

The remedy which the gospel provides will be understood only in the light of the relation in which sinful man stands to God. God is a ruler; man is a transgressor. These simple statements are pregnant with awful meaning. They describe the relation which now unhappily subsists between the Creator and his creature, the Father and his child. Whether the transgressor may ever escape the penal consequences of his transgression must depend entirely on the will and grace of the Ruler; and if he may, *how* he shall escape must depend on the will and wisdom of the Ruler. That he may, and how he may, have both been revealed. The redemption of man is not an immediate act of sovereign prerogative; it is the result of a process, originating in love, but wisely involving mediation, and the death of the Mediator. In the death of Jesus Christ, the blood of a sinless man, on whom the divine law had no claim, and could have none, was poured out as a vicarious offering. "First in systematic order as well as in magnitude," says Mr. Isaac Taylor, "is the doctrine of the Propitiation effected by the Son of God—so held clear of admixtures and evasions, as to sustain, in its bright integrity, the consequent doctrine of THE FULL AND ABSOLUTE RESTORATION OF GUILTY MAN TO THE FAVOUR OF GOD, on his acceptance of this method of mercy; or, as it is technically phrased, JUSTIFICATION THROUGH FAITH. A doctrine this, which in a peculiar manner refuses to be tampered with or compromised, and which will hold its own place or none. It challenges for itself, not only a broad basis on which it may rest alone, but a broad border, upon which nothing that is human may trespass. . . . .

"In the justification of man through the mediation of Christ, man individually as guilty, and his divine sponsor, *personally competent to take upon himself such a part,* stand forward in the court of heaven, there to be severally dealt with as the honour of law shall demand; and if the representative of the guilty be indeed thus qualified in the eye of the law, and if the guilty on his part freely accept this mode of satisfaction, then, when the one recedes from the position of danger, and the other steps into it, justice, having already admitted both the competency of the substitute, and the sufficiency of the substitution, is itself silent.

"Such a transaction does indeed originate in grace or favour; but yet if it satisfy law, it can be open to no species of after interference. Now, in the method of justification through faith, God himself solemnly proclaims that the rectitude of his government is not violated, nor the sanctity of his law compromised. It is he who declares that, in this method, he may be just while justifying the ungodly. After such a proclamation from heaven has been made, 'Who is he that condemneth? It is God that justifieth.'

"A sacred doctrine this! most honoured, assuredly, when admitted with a simple hearted and joyful gratitude! If it be asked, 'Is it a truth?' in reply, besides citing the apostolic authorities, which are most explicit, we might well ask, whence such a doctrine might proceed if not from God? Which of the creations of the human mind does it resemble? Whether we regard that aspect of it which is thoroughly intelligible, or that in which it presents an inscrutable mystery, it stands equally remote from the customary style of human speculations; besides that it contravenes the pride and prejudices of the heart. Clear and bright as noon is this truth: vast and deep as infinity."

The moral influence of this truth on the hearts of men is, as our facts and histories show, not only salutary but converting. To use the words of Dr. Duff, the doctrine of the cross, brought home to the heart and conscience, is "the only antecedent to the conversion of a soul towards God." The character of

God is exhibited in the mediation and sacrifice of Christ as all-glorious, both in its purity and in its love. But this alone would not account for the peculiar effects which the truth as it is in Jesus produces. The words of an ancient psalm touch the very philosophy of the connection between the belief of that truth and the spirit of loving obedience to God which follows it—"There is forgiveness with thee, that thou mayest be feared." The heart of the sinner is estranged from God, and this estrangement is confirmed and strengthened by the dread of God's righteous displeasure. While haunted by a sense of unpardoned sin, there can be no free, or willing, or ingenuous obedience. "There might be," says Dr. Chalmers, "a service of drudgery, but not a service of delight—such obedience as is extorted from a slave by the whip of his overseer, but not a free-will offering of love or of loyalty. It makes all the difference between a slavish and a spontaneous obedience. . . . . And yet how shall this translation be effected from the spirit of bondage to that of liberty? How shall we get quit of that overwhelming terror, wherewith it is impossible that either affection or confidence can dwell; and which, so long therefore as it subsists, must cause the religion of a man upon earth to be wholly dissimilar to that of an angel in heaven? For this purpose, and to appease the terror of our own spirits, shall we shut our eyes to what is really terrible in the character of God? Shall we view him otherwise than as a God of holiness? Shall we dismantle his character of its justice, and righteousness, and truth? Shall we conceive of him as descending to a compromise with sin, and as relenting in aught from his hatred and hostility against it? To soften the Divinity into an object of our possible tenderness and truth, shall we strip him of all his moral attributes but one; and, in the midst of this wild and wasteful anarchy, shall mercy abide as the only surviving perfection of that God whom we deemed to be unchangeable? Oh, we feel that the constitution of the Godhead cannot be so tampered with; and that the principles of his everlasting government can never be set aside, nor make way to suit the wishes or the convenience of sinful man. And the question remains, How shall man ever be divested of that terror which is inspired by the thought of an angry God; and which at the same time is increased by the consciousness of impotency in all the efforts of nature to love God, or to impregnate with a right spirit any part of the obedience which it renders to him?

"It is reserved for the gospel of Jesus Christ to do away this terror from the heart of man, and yet to leave untarnished the holiness of God. It is the atonement that was made by Christ which solves this mystery, providing at once for the deliverance of the sinner, and for the dignity of the Sovereign. . . . . This is that great transaction, by which the broken fellowship of earth and heaven is re-adjusted; and through this, as a free and open communication, can God rejoice as before in all kindness over man, and man again place his rejoicing confidence in God. On doing this, he is disburdened from the terror that had enslaved him, and that had given the spirit of a crouching pusillanimity to all his obedience. He from this moment enters into liberty. He is no longer haunted by degrading apprehensions about self and safety. He sees God to be at peace with him, but in such a way as to enhance the sacredness of his now vindicated character; and in the very act of receiving his forgiveness through the hand of a Mediator, man beholds, throughout the whole of the august ceremonial, the heightened lustre that is thrown over the truth, and the justice, and the majesty of the Godhead. But while this view of God in Christ extinguishes one fear—the fear of terror, it awakens another and an altogether distinct fear—the fear of reverence." And with a "heart enlarged," the pardoned man "can run in the way of God's commandments." "The doctrine of faith alone," says professor Butler, "laying deep its foundations in self-abasement, bestows a blessed confidence, without which the Christian may be the inconsolable penitent, the mortified ascetic, the prostrate trembler before an offended God; but without which he is, nevertheless, but half a Christian."

CONCLUSION.

OUR facts are now before the reader. We have already "asked questions" of them, to use the significant language of lord Bacon, and we have received no dubious answers. The painful truth that man is morally estranged from his Maker was elicited from the first "instances" which we adduced, and has been confirmed by all that have followed. "As the greatest and highest of all blessings, God made him, who was to be lord over all the rest of the creation, in his own image. This was the greatest blessing which God could bestow on any creature, his own image, a shadow of his own eternal power and truth, a shadow, and likeness, and capacity of his own holiness and love; and this he bestowed upon man. But this, the greatest of all blessings which it can enter into man's heart to conceive, man wilfully cast away. He would not have it. . . . He bowed his neck to the yoke." "It is this that marks, even in noble spirits, the profound and general depravity of the human race. This is the seal of our reprobation, that we have forgotten why and for what we were sent into the world. All evil comes from this; and each particular sin disappears in this great and primal sin."*

But although no truth rests on a wider or more

* Vinet.

solid basis of facts than this, there is none which men are more unwilling to admit. "Even now, with all the light of the Scriptures shining around us, with the law of God ever sounding in our ears, and the life of Christ set continually before us, how prone are we to forget our sinfulness, to turn away from the thought of it, to fancy that we are as good as we need be, and that though we might certainly be better, yet it does not matter much! How apt are we still to forget that we are 'concluded under sin!' To forget that we are shut up in it as in a prison! How readily do we still let ourselves be dazzled by the gilded glaring walls, and the gaudy flaring flowers! . . . . Although the souls of so many millions are lying around us, bloated with the poison of sin, how tardily do we acknowledge that the poison by which they perished must also be deadly to us! . . . This is the craft and subtlety of the evil one, that he makes us fancy we are free, when we are in prison; he makes us fancy we are at liberty, when we are in bondage; he makes us fancy we are our own masters, when we are his slaves; he blinds and cheats, and stupefies us, until we deem we are doing our own will and pursuing our own pleasure, when in fact we are drudging in his toils, and rushing into the jaws of destruction before his lashing scourge. Therefore, in order that our eyes might be open to the misery of our condition, that we might see our danger before it was too late, God was mercifully pleased to give us his Scriptures, wherein he declares in the ears of all mankind, that one and all are concluded under sin; that, however its appearance may deceive us, sin is not a palace but a prison, that in that prison we are all shut up, and that no earthly power can deliver us from it."

The facts of the inner world which this book relates, and which are as real as those of the outer world, are perpetual witnesses of the power and presence of God in the government of mankind. In "questioning" them we have ascertained the means by which those that are "without God" may be reconciled to him, restored to fellowship with him, and brought into a state of loving, child-like obedience to his authority. and in these means we discover no light argument for the divinity of the christian faith—the divinity especially of those truths which are "mighty" to the conversion of men's hearts to God. The argument which Joseph John Gurney addressed to the mechanics of Manchester, on the correspondence of Old Testament prophecy and New Testament history, is equally applicable to our theme. "When a lock and key (he said) are well fitted, a fair presumption arises, even though they be of a simple character, that they were made for each other. If they are complex in their form, that presumption is considerably strengthened. But if the lock is composed of such strange and curious parts as to baffle the skill even of a Manchester mechanic—if it is absolutely novel and peculiar, differing from everything that was ever before seen in the world—if no key in the universe will enter it, *except one,* and by that one it is so easily and exactly fitted that a child may open it, then indeed are we absolutely certain that the lock and the key were made by the same master-hand, and truly belong to each other. No less curiously diversified, no less hidden from the wisdom of man, no less novel and peculiar, are the prophecies contained in the Old Testament respecting Jesus Christ. No less easy, no less exact, is the manner in which they are fitted by the gospel history.

Who then can doubt that God was the author of these predictions, of the events by which they were fulfilled, and of the religion with which they are both inseparably connected?"

The gospel of Jesus Christ is the only key that opens the lock of the human heart. The adaptation of the one to the other is attested by its efficiency in instances happily too numerous to be told. In whatever other respects the hearts of men are dissimilar, they have been found alike in this, that they have been opened by the gospel of Christ to receive divine principles and affections which have made them the home of a holy happiness. And in this lies evidence that the gospel is of God. "That is the best key," says Richard Baxter, "that will open the lock, which none but that of God's appointing will do."

The historic evidence of Christianity can never be relinquished or treated as of little importance. But it will meet the wants of these times only as it is associated with the gospel itself. "It is my steadfast conviction," says the author of "The Restoration of Belief," "that Christianity will not henceforth maintain its ground, as related to the present intellectual condition of instructed communities, so long as Christian apologists (so called) take up a position upon the outworks, or spend their efforts upon the well meant but fruitless endeavour to put forward the 'historic evidences' apart from the PRINCIPAL TRUTH, which forms the substance of the gospel. So long as this principal truth does not occupy its due position in the mind and faith of the writer, and so long as it is not boldly presented to the mind of the reader, there is a consciousness on both sides of an interior incoherence in the system itself: there is a painful and perplexing feeling of incongruity, which sets these evidences jarring, as well in a logical as in a moral sense, one against another. . . . . For my own part I could not attempt, and in fact should fail to have any motive sufficiently impulsive for attempting, to set forth the Christian evidences on any other ground than that of an amply expressed and unexceptive ORTHODOXY." The Godhead and atoning sacrifice of Jesus Christ constituting the substance and soul of Christianity, "Let it be argued," this able writer says, and says with a boldness which the Scripture testimony warrants, and which is sustained by innumerable facts like those that are contained in this volume—"Let it be argued . . that the Christian doctrine of Propitiation for sin (stated without reserve) . . is every thing that ought to be reprobated, and to be met with an indignant rejection; let all such things be said—and they will be said to the world's end—it will to the world's end also be true that each human spirit, when awakened toward God, as to his moral attributes, finds rest in that same doctrine of the vicarious sufferings of the Divine Person, and finds no rest until it is *there* found."

If we "question" our facts again, and interpret their answer correctly, we shall understand better than by definitions the true nature of the divine life which follows the conversion of the heart to God. Conversion does not impart new mental powers to men. It may stimulate those which they possess naturally, quicken them into activity, increase their strength, and enlarge their sphere of exercise by the new motives with which it inspires the heart, and the new tastes which it imparts to the soul; but it neither changes their essential character, nor adds to their number. The memory, imagination and judgment of the unconverted man go with him into the new spiritual world into which conversion introduces him. And all that constitutes his intellectual idiosyncracy and individuality survives the moral transformation by which he has become a Christian. There are "the same faculties, but not the same uses; even as the breathing organs of a human body are still substantially the same, when at one hour inhaling pestilence and ruin, at another drawing the pure and reviving air of morning in the open landscape, and with all the happy consciousness of life, and health, and vigour."

This is true likewise of all a man's natural susceptibilities of affections. Hope and fear, love and hatred, are not uprooted or destroyed; they only find new objects. The "old machinery of humanity" is not discarded by the gospel, there is not provided for us a "new organization of passions and affections." It is an error to suppose "that in the work of renewal new faculties are given to us, instead of a new direction to the old ones; that God annihilates human nature when he only perfects it; and that the proper office of the Holy Spirit is to evacuate our former being, instead of taking it as the basis of his mighty work; to destroy the channels themselves, instead of cleansing their polluted streams, and then replenishing them for ever with the waters of paradise."* The change is purely moral. The heart's love is set on worthier objects, the soul's desires are set on

* Professor Butler's Sermon. "Human Affections raised, not destroyed by the Gospel."

worthier ends, the whole man finds his rest in God. And thus out of the common materials of intellect and affection, there is framed a "temple of the Holy Ghost" for time and eternity.

On the other hand, this divine life is something distinctively new, and not something whose germ was always in the heart, and needed only the sunshine of favourable circumstances to make it germinate into visible existence. The oak exists in the acorn, and a suitable soil and time will make it grow. It often happens that mental powers, whose existence is unsuspected, lie dormant till culture or circumstances wake them from their slumber. But it cannot be said of the divine life that it lies concealed beneath the crust of worldliness, that its germ is in every bosom, and that fitting time and opportunity alone are required to call it into visible and practical exercise. There is no seed of love to God in the unregenerate heart. It is not a moral slumber or stupor that has overtaken it, but a moral death.

The terms "flesh" and "spirit" are not, as some think, equivalent to passion and conscience, between which there is oft-times a conflict, even in the unconverted heart. "That which is born of the flesh is flesh, and that which is born of the Spirit is spirit." The "flesh," as used in these words of the infallible Teacher, consists in the moral nature of man, as born of man; the spirit the moral nature of man as "born again" of the Holy Spirit. In the former, if Paul may be regarded as a true type of the species, "there dwelleth no good thing." To use the words of Dr. John Brown in his Commentary on Galatians v. 17—"The 'flesh' here is just a general term for that mode of thinking and feeling which is natural to man in his present depraved state, and which, although modified by an infinite variety of circumstances in individuals, is in its grand substantial character the same, common to the species; and the 'spirit' as opposed to it, is just a general name for that mode of thinking and feeling which is produced in the mind by the agency of the Holy Spirit, through the instrumentality of Christian truth, which, differing in degree, is substantially the same in all true Christians. 'The flesh' is a phrase of equivalent meaning with 'the old man,' and 'the spirit' with 'the new man.' These two modes of thinking and feeling are here, as in many other parts of the apostle's writings, personified and spoken of as if they were living beings."

The lusting of the flesh against the spirit, and of the spirit against the flesh, is one of those subjects which, as Dr. Brown says, are best illustrated by examples. Take one: "Under the influence of that mode of thinking and feeling which the faith of the gospel and the operation of the Holy Ghost produce, the Christian earnestly wishes to acquiesce in the most severely afflictive dispensations of Divine Providence —to have no will but the will of God; but, under the influence of that impatience of suffering, and that opposition to the divine will, which are natural to man, he finds such acquiescence no easy attainment, and feels in extreme hazard of becoming fretful or sullen. This is 'the flesh lusting against the spirit.' On the other hand, when a Christian meets with unmerited ill-treatment from his fellow men, he is very apt, under the influence of his natural mode of thinking and feeling, to cherish resentment and seek revenge; but his new mode of thinking and feeling opposes this, and, remembering how God for Christ's sake forgave him all his trespasses, he is made, in opposition to the lustings of nature, to forgive his brother his trespasses. This is 'the spirit lusting against the flesh.'"

In conversion there is, then, not the awakening of principles that were dormant, but the communication of principles which did not exist—the principles of a grateful and loving obedience to the Father that is in heaven. The changed man is a "new creature." Of the divine moral image, "righteousness and true holiness," no part had survived the fall. And its re-creation is of God himself.

This last sentiment, the agency of God in conversion and in the production of the divine life, rests on the authority of Holy Scripture; and it is strongly corroborated by our facts, in which we find, to use the words of Neander, "the standing miracle of the church," that which was to be wrought among all men and in all time. "Let us pause for one moment," says the biographer of Dr. Hope, in relating the humble and happy experience of this distinguished physician in the prospect of an early grave—"Let us pause for one moment to consider this remarkable change, and inquire into its causes. Can this be the same individual who, filled from the earliest childhood with bright visions of earthly honour, wealth, and distinction, so perseveringly struggled for their attainment, and for nearly thirty years sacrificed every personal consideration to gain those very treasures which he now prizes so lightly? Strange, incredible as it may seem, it is indeed he. Whence, then, this change? Has the world frowned on him, and has he learned, by hard necessity, to despise the smiles of fortune? No—the world before him is brighter and more inviting than it ever was before. Is it the madnesss of enthusiasm, or the sickly dream of an exhausted brain? No—for his intellect is clear, his judgment cool, and his present feelings, far from being the growth of temporary weakness, date their commencement from the time when health was un impaired. The Christian alone can discover the cause in the Book of God. He will there find that, through the divine agency, man becomes a new creature; old things pass away, and all things become new. To the transforming influence of the Holy Spirit alone can we ascribe a change of sentiment and feeling which human motives would have been too weak to have effected. The infidel philosopher may nerve himself to regard with stoic indifference the approach of death; he may reason himself into a belief of the worthlessness of those joys which he had found insufficient for his happiness; but he cannot, like our Christian philosopher, enter into the feelings, and appreciate the blessings of this world, and yet resign them joyfully, because there are within his grasp richer treasures, surpassing honours, purer joys, which shall never fade, never cloy, but endure for ever and ever. This higher excellence is reserved for him who, justified by faith in Christ, and sanctified by the Spirit, has fought a good fight, has finished his course, and knows that henceforth there is laid up for him a crown, which the Lord shall give at his appearing."

In reference, then, to this "standing miracle" of Christianity, let us ever (to use the language of professor Butler) "maintain for the Spirit of truth—and more than ever in these days, in which we are wont to hear the gravest truths of revelation questioned, or diluted, or overlooked—his own unparticipated right to illuminate man; not indeed by making man no longer man, but by feeding the affections with holy food, by inviting them to holy objects. In this work, he is alone. 'It is the Spirit that quickeneth.' The old and the new creation are alike exclusively divine. The revelation of God itself, as delivered in books, dares not dispute this honour with the everlasting Spirit. That revelation is written in a language familiar to our daily thoughts and converse; it speaks of life and death, and faith, and hope, and love—all household words, which, in their earthly acceptation, every man can speak of and define; but to pass from the earthly term to the heavenly purport, from the natural object to the supernatural, from the life of the flesh to the life of the spirit, from the faith which trusts in the brother-man to the faith which trusts in the 'First-born among many brethren,' from the love and hope that are entangled among creatures of clay to the love and hope that are busy among the immortal realities of heaven—this is an art which the Spirit that inspired the Scriptures alone can teach to the man who reads them."

If these conclusions are according to truth, they may not be laid aside or forgotten, like those of material science, while we attend to things of more immediate importance. "The eternal Ruler of the universe declares himself a party in a controversy in which each individual of the human race separately sustains the opposite position. No liberty is granted to us to recede from the high but ominous dignity of thus waging battle with the Almighty; and if in no other manner, yet by acts of wilful rebellion, have we singly accepted the distinction, and stand pledged to the consequences." Has the reader awakened to see this to be his condition in relation to God? Has he returned to his heavenly Father through the one Mediator? or does he flatter himself that a more convenient season will come? If he does, let him ponder the following tale of mournful truth.*

An accomplished and amiable young woman had been deeply affected by a sense of her spiritual danger. She was the only child of a fond and affectionate parent. The deep depression which accompanied her discovery of guilt and depravity awakened all the jealousies of the father. He dreaded the loss of that sprightliness and vivacity which constituted the life of his domestic circle. He was startled by the answers which his questions elicited; while he foresaw, or thought he foresaw, an encroachment on the hitherto unbroken tranquillity of a deceived heart. Efforts were made to remove the cause of disquietude; but they were such efforts as unsanctified wisdom directed. The Bible, at last—oh, how little may a parent know the far-reaching of the deed when he snatches the word of life from the hand of a child!—the Bible, and other books of religion, were removed from her possession, and their place was supplied by works of fiction. An excursion of pleasure was proposed, and declined. An offer of gayer amusement shared the same fate. Promises, remonstrances, and threatenings followed; and the father's infatuated perseverance at last brought compliance. Alas! how little may a parent be aware that he is decking his off-

* From "Letters to a Friend," by Dr. Henry.

spring with the fillets of death, and leading to the sacrifice, like a follower of Moloch. The end was accomplished. All thoughts of piety and all concern for the immortal future vanished together. But, oh, how in less than a year was the gaudy deception exploded! The fascinating and gay L. M. was prostrated by a fever that bade defiance to medical skill. The approach of death was unequivocal; and the countenance of every attendant fell, as if they had heard the descent of his arrow. "I see even now," said one who was present, "that look directed to the father by the dying martyr of folly. The glazing eye was dim in hopelessness; and yet there seemed a something in its expiring rays that told reproof and tenderness and terror in the same glance. And that voice—its tone was decided, but sepulchral still—'My father! last year I *would* have sought the Redeemer. Father—your child is'——eternity heard the remainder of the sentence, for it was not uttered in time. The wretched survivor now saw before him the fruit of a disorder whose seeds had been sown when his delighted look followed the steps of his idol in the maze of a dance. Oh how often, when I have witnessed the earthly wisdom of a parent banishing the thoughts of eternity, have I dwelt on that expression which seemed the last reflection from a season of departed hope, 'Last year I *would* have sought the Redeemer!'"

The poet shall be our last teacher. "The Sand and the Rock," by Mr. James Montgomery, is founded on the solemn words of our Lord in the sermon on the mount, and represents, in characteristic form, the spiritual history of a converted soul. God grant that every reader of these pages may be the subject of a like history.

PART I.—DESTRUCTION.

I BUILT my house upon the sand,
And saw its image in the sea,
That seemed as stable as the land,
And beautiful as heaven to me. . . .

I said unto my soul, "Rejoice
In safety, wealth, and pleasure here;"
But while I spake a secret voice
Within my bosom whispered, "Fear."

I heeded not, and went to rest,
Prayerless, once more, beneath my roof,
Nor deemed the eagle on his nest
More peril-free, more tempest-proof.

But in the dead and midnight hour
A storm came down upon the deep;
Wind, rain, and lightning, such a stour,
Methought 'twas doomsday in my sleep.

I strove, but could not wake,—the stream
Beat vehemently on my wall;
I felt it tottering in my dream;
It fell, and dreadful was the fall.

Swept with the ruins down the flood,
I woke; home, hope, and heart were gone;
My brain flash'd fire, ice thrilled my blood;
Life, life, was all I thought upon.

Death, death, was all that met my eye;
Deep swallowed deep, wave buried wave;
I look'd in vain for land and sky;
All was one sea—that sea one grave.

I struggled through the strangling tide,
As though a bowstring wrung my neck;
"Help, help!" voice failed—I fain had cried,
And clung convulsive to the wreck.

Not long—for suddenly a spot
Of darkness fell upon my brain,
Which spread and pressed, till I forgot
All pain in that excess of pain.

PART II.—TRANSITION.

Two woes were past; a worse befell;
When I revived, the sea had fled;
Beneath me yawned the gulf of hell,
Broad as the vanished ocean's bed.

Downward I seemed to plunge through space,
  As lightning flashes and expires,
Yet—how I know not—turned my face
  Away from these terrific fires;

And saw in glory throned afar
  A human form, yet all divine;
Beyond the track of sun or star,
  High o'er all height it seemed to shine.

'Twas He who in the furnace walked
  With Shadrach, and controlled its power;
'Twas He with whom Elias talk'd,
  In his transfiguration hour.

'Twas He whom, in the lonely isle
  Of Patmos, John in spirit saw;
And at the lightning of his smile
  Fell down as dead, entranced with awe.

From his resplendent diadem
  A ray shot through my inmost soul;
"Could I but touch his garment's hem,
  Methought, "like her whom faith made whole!"

Faith, faith was given; though nigh and nigher
  Swift verging towards the gulf below,
I stretched my hand; but high and higher,
  Ah me! the vision seemed to go.

"Save, Lord, I perish;" while I cried,
  Some miracle of mercy drew
My spirit upward; hell yawned wide,
  And followed; upward still I flew;

And upward still the surging flame
  Pursued; yet all was clear above,
Whence brighter, sweeter, kindlier came
  My blessed Saviour's looks of love.

Till with a sudden flash forth beamed
  The fulness of the Deity;
Hell's jaws collapsed; I felt redeemed;
  The snare was broken, I was free.

What follow'd, human tongue in vain
  Would question language to disclose;
Enough that I was born again,
  From death to life that hour I rose.

PART III.—RESTITUTION.

I BUILT once more, but on a rock,
  Faith's strong foundation firm and sure
Fixed mine abode, the heaviest shock
  Of time and tempest to endure.

Not small, nor large, not low, nor high,
  Midway it stands upon the steep,
Beneath the storm-mark of the sky,
  Above the flood-mark of the deep,

And here I humbly wait, while He,
  Who plucked me from the lowest hell,
Prepares a heavenly house for me,
  Then calls me home with him to dwell.

"For ever with the Lord!"
  Amen; so let it be;
Life from the dead is in that word,
  'Tis immortality.

Here in the body pent,
  Absent from him I roam;
Yet nightly pitch my moving tent
  A day's march nearer home.

INDEX.

Page

Anderson, Christopher . . 145

Banerji, Krishna 307
Baxter, Richard 346
Bengel, Albert. 126
Berridge, John 345
Bilney, Thomas 167
Birrell, Ebenezer 82
Blackader, Colonel . . . 130
Boos, Martin 172
Budgett, Samuel 257
Bunyan, John 148
Burn, Andrew 158
Butler, W. Archer . . . 170

Cecil, Richard 274
Chalmers, Thomas . . . 239

Doddridge, Philip . . . 240

Edwards, Jonathan . . . 198

Fletcher, Joseph 137
Foster, John 117
Fry, Caroline 90
Fuller, Andrew 350

Gifford, Andrew 218
Graham, Mrs. Isabella . . 139
Gurney, Joseph John . . 133

Page

Haldane, Robert 241
Hervey, James 338
Hewitson, W. H. 258
Hope, Dr. James 260
Howels, William 269
Huntingdon, Lady . . . 221

James, Mons. 244
Jenyns, Soame 178
Judson, Adoniram . . . 251

Kiffin, Alderman 219
Knibb, William 121

Latimer, Hugh 68
Loyola, Ignatius 58
Lyttleton, Lord 177

MacAll, Robert 353
Merle D'Aubigné 245
Morrison, Robert 119

Newton, John 279

Phelps, Mrs. Stuart . . . 204

Richmond, Legh 238
Rieu, Charles 244
Robinson, Thomas . . . 223
Rochester, Earl of . . . 178

	Page
Scott, Captain	221
Simeon, Charles	226
Stewart, Alexander	229
Toplady, Augustus	343
Urquhart. John	78
Waldo, Peter	277
Walker, Samuel	341
Wesley, Charles	315
Wesley, John	312
West, Gilbert	177
White, H. K.	188
Whitefield, George	326
Wilberforce, William	233
Williams, John	247
Brahmins, The	305
Greenlanders, The	299
Kingswood Colliers, The	335
South Sea Islanders, The	303

PUBLICATIONS OF THE BOARD.

Books published by the Presbyterian Board of Publication, No. 821 Chestnut St., Philadelphia.

Jos. P. Engles, Publishing Agent.

The Life of the Rev. Richard Baxter, abridged from Orme's Life of Baxter. 18mo. 25 and 30 cents.

Who has not read Baxter's Call to the Unconverted, and the Saint's Everlasting Rest, by the same author? And who that has read these, has not felt a desire to become personally acquainted, as it were, with the author? Biography affords the necessary introduction, and we may here see the author practically illustrating in his own life, the principles which he taught to mend the hearts and reform the lives of others.

The Life of Major-General Andrew Burn, of the Royal Marines. With a likeness. 18mo. 25 and 30 cents.

The biography of General Burn is instructive. He narrates with great simplicity and piety the dealings of the Lord with his soul. His profession of religion under inadequate impressions; his subsequent apostasy; the dreadful effects on his character, produced by a residence in France; his subsequent deliverance; his true conversion, and his steadfast piety to the close of a protracted life, are topics which will all furnish food for serious reflection.

LIFE OF LIEUTENANT-COLONEL BLACKADER. Born 1654—Died 1729. 18mo. 20 and 25 cents.

This biography furnishes strong proof that divine grace can sustain the soul and preserve Christian consistency of character in the most untoward situations of life. Burn and Blackader, in those two schools of vice, the British navy and army, were pleasing examples of the truth and power of true religion. Blackader, as a brave soldier, exposed to innumerable perils in some of the bloodiest battles which have afflicted humanity, never seemed to forget that his dependence was in God. Let those who excuse their negligence on the ground of want of opportunity for cultivating religious principles, read this memoir, and see how piety can be cultivated in the most unpropitious situations.

THE BEDFORDSHIRE TINKER; or, The History of John Bunyan. Written for young children by E. G. Sargent. 18mo. with an engraving. 15 and 20 cents.

The Bedfordshire Tinker was no less a personage than John Bunyan, the author of the celebrated Pilgrim's Progress. This is a brief sketch of his wonderful life, during which he was rescued from the deepest profligacy and degradation, to be made an eminent minister of the Gospel, and one of the most famous among authors.

THE LIFE OF THE REV. JAMES HERVEY, M. A., Rector of Weston Favel. And the Life of the REV. AUGUSTUS M. TOPLADY, Vicar of Broad-Hembury. 18mo. 30 and 35 cents.

The eminent piety of these two distinguished divines is generally known. Although in the English Established Church, they were free from exclusiveness, not in bondage to forms, and strongly Calvinistic in their doctrines. These memoirs form a volume of truly delightful biography for the edification of all true Christians.

MEMOIRS OF THE REV. JOHN NEWTON, formerly Rector of St. Mary Woolnoth, &c., with selections from his correspondence. 18mo. 35 and 40 cents. With a mezzotint likeness.

As John Newton was among the most useful and distinguished ministers of the gospel, so his early life was most remarkable. Rescued from the deepest degradation of sin, he rose to be one of the brightest monuments of divine grace. This memoir of him is much more complete than those which are more commonly known.

MEMOIRS, INCLUDING LETTERS AND SELECT REMAINS OF JOHN URQUHART, late of the University of St. Andrews. By William Orme. With a prefatory Notice and Recommendation, by Alexander Duff, D.D. LL. D., 12mo. pp. 420. With a portrait. Price 65 cents.

This volume contains an interesting memoir of a young Scottish student of remarkable talents, attainments, and piety. At a very tender age he devoted himself to the work of preaching the gospel to the heathen, but owing to various obstacles, his intentions were never carried out. From the age of twelve years onward he was a fellow-student and intimate associate of the present distinguished missionary Dr. Alexander Duff, who has revised the work; and written an introductory essay on the life and character of his friend.

GEMS FROM THE CORAL ISLANDS. WESTERN POLY NESIA. Comprising the New Hebrides Group, the Loyalty Group, and the New Caledonia Group. By the Rev. William Gill, Rarotonga. 12mo. pp. 232. Price 60 cents.

This volume may be confidently commended as containing an intensely interesting record of missionary labours, trials, and successes in that part of the Pacific indicated by the title. It is written by one who has himself been more than seventeen years engaged in the work about which he writes. The volume is issued in beautiful style, and is illustrated with many wood cuts.

GEMS FROM THE CORAL ISLANDS; or Incidents of Contrast between Savage and Christian Life of the South Sea Islanders. By the Rev. William Gill, Rarotonga. Eastern Polynesia, comprising the Rarotonga Group, Penrhyn Islands, and Savage Island. 12mo. pp. 285. Price 75 cents. With illustrations.

This volume like the above, is filled with most interesting accounts of the wonderful works of God, and triumphs of his gospel, in that distant and until lately debased and savage portion of the world. No one can read these two books on Polynesia without finding his interest in the work of missions increased, or without becoming more hopeful in regard to the future and rapid progress of the gospel.

REMAINS OF REV. RICHARD CECIL, with a view of his character. By Josiah Pratt. 18mo. 35 and 40 cents.

A truly suggestive book for thinkers, and an excellent summary of gospel truths, pleasantly and instructively spoken.

A History of the Work of Redemption, containing the outlines of a Body of Divinity, in a method entirely new. By the Rev. Jonathan Edwards, President of the College of New Jersey. Accurately copied from the third American edition, without abridgment. 12mo. 60 cents.

The high estimation in which President Edwards's work on Redemption has always been held, has led to the publication of this full, correct, and unmutilated edition. It presents a judicious, solid, and scriptural view of the great work of Redemption, and is perhaps the best adapted of all the author's admirable productions for general usefulness.

Daily Readings. Passages of Scripture, selected for social reading, with applications. By Caroline Fry. 12mo. 60 cents.

This is a casket filled with gems of thought and piety. Like the holy Book whose truths it is designed to elucidate and enforce, it may be read and re-read with undiminished interest.

Annals of the Poor. By the Rev. Legh Richmond, A. M., late Rector of Turvey, Bedfordshire. A new edition, enlarged and illustrated with engravings. 12mo. 50 cents.

The Annals of the Poor, written in the graceful style of the excellent Legh Richmond, has become so generally known as to need no recommendation. It may be truly said of this edition, that it is more complete than any extant, and unsurpassed in the beauty of its typography and embellishments.

Death-Bed Triumphs of Eminent Christians, Exemplifying the Power of Religion in a Dying Hour.—12mo. pp. 191. Price 40 cents.

In this volume we have the dying testimony of quite

a number of eminent christian men, to the truth and power of religion. The reading of the dying experiences of these christians will teach the true believer to contemplate death, as one of them expressed it, as "a great blessing"—as the messenger sent to release us from earth, and introduce us to heaven.

Leila Ada, the Jewish Convert, an authentic Memoir. By Osborn W. Trenery Heighway. Revised by the Editor. 12mo. pp. 230. 55 cents. With a portrait.

The history of a cultivated Jewess, struggling after the truth, and at length finding it in Jesus. A work of absorbing interest.

Children of Abraham, or Sketches of Jewish Converts, being in part a sequel to "Leila Ada." 18mo. pp. 120. Price 20 and 25 cents.

This volume contains sketches of the lives and especially of the dying scenes of six converts from Judaism, and one unconverted Jewess, by way of contrast. The readers of "Leila Ada," will be pleased to learn something more about her cousin Isaac, who stood by her so nobly at the time of her fiery trial.

www.ingramcontent.com/pod-product-compliance
Lightning Source LLC
La Vergne TN
LVHW020124110826
845151LV00001B/267

* 9 7 8 1 4 2 5 5 4 1 4 1 5 *